HOW TO TRAVEL ROUND TH

GW01071873

In this Series

Other titles in preparation

TRAVEL ROUND
THE WORLD

Your practical guide to the experience of a lifetime

Nick Vandome

How To Books

Other books by the same author
How to Find Temporary Work Abroad
How to Get a Job in Australia
How to Spend a Year Abroad

British Library Cataloguing in Publication Data
A catalogue record for this book is available from the British Library.

© Copyright 1995 by Nick Vandome.

First published in 1995 by How To Books Ltd, Plymbridge House, Estover Road, Plymouth PL6 7PZ, United Kingdom. Tel: (01752) 735251/695745. Fax: (01752) 695699. Telex: 45635.

All rights reserved. No part of this work may be reproduced or stored in an information retrieval system (other than for purposes of review) without the express permission of the Publisher given in writing.

Note: The material contained in this book is set out in good faith for general guidance and no liability can be accepted for loss or expense incurred as a result of relying in particular circumstances on statements made in the book. Travel information is complex and liable to change, and readers should check the current position with the relevant authorities before making personal arrangements.

Typeset by PDQ Typesetting, Stoke-on-Trent
Printed and bound by The Cromwell Press, Broughton Gifford, Melksham, Wiltshire.

Contents

SECTION TWO: THE GLOBETROTTER'S WORLD

LIST OF ILLUSTRATIONS

Preface

No traveller can survive for long without help from others and I am indebted to numerous people who helped me during my times in weird and wonderful places – I have received so much generosity and kindness that it would be unfair to single out individual people. In addition, fellow travellers have helped fill in gaps in my own global education and some of their thoughts and experiences are used here. I am also grateful to dozens of embassies and their staff for invaluable information regarding specific countries. Special thanks goes to Christine Stewart for facts and figures regarding round the world air flight.

I am always on the lookout for views and opinions from fellow travellers and all contributions will be gratefully received. Send them to the author, c/o How To Books, Plymbridge House, Estover Road, Plymouth PL6 7PZ.

Nick Vandome

1
Introduction

THE LURE OF TRAVELLING ROUND THE WORLD

It is over a hundred years since Jules Verne wrote *Around the World in Eighty Days* and the idea of travelling round the world is one that still conjures up exotic and romantic images. The thought of the deserts of the Sahara, the wildlife of Africa, the beaches of the Caribbean, the Great Barrier Reef and the oriental delights of southeast Asia is enough to give even the most settled individual a hint of itchy feet.

But while travelling to one specific destination is an exciting and eye-opening experience there is something special about travelling to a variety of destinations. It not only provides the traveller with a wealth of experience but it is like a huge international embrace: throwing your arms around the world to try and come to a better understanding about the different cultures and religions which inhabit the earth.

Of course, travelling can be just as enjoyable if you visit only one place. But if you feel it in your blood to go as far and as wide as you can then your wanderlust will probably never be satisfied until you give it a go. Even if you do not complete the round the world circuit, and there is nothing to say that you have to, it at least gives you a starting point to aim for and plan around. Any type of travel needs a focus and a global tour is as good a target as there is.

While the goal of completing the round the world link is a good base on which to plan your travelling it is not something that should be stuck to rigidly. One of the benefits of travelling is that you can change your plans on the spur of the moment – consider your round the world mission as a very flexible creature. It takes determination, a single mindedness and, usually, a certain amount of time, to circumnavigate the globe, but it is something that most travellers will have thought of at some time.

SOME ROUND THE WORLD TRAVELLERS

Just as with walking from John O'Groats to Land's End people have travelled round the world in a variety of weird and wonderful ways, and sometimes by a combination of weird and wonderful methods of transport.

Some people, such as Phileas Fogg, have travelled round the world through the pages of literature. Others, such as Michael Palin who tried to emulate Fogg's exploits, chose to do it in considerable comfort and in the very public glare of the television cameras. Methods of transport have differed too, with the likes of Sir Francis Chichester opting for a nautical round the world trip. Other, less celebrated, individuals have undertaken their travels on bicycles, on foot, by hot air balloon and even by a microlight aircraft.

The above examples only serve to show that the possibilities for travelling round the world are only as limited as someone's imagination – discard all your preconceptions and start thinking about your travels from a global viewpoint.

THE NEEDS OF THE ROUND THE WORLD TRAVELLER

Due to advances in modes of transport, health care and equipment the days of world travel being major expeditions have long gone. With a little planning anyone can undertake an extended period of travel and once you are on the road you will soon realise that in many cases the less you have with you then the easier it is to travel.

Personal qualities are just as important for travellers as malaria tablets, plane tickets and backpacks. An open mind, a sense of humour, bucket-loads of patience and an international outlook are indispensable for the traveller and, as with a famous credit card, travellers should not 'leave home without it'.

THE GLOBAL BENEFITS OF WORLD TRAVEL

How long is a piece of string? It is hard to assess the benefits from people of different nationalities and cultures mixing and learning from each other. However, for this process to work properly the traveller has to possess a certain amount of humility and be prepared to learn from others and not force their own opinions and way of doing things onto other people. As soon as you leave home you are on unfamiliar territory and the role of the visitor should never be forgotten.

If travellers adopt an understanding and receptive manner then they will be more fully accepted in the places they visit and the two-way process of international communication can begin.

This may sound like commonsense but it is surprising how many people have an intransigent attitude when they are abroad – they think they are trying to help the locals but in fact they are doing them a great disservice, as a traveller in Pakistan explains:

'While I was walking through Lahore I saw a group of teenagers playing cricket in the corner of a park. It was a fairly disorganised affair, with no order to who was batting or bowling. Despite this the kids were having a great time and there were frequent shrieks of laughter. Halfway through the game an English traveller stopped to watch and he was invited to join in. After about fifteen minutes he couldn't stand the disorganisation any longer and suggested that two teams were created. The local boys were too polite to object and although the game became a lot more organised the laughter became conspicuous by its absence.'

The missionaries in Africa in the 19th century are a good example of how good intentions can be misplaced. Travellers should remember that they are pupils in the international scene and not teachers.

THE DRAWBACKS OF WORLD TRAVEL

Obviously if you are away from home for several months there will be some drawbacks:

- Homesickness. This is an occupational hazard for any traveller, but then you can be homesick if you are only 10 miles from home. One good way to overcome homesickness is to ask yourself if you would rather give up your travels and return home. The answer is invariably no and sometimes you have to keep reminding yourself that you are involved in a once in a lifetime experience. Keeping in touch with people at home at regular intervals can reassure you that nothing too dramatic is happening in your absence.

- Missing out on friends/jobs and careers. Travellers can sometimes feel cut off and this can generate a feeling that they are being forgotten about. Although it is difficult to feel part of your home life when you are thousands of miles away it is amazing how easy it is to catch up when you get home. A few days at home and a night or two in the pub with your friends and you, and they, will feel as if you have never been away. As for jobs, the situation is so difficult at the moment that an example of world travel on your CV will only be an advantage and any forward looking employer will appreciate this.

THE INDIVIDUAL BENEFITS

This is best summed up by Calum Thomson who spent a year travelling once he finished college.

'I had a reasonably conventional upbringing – school, exams and then onto college. Everyone presumed that I would then progress into a

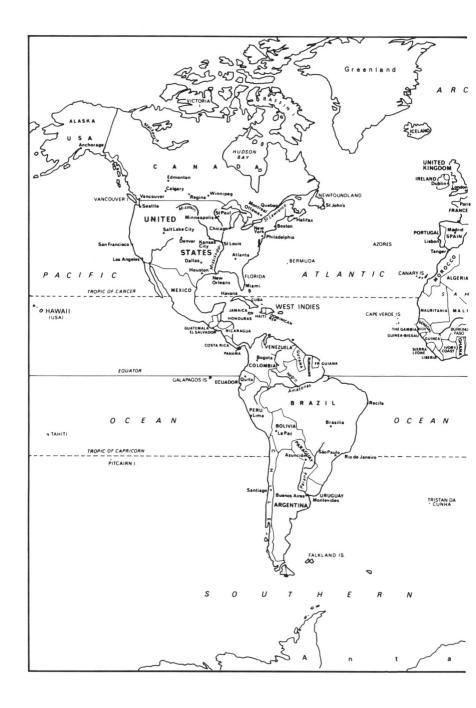

Fig 1. Outline map of the world.

job, get married, buy a house and then shuffle off into the suburban sunset. Although this sounded reasonable enough there was something at the back of my mind that kept nagging away at me, goading me into see what else there is on this planet of ours. So I sold everything I had and worked flat out for a year to earn enough money for my trip.

'I bought a round-the-world air ticket and flew to Bangkok in Thailand. For the next three months I travelled around southeast Asia and China, using local transport and trying to find as many remote places as possible. I tried to keep away from cities and large towns because I had experienced enough of them at home. My next stop was in Australia and I worked my way across the country and also spent a few weeks in New Zealand. I then managed to get a lift on a yacht to Tahiti and from there I was able to use my RTW ticket to hop to Hawaii and then Los Angeles. This opened up America and Canada and I bought a beat-up car and drove through North America for the rest of the trip.

'It is hard to quantify what I got from the trip but I can honestly say I will never be the same again. The main benefit was that it has put everything in perspective – after seeing people in a Chinese village working 12 hours a day just to feed their family it is a bit difficult to get upset when a pint of beer goes up in price. It has also made me realise how small Britain is, both in terms of size and attitudes – perhaps everyone should have a period of world travel.

'Since I have come home I feel a lot more relaxed and comfortable with myself. I have also got a job with a company whose managing director did exactly the same as me when he was in his twenties, so it has had a material benefit too. I would honestly recommend it to anyone who has ever wondered what happens on the other side of the fence.'

2
Smoothing Out Official Matters

Anyone who travels round the world will notch thousands of miles under their globetrotting belt. However, there are a number of areas to look at before you set off:

- passport
- visas
- insurance
- health
- money

If any of these items are neglected you may find your plans are grounded before you even get to the runway.

HOW DO I APPLY FOR A PASSPORT?

Everyone knows you need a passport to travel overseas but it is surprising how many people leave it to the last minute to apply for one, or suddenly realise that it will run out halfway through their trip. Even if your passport is valid until after your proposed date of return it may be necessary to apply for a new one: some countries, including Australia and Thailand, require a passport to be valid for a period of time beyond the length of your intended stay. This varies from three to six months but to be on the safe side it is best to have twelve months leeway just to prevent any unnecessary hassle.

It is a good idea to memorise your passport number – it will save you a lot of time while filling in visa forms and the such like.

Passport offices in the UK

London Passport Office, Clive House, 70 Petty France, London SW1H 9HD. Tel: (0171) 279 3434. This office is for personal callers only – applications from Greater London and Middlesex should be sent to the Glasgow Office.

Liverpool Passport Office, 5th Floor, India Buildings, Water Street, Liverpool L2 0QZ. Tel: (0151) 237 3010.

Newport Passport Office, Olympia House, Upper Dock Street, Newport, Gwent NP9 1XA. Tel: (01633) 244500.

Peterborough Passport Office, Aragon Court, Northminster Road, Peterborough, Cambs PE1 1QG. Tel: (01733) 894445.

Glasgow Passport Office, 3 Northgate, 96 Milton Street, Cowcaddens, Glasgow G4 0BT. Tel: (0141) 332 0271.

Belfast Passport Office, Hampton House, 47-53 High Street, Belfast BT1 2QS. Tel: (01232) 232371.

Passport application forms are available from Post Offices and larger travel agents. The fee for a standard 32 page passport is £18; for the larger 48 page version it is £27. Both are valid for 10 years.

Make sure you apply for your passport in good time – months, rather than weeks, before your departure. Processing of your application will take longer over Christmas and the height of summer.

CHECKING OUT VISA REQUIREMENTS

Visas are the magic stamps in your passport which allow you to enter and leave foreign countries. Although you do not need them for EU member states (and in some instances the USA and certain Eastern Bloc countries) you will for most other countries. Visas invariably cost money so you will have to include this in your travel budget.

Where do I get them?

In Britain visas are issued from foreign embassies, most of which are located in London. Visas can also be obtained as you are travelling but you must have one before you can enter a particular country. It is often tempting to try and get as many visas as possible before you begin your travels, but in reality it is more effective to pick them up as you go along. One of the main reasons for this is that most visas are for a specific period of time and so you would have to follow a strict timetable if you already have several visas. If you are planning to get visas as you travel then make sure that you have at least three dozen passport-sized photographs of yourself – the visa monster devours photos with alacrity.

CHOOSING THE RIGHT INSURANCE

Insurance may seem like an expensive luxury, but it is not – it is an absolute necessity, as was shown by a couple who went on holiday to America. The woman was seven months pregnant but she unexpectedly had the baby prematurely while on holiday. The hospital bill came to £80,000 and her husband said that the couple of hundred pounds they paid on insurance was the best investment they had ever made.

These are some areas you should have on your insurance policy:

Medical expenses

This is the most important part of your insurance policy and you should not set foot overseas if you do not have this. The range of cover varies but a minimum of £250,000 would be recommended while a sum of £2 million should be considered seriously, particularly if you are going to be travelling in North America where medical insurance can, quite literally, be bankrupting.

Personal accident

This allows for the payment of a lump sum to the policy holder in the event of an accident, such as the loss of a finger or serious disablement. The sum varies depending on the injury and most policies have set amounts.

Loss of baggage and money

It is a good idea to be insured against the loss of your belongings and your money.

Personal liability

This insures you against sums payable if someone decides to sue you for injury, loss or damage to other people or their property.

Cancellation

If the policy holder has to cancel a journey for a genuine reason such as ill health then any money already paid as a deposit will be insured.

Strikes and delays

This will mean you are compensated if your journey (from Britain) is delayed or affected by a strike.

Travel insurance companies

Trailfinders Travel Centre, 42-50 Earls Court Road, London W8 6EJ. Provide excellent longterm travel insurance, including up to £2 million worth of medical cover. From £436 for 12 months cover.

Automobile Association, Fanum House, Leicester Square, London W1. Tel: (0345) 500600. Provide cover for overland travel abroad.

Campbell Irvine Ltd, 48 Earls Court Road, Kensington, London W8 6EJ. Tel: (0171) 937 6981. Offer personal and vehicle insurance.

Hanover Insurance Brokers, 80-86 Westow Street, Upper Norwood SE19 3AQ. Tel: (0181) 771 8844. Offer personal and extensive vehicle insurance.

International Student Insurance Service. Available from Endsleigh Insurance Services Ltd, Endsleigh House, Ambrose Street, Cheltenham Spa, Gloucester GL50 3NR. Good all-round travel insurance policies at very competitive prices.

WEXAS International, 45-49 Brompton Road, London SW3 1DE. Tel: (0171) 589 0500. Offer members comprehensive insurance at very competitive prices.

LOOKING AFTER YOUR HEALTH

Health, or to be precise ill-health, is one of the biggest worries for any world traveller. There are a number of actions that a traveller should take before setting foot on foreign soil – such as certain vaccinations that are essential – and a number of areas which they should be aware of. One point to remember though: the majority of people who travel round the world are not struck down by life-threatening diseases. People should be aware of the risks but there is no point in making yourself sick with worry before you even step out of your front door.

See Chapter 5 for in-depth coverage of how to take steps to stay healthy abroad.

HOW TO DEAL WITH MONEY MATTERS

Money seems to be a constant problem for most people and the traveller is not exempt from this. What you will have to decide before you go is:

1. In what form do I want to take my money?
2. Do I want to leave some at home and have it sent out to me?
3. How do I want to carry it while I am travelling?
4. Do I want to take a credit card?
5. Do I have a back-up if I lose all my money?

If you intend being overseas for a year, particularly if a large part of that time will be taken up with just travelling, you will need to take a substantial amount of money with you. This can be done in a number of forms:

Travellers cheques
Thomas Cook and American Express travellers cheques are the most widely accepted around the world, with the latter being the best in terms of fast replacements if your cheques are stolen. You should get your cheques in a variety of small and large denominations – if you need money for your last day in a country whose currency is worthless outside

its borders you do not want to have to cash a £50 travellers cheque. They should be in dollars or pounds sterling and make sure you leave a list of the numbers with a reliable contact at home. The safest way to carry large sums of money while travelling.

Cash

Every traveller should take some money in cash (approximately £100) – the American dollar is the most widely accepted currency abroad. This can be used if you are dealing in the black market (see below) or if you need to offer bribes, since hard currency is much sought after.

Credit cards

These are not only the traveller's flexible friend but sometimes their lifeline. If you have Visa and Access it is a good idea to take both since some outlets worldwide only take one or the other. An American Express card is also a valuable asset – if you can afford one. The important thing with credit cards is to use them for emergencies or the occasional luxury, and not rely on them for everyday expenses. If you do you will inevitably come across a country that has very few outlets for any credit cards, such as Pakistan. In order to pay off your credit cards you can leave some money in your bank at home and have a standing order to pay a specific sum each month or a direct debit to pay the whole amount due. The former may be the best idea – if you have to unexpectedly pay for an expensive item such as a flight there may not be enough in the bank to cover the total amount.

Using different methods

It is a good idea to spread your finances between different methods. A suggested combination could be (for every £1000): £600 in travellers cheques of different denominations; £100 in cash (dollars and sterling); £300 left in a bank at home to pay off credit card bills.

Another method of obtaining money is to leave a large lump sum in your bank at home and have it wired to you at various destinations where the bank has a contact branch. Obviously, you need a bank that has contacts around the world (Standard Chartered offer this type of service) but there are a number of drawbacks with this method:

- It can be very expensive – bank charges of £60 for £500 transferred are not unheard of.

- It can be time consuming – you may have to wait several days in one place while the transfer is being completed.

- It can be unpredictable – not all banks around the world are computerised and telexes have been known to get lost and money to have gone missing.

Carrying your money

You should treat your money in the same way as your passport and carry it on your person at all times. This may lead to a bulky package in your money belt but this is preferable to having it in a pocket or backpack.

Your money checklist

1. Have you spread your finances over a number of methods?

2. Have you left a list of your travellers cheque numbers with a contact at home?

3. Do you know where to go abroad to claim replacement travellers cheques if necessary? (American Express and Thomas Cook issue booklets with the addresses of their overseas branches and outlets.)

4. Have you left sufficient money at home to pay off any credit card bills, and is it a standing order or direct debit?

5. Is there a family member or friend who could send you emergency funds if you were destitute? (This can be done by telegraphic or mail transfer to a bank overseas. It can take several days.)

DO'S AND DONT'S BEFORE YOU GO

Do

- Make sure your passport is up to date – and valid for at least three months after your intended date of return.

- Make sure you have adequate insurance – organise it in good time before you leave and ensure that you are covered for the entire period you expect to be overseas.

- Have a contingency plan in case you spend more time overseas than you expected. Ask a relation or a friend to extend your insurance if possible – and leave them some money to pay for it.

- Go to your doctor and dentist before you leave. Check on any vaccinations that you need.

- Write to the embassies of the countries you intend to visit. They will be able to tell you the latest situation with regard to visas.

Don't

- Leave things to the last minute.

- Rely on the 'I'll buy it when I get there' philosophy. Invariably you will suffer from the 'Sorry we've just sold the last one' syndrome.

- Cut any corners as far as health is concerned – being ill abroad can not only cost you time and money, it could ultimately lead to you returning home.

SELF-ORGANISATION ROUTE

Question 1. Do I have a passport? Does it need to be renewed? How long will I have to renew it before I leave?

Question 2. Do I have health insurance? Does it provide cover for the worst possible scenario? Will someone at home have a copy of the policy?

Question 3. Have I checked on the medical requirements for the countries I will be visiting?

Question 4. Do I know if I will require any work permits or visas? Can I get them before I go? How long will they take?

Question 5. Do I have enough money? Do I have my money in travellers cheques? Have I left a copy of their numbers? Do I know how to claim a refund if they are lost or stolen? Have I a way of paying off my credit cards if I use them? Is there a way for money to be sent to me if I lose everything?

Question 6. Do I have a contact address in the country I am going to?

Question 7. Is there someone at home I can contact quickly in an emergency?

Question 8. Do I have a St Christopher and a rabbit's foot with me?

3
Planning Your Travel Arrangements

When considering the best way to get yourself round the world there are two types of travel to consider:

1. Long haul travel – for large distances in one go.
2. Short haul travel – for local travel once you get somewhere.

LONG HAUL TRAVEL

There are a number of methods of travelling long distances. Some people undertake the task on a unicycle or a hot-air balloon but for the sake of normality we will stick to the conventional choices of:

- air
- rail
- sea
- road

TRAVELLING BY AIR

Although air travel can be frustrating and uncomfortable it is undoubtedly the quickest way to get from A to B, particularly if B happens to be several hundred miles away. Airline seats, like every other commodity, are sold at a variety of prices for the same item and it is important to shop around for the best offers.

Where are the best places to buy tickets?

Bucket shops
In the 1970s 'bucket shops' – named after dubious activities on the US stock market in the 19th century – appeared in Britain, selling illegally discounted airline tickets. Although it is still theoretically against the law to sell discounted tickets in this way no action is ever taken by the government and it has become an accepted part of airline ticket sales.

Most bucket shops are located in London and they advertise regularly in the national press as well as *City Limits*, *TNT*, *Time Out*, and the

Standard. Although there is still a slight stigma of doubt attached to bucket shops the vast majority of them are highly reliable. But if you are booking a ticket through them make sure they are a member of the Association of British Travel Agents (ABTA), or licensed by the International Air Transport Association (IATA). An additional safe-guard of reliability is if they accept Access or Visa – these companies check their credibility very carefully before dealing with them.

The Air Travel Advisory Bureau (Tel: (0171) 636 5000) will provide you with telephone numbers of reputable bucket shops dealing with your desired destination.

Trailfinders
A wonderful organisation for the independent traveller – they offer a wide range of cheap flights to most parts of the world and will arrange your itinerary according to your needs. They also offer very reasonable travel insurance and can arrange visas for countries worldwide. Trailfinders have offices throughout the country:

42-50 Earls Court Road, Kensington, London W8 6EJ. Tel: (0171) 938 3366 (Longhaul).

194 Kensington High Street, Kensington, London W8 7RG. Tel: (0171) 938 3939 (Longhaul).

58 Deansgate, Manchester M3 2FF. Tel: (0161) 839 6969.

48 Corn Street, Bristol BS1 1HQ. Tel: (0117) 929 9000.

254-284 Sauchiehall Street, Glasgow G2 3EH. Tel: (0141) 353 2224.

Other good suppliers of cheap air tickets are Campus Travel whose head office is at 52 Grosvenor Gardens, London SW1W 0AG. Tel: (0171) 730 6525 and STA, 74 Old Brompton Road, London SW7 3LH. Tel: (0171) 937 9921.

High street travel agents
Since the appearance of bucket shops the major travel agents have cottoned on to the importance of discounted tickets. They now all offer various discounts on 'flight only' tickets, but they will invariably be higher than the bucket shops. Sometimes travel agents will quote you the first price that comes up on their computer. In some cases there will be other seats at lower prices so it is worth asking if this is the only price available.

For many people the advantage of a local travel agent outweighs the lower prices of the London bucket shops.

What is the best type of ticket?
Round the world (RTW)
In many ways these are ideal for the round the world traveller as they

offer good value, you can pick a route that goes completely round the world and you have the security of knowing that you have a ticket for your whole journey. Most of them are operated by two or three airlines teaming up for the relevant parts of the world. With some RTW tickets you can buy additional travel passes for travel within individual countries, such as America or Australia. However, certain points should be kept in mind before buying a round-the-world ticket.

- You have to keep travelling in the same direction as the one you started – you cannot backtrack.

- The tickets are usually valid for a year, so if you are planning to take longer then you may need to make additional arrangements.

- Once you have chosen your route there is not much flexibility to change your mind. If you decide to go to another country on a whim (as frequently happens when you are travelling) then you will have to pay for additional transport.

Having said this a round-the-world ticket should be seriously considered. Some examples of carriers, routes and prices are (prices are correct as of mid-1994):

- Singapore Airlines, Air New Zealand and Virgin Atlantic. London-Bombay-Singapore-Australia-New Zealand-Fiji-USA-London (from £862).

- Garuda Indonesia, Malaysia Airlines, Thai Airways, Cathay Pacific and United Airlines. London-Abu Dhabi-Kuala Lumpur-Indonesia-Bali-Australia-New Zealand-USA-London (from £885).

- KLM and Northwest Airlines. London-Amsterdam-Thailand-Australia-USA-London (from £734).

- Air France. London-Singapore-Indonesia-Australia-New Zealand-Tahiti-USA-London (from £1485).

- African Airways, Air New Zealand and Virgin Atlantic. London-South Africa-Australia-New Zealand-Fiji-Honolulu-USA-London (from £975).

- Aerolineas Argentinas and Qantas. London-Hong Kong-Australia-New Zealand-Argentina-Brazil-London (from £1237).

Trailfinders, Campus Travel and STA (see above) all offer good value RTW tickets. A good investment is also the *Round the World Air Guide* by Katie Wood and George McDonald (Fontana).

Most airlines will do their best to accommodate your itinerary but in general the more stops you want to make then the more expensive the ticket. In some cases, such as southeast Asia, it would be advisable to take one flight there and then make the rest of your way on local transport.

Apex/Super Apex (Advance Purchase Excursion)
One of the best options for the traveller looking for the best deal. It is the method whereby airlines offer officially discounted seats. There are certain restrictions with APEX tickets – they must be booked and paid for well in advance of departure, varying between seven days and a month, a minimum stay abroad is required and there are no stopovers allowed. However, these are minor considerations for the committed traveller with a relatively flexible agenda. They are well worth the reductions of up to sixty per cent.

Standby fares
Cheap seats on the day of departure – available mainly on routes to North America. Although the tickets can be bought three months before departure, it will depend on the availability on the day. A reasonable option if you can wait around until a seat becomes available.

Quality of airlines

Airlines around the world vary in terms of service, punctuality and flight times. For most independent travellers cost will be the main consideration and in this regard you should not be afraid to use less well-known airlines, such as some of the eastern European and Asian carriers. Particularly if it is a one-off then the low price will be well worth the few moments of discomfort you may experience. However, you may dispute this if you have just spent 40 hours, including numerous delays, getting to Australia.

Things to check with your ticket

When flying it is important to take a few simple steps to make sure you have been properly booked onto the flight:

- Ensure you confirm your ticket at least 72 hours before your departure date. This applies wherever you are flying from in the world.

- Ensure that your ticket has OK in the 'Status' box. This means the ticket has been confirmed. If the letters RQ appear then it means the flight has been requested but not confirmed. WL means you have been 'wait-listed'. OPEN indicates you have not yet decided when you want to travel.

- In Third World countries make sure you buy your ticket in person, not over the phone. Check and re-check your ticket: in some countries where there is no computerised system there is a tendency to over-book flights.

The pros and cons of air travel

Pros

- Quick – you can be in a foreign country in the time it would take to cross London in the rush-hour.

- Value for money – if you are prepared to be discriminating in your choices.

- Relatively safe – in 1990 air passengers worldwide made 1.3 billion flights. During that period there were 300 deaths in 12 jet airliner accidents. This means, on average, you would have to make 4.3 million flights before a fatality occurred. Compare this with the fact that in Britain, in 1990, 5000 people died in motoring accidents. However, some airlines have a worse safety record than others, with China and Russia having particularly poor records. In general, internal flights within a country are more prone to accidents than international ones.

Cons

- Uncomfortable – unless you can afford the luxury of flying First or Business Class, then aircraft seats are among some of the smallest ever designed. And as for the food...

- Disconcerting – being transported from Britain to somewhere on the other side of the world in a matter of hours can be unsettling both physically and emotionally. Time must be taken to overcome this almost instantaneous change.

- Loss of luggage – backpacks and suitcases have an unfortunate propensity for becoming detached from their owners during air travel. Although they are frequently reunited it is a good idea to carry all your valuables in your hand luggage.

TRAVELLING BY RAIL

Many travellers consider the train to be the ultimate form of travel, looking at it as an experience in itself as well as a means of getting from A to B. This may not be the case if you have to commute to work by train but for someone with time to spend it is one of the most exhilarating ways to get around. You only have to read Paul Theroux's *The Great Railway Bazaar* to be persuaded about the merits of rail travel.

For the long-haul traveller rail travel can be over-crowded, infuriatingly slow, and unhygienic – but it is ultimately one of the greatest experiences when travelling. The thing to remember is that you will have to shed all your previous notions about travelling by train.

Rail ticketing around the world

When buying a train ticket in most Third World countries (where rail travel is extremely cheap and therefore used widely) you will need initiative, patience and at times physical strength. Queuing takes place in something akin to an expanded rugby scrum and you may have to visit several ticket offices before you achieve your objective. Don't be afraid to use your elbows, otherwise you may never reach the ticket office. Even so, expect to spend at least two hours buying a ticket in a busy station.

It is a good idea to enlist local help when trying to buy rail tickets in countries like Peru, China and India. There is a strict procedure to follow and without local knowledge you may be totally lost. For instance, the task of getting a rail ticket in China is one that is akin to completing an army assault course blindfolded.

At smaller stations the hardest thing is sometimes galvanising the station master, as one traveller in India explains: 'While travelling from Amritsar to Jaipur I stopped off on the way at a small town. When I tried to continue my journey I had to contend with a station master who was more concerned with playing cards with his friends than issuing me with a ticket. I asked him half a dozen times during the course of a morning and when I eventually got my ticket the train had arrived and was on the verge of departing. As I ran after it, dozens of people on the roof (they are standard issue on Indian trains) cheered me on board.'

Timetabling

Dar-es-Salaam, in Tanzania, has one of the most impressive-looking stations in Africa. Unfortunately, it only has three or four trains leaving it every week. Because of this the best way to find out when the train is leaving is to go to the station and ask at the ticket office. In general, verbal information is preferable to written timetables, which can be hopelessly out of date. Make sure you ask a number of people – officials as well as fellow travellers.

Always try and get to the station well in advance of the departure time. This not only safeguards you against the possibility of the train leaving early but it will give you a chance to get ahead of the crowds that will be trying to cram themselves onto the train when it arrives.

Should I travel first, second or third?

Choosing which class to travel is a major consideration. Due to the low prices first class will be in reach of almost every traveller and on occasions this should be tried just for a little luxury. Even second class is of a high standard, particularly in ex-colonial countries where the old rolling stock is still in use. In Kenya, for example, second class compartments have your own name on the outside of the carriage, and beds and washing facilities inside. The dining car provides good quality food, served by waiters in white, starched jackets.

Third class is invariably very cheap, very crowded and can test the patience of even the most even-tempered traveller. Unless you are very hard-up you may prefer to keep your third class travel to a minimum.

Seeing different aspects of life
The great joy of rail travel is the people you meet, the sights you see and the feeling that you are moving through an area at a pace that is conducive to absorbing your surroundings. In countries such as India, the accepted Mecca of rail travel, you will see, hear and feel all aspects of humanity; from the teeming community that is an Indian station to the chai-sellers who descend on the trains, whenever they stop. You may find yourself being woken at 4am by an impromptu concert on board but join in, make the most of it and treat the train as an experience, not just a mode of transport.

Buying International Rail Tickets
Campus Travel, 52 Grosvenor Gardens, London SW1W 0AG, tel: (0171) 730 6525, offer a variety of rail ticket, some just for Europe but others that extend to Thailand, Malaysia, Singapore and the USA. An example of the prices are: Thailand, 21 days, £33; Singapore, 21 days, £37; USA, 15 day off-peak, $318.

The rail traveller's library
- Thomas Cook's Overseas Timetable, Thomas Cook Publications, PO Box 36, Thorpe Wood, Peterborough PE3 6SB; or BAS Overseas Publications, 45 Sheen Lane, London SW14 8LP – indispensable for the serious rail traveller outside Europe. (Also includes road and shipping services.)

- Thomas Cook's European Timetable, as above.

- The World Train Travel Guide 1994-95, Kuperard, 9 Hampstead, 224 Iverson Road, West Hampstead, London NW6 2HL. Tel: (0171) 372 4722.

- Newman's Indian Bradshaw – covers every passenger train on the 35,000 miles of India's rail network.

Classic railway journeys to consider

There are several glamorous, and expensive, tours available around the world but sometimes the ordinary passenger trains are better value for money:

- The Trans Siberian Express – desolate, but a must for the enthusiast.

- The Indian-Pacific – Sydney to Perth, across the Nullabor desert.

- Central Railway of Peru – rises to 15,500 feet above sea level, the highest point in the world reached by a passenger train. Oxygen masks available on request.

- Nairobi to Mombasa – short but sweet. Travel by day to catch a view of the game at the side of the track.

- Anywhere in India.

Pros and cons of rail travel

Pros
- Cheap if you travel on the right trains in the right countries
- Easy pace of travel
- Good way to meet people

Cons
- Buying tickets can be a hassle
- Possibility of theft of luggage
- Can be frustatingly slow if you are in a hurry. (There are exceptions to this of course, most notably in Japan.)

TRAVELLING BY SEA

Commercial shipping

Unfortunately for the intrepid voyager, the days of working a passage on commercial shipping sailing under a British flag have all but passed. Union and nautical regulations mean that unless you are a registered seafarer (*ie* a qualified Merchant Seaperson) you will not find casual employment and a ride over the ocean waves with a British registered ship.

However, all is not lost. Various nations do still allow their shipping lines to take on unqualified, casual workers. These include ships flying the flags of Panama, Liberia, Liechtenstein and several Far East countries. This may not be ideal for transport from Britain but it could be utilised once you are in other parts of the world. Cargo vessels go regularly between the Americas and the Antipodes and employment is available occasionally. A direct approach is best: find the captain of a commercial ship (medium sized cargo ships are best) and ask him if he requires any working passengers.

If you do obtain a job on a commercial line you will work long hours and do all the dirty jobs going. You will need to have full travel insurance for the duration of the voyage, a visa for the country you are heading to, a certificate of good health including proof of relevant inoculations and a cash bond of approximately £200.

One company that has taken on working passengers in the past is Columbus Maritime Services, Ost-West Strasse 59, 2000 Hamburg 11, Germany.

Freighter

One way of travelling by ship is to pay for a cabin on a freighter. Despite the fact that this is an expensive way to travel it is proving increasingly popular, particularly with the over 60s, and some companies have long waiting lists. For the independent traveller with limited means it may not be the most practical mode of transport.

A list of companies carrying passengers, and all other matters nautical, can be found in the *ABC Passenger Shipping Guide*, ABC International, Church Street, Dunstable, Bedfordshire. Tel: (01582) 600111.

Yachting

Travelling on a private yacht is a definite possibility if you are in the right area. Yachtsmen and women are not subject to the same strict regulations as commercial shipping and they can, and do, take on passengers cum general dogsbodies. This may involve painting the deck while sailing through the South Sea Islands or keeping watch on a voyage to the Caribbean – wherever there are yachts on the water there will be people looking for crew. Because of this it is best to make some simple preparations before you commit yourself to a trip under sail:

1. Find out if you actually enjoy sailing. If you do not have much experience get some before you go. Find the nearest yachting club to you and ask if you can join them for a day or two.

2. Undertake some basic nautical training: learn how to tie a sheepshank, know your port from your starboard and familiarise yourself with the various shipping signs and terminology. Even with this rudimentary information you will be an asset to the skipper of a yacht rather than a mere passenger.

3. Take a short sailing course. This is not essential but could be invaluable to you. The Royal Yachting Association, Romsey Road, Eastleigh, Hampshire SO5 4YA, offer courses at their centres

around the country. The grade of Competent Crew can be reached in approximately a week and costs in the region of £220.

4. Buy suitable waterproofs.

With this preparation you can feel reasonably confident of finding a yacht skipper somewhere in the world to take you on. You can either do this by looking for 'Crew wanted' notices in 'yachtie' areas or else there are various organisations who specialise in finding crew for yachts:

Cruising Association Crewing Service, Ivory House, St Katharine Dock, London E1 9AT. Tel: (0171) 537 2828. £18 registration fee for the crewing service.

Club Crewit, PO Box 34, Wokingham, Berks RG11 4PW. Tel: (01734) 731616. £30 registration fee but for this you receive a high quality service that provides crew to and from anywhere in the world.

Pros and cons of going by sea
Pros

- An entirely new environment compared with travel on firm ground.

- Opportunities for casual employment on private boats.

- A challenging way to travel – you will learn a lot more than if you were sitting on a plane for a few hours.

- A wide range of 'characters' inhabit the seafaring world.

Cons

- Slow and occasionally erratic form of transport.

- There is nowhere to hide on a ship or yacht if you do not get on with your fellow crew members.

- Single women should be very careful because sometimes they are taken on as crew for all the wrong reasons. Establish the ground rules before accepting an offer of a place on board.

- Piracy is a very real threat in some parts of the world, most particularly the South China Sea and, increasingly, areas of the Caribbean.

- Seasickness is one of the worst feelings known to mankind.

TRAVELLING BY ROAD

For the traveller who is keen on motorised transport by road there are two options for longhaul travel:

- conventional car
- overland vehicle

Going by car

Some people swear by the joys of having a car abroad, others would not touch it with a ten foot dipstick. As a rule, if you are not a driving enthusiast when you are at home then it is not a good time to start when you go abroad.

If you are a confirmed motor-addict then you could take a car from Britain. However, this is perhaps not the best idea unless you are driving to Europe. A better plan, particularly if you are in North America or in the Antipodes, is to buy a car when you get there. This can be done relatively cheaply and once you have finished your travels you can sell it and recoup some of your money. One of the great advantages of this is that you can arrange technicalities like insurance and tax on a local basis and not worry about the problems of crossing borders and the red-tape that this entails.

Using overland companies

A number of companies, such as Encounter Overland, Guerba and Exodus Expeditions, specialise in long-haul overland expeditions. These usually take place in converted Bedford trucks and the most popular routes are through Africa and Asia. These tours normally take several weeks and visas and injections are organised for you. Food is bought through a kitty system and cooked by one of the employees of the tour company.

Pros and cons of going by road

Pros

- Experienced staff who know all the best areas to visit and some of the dodges to make life run more smoothly.

- You get the benefits of an organised tour while still retaining the rough edges that distinguishes the traveller from the tourist.

- A happy band of travelling companions – hopefully!

Cons

- You will be travelling in cramped conditions with at least a dozen other people. If you fall out with any of them there is nowhere to hide. Some travellers have been known to 'jump truck' halfway through these tours and make their own way.

- It is a relatively expensive way to travel through these countries.

- You have to go where the truck takes you.

Overland on your own

Only the experienced off-road driver should consider an overland journey by car. Even if you have been driving in Britain for a long time this does not necessarily mean you could jump into a Land Rover and drive across the Sahara: some people are horrified by driving standards on the Continent but overland driving is an expedition rather than a Sunday afternoon outing.

If you do have an adventurous, motorised spirit you will have to buy a suitable vehicle. Your best bet would be a short wheelbase Land Rover, Toyota Land Cruiser or Land Rover Discovery. You will need to fill this with virtually every spare part imaginable and enough provisions for *twice* the length of your proposed trip.

An overland journey is not for the novice and even for the experienced off-road driver expert advice should be sought before leaving. The two most important things to remember are:

1. Make sure you have enough drinking water.
2. Never leave your vehicle if you break down.

For more detailed information on off-road driving consult chapter 5 of *The Traveller's Handbook* (WEXAS).

MAKING THE BEST OF LOCAL TRANSPORT

Once you get to your destination one of the best methods of getting around is local transport. This usually means buses, which are a wonderful way of meeting people (sometimes because they are sitting on your lap), getting around for next to nothing, and seeing a country as its inhabitants see it. However, a word of warning: newspapers in Third World countries frequently have headlines declaring 'Bus crashes into ravine – 34 killed, 76 injured'. This highlights the fact that it is not necessarily the safest form of transport and also that these vehicles tend to be slightly overloaded.

There is no way of assessing the safety potential of local buses – most of the vehicles are at least twenty years old and the drivers seem to have invariably been trained by Nigel Mansell. It is one instance of taking your life in your hands and hoping that it will not be you making the headlines the next morning.

As for catching local buses the best idea is to rely on local knowledge. Always check with the driver that the bus is going to the desired destination. Luggage is frequently stored on the roof so make sure that you have all your valuables about your person.

Other forms of local transport that should be used if possible are:

• Converted mini-buses. These have different names in different countries and operate in cities and also further afield. There is a constant competition to see how many people can be crammed into these vehicles so do not be surprised if you find yourself on the outside of the back door, hanging on for dear life.

- Rickshaws. These are generally bicycle-powered or motorised these days.

- Tuk-tuks. A large, covered seat with a motorbike attached. Not good for the life expectancy.

- Ferries. Tend to be grossly overloaded too.

- Tongas. Down-to-earth, horse-drawn carriages.

Hitchhiking

Most people will turn to hitchhiking at some stage of their time abroad. In developed countries it is best to look clean and fresh (even if you do not feel it), hitch in small numbers (but preferably not alone), stay away from other hitchers, and do not hitch in towns as the police may take a dim view of this.

In Third World countries hitching is a slightly different ball-game. Motor vehicles are often at a premium and it is a much more accepted fashion of general transport than in the West. In some countries, such as El Salvador where the public transport system has virtually disappeared, it has all but replaced the public buses and equivalent fares are expected from hitchers. This is true for most Third World countries – do not be surprised, or offended, if you are asked for money for your lift. This is just the accepted norm and the price will probably be nominal – but make sure you agree on it before you get in.

Although there are some horror stories about hitching the risks can be lessened greatly:

Don't – accept a lift from anyone who is obviously drunk or high on drugs.
  – hitch after dark.
  – hitch alone if you are a woman – unfortunately this is a problem all over the world.
Do – find out the correct hitching sign for the country you are in.
  – offer to pay for a lift if this is expected.
  – be wary of any offers of accommodation. But do not be afraid to accept if they seem genuine.

Travelling successfully with children

Some people say that travelling with children is an invigorating experience while others claim it would be easier to travel with a poisonous snake. A traveller in Nepal summed up the problem of attitudes when travelling with children:

'At the border post from India there was a charge for entering into Nepal. The couple in front of me had a five-year-old boy with them and they were told that they would have to pay for him too. The woman pointed out that under-fives were free. The official agreed with this but explained, perfectly reasonably, that the child was over five. The woman became incredibly indignant and started abusing the official. All through this the child in question stood quietly in a corner, making no fuss. Cases such as this lead me to believe that it is the adults that are the problem and not the children.'

Points to remember if you are considering travelling with children are:

- You have responsibilities for another person, not just yourself – always have a contingency plan for lost children etc.

- You will need to take things more slowly.

- You will have to be patient and always offer explanations for what is going on.

- You will need to take different equipment – nappies, toys etc.

- You will have to be doubly conscious of health hazards.

- You will have to be prepared for prejudice in restaurants, on transport and virtually any other place where people can become impatient.

- You will have to plan everything in about ten times greater detail.

GLOBETROTTING FOR THE DISABLED

It is impossible to set down guidelines for every disability as far as travel is concerned. The important point to remember is that disabled people do travel, and travel very successfully.

Useful organisations and publications dealing with travel and the disabled include:

The Royal Association for Disability and Rehabilitation (RADAR), 250 City Road, London EC1V 8AS. Tel: (0171) 250 3222. They produce a number of publications related to travel for the disabled.

Holiday Care Service, 2 Old Bank Chambers, Station Road, Horley, Surrey RH6 9HW. Tel: (01293) 784535.

Airline Users' Committee, 2nd Floor, Kingsway House, Kingsway, London WC2B 6QX. They produce a booklet called *Care in the Air*.

Nothing Ventured (Rough Guides).

SUGGESTED ROUND THE WORLD ROUTES

- Bucket shop flight from London to India. Overland through India, Pakistan and Nepal. Flight to Thailand. Overland by coach through Malaysia and Singapore. Flight to Perth, Australia. Coach to Melbourne and then crew on a yacht to New Zealand. Flight to USA. Internal travel in North America and back to London.

- Round-the-World ticket to South Africa (side trip through East Africa and back), Australia, New Zealand, Fiji, Argentina (side trip through South America and up to Central America), back to London.

- Overland from Britain to Morocco. Overland by local transport to West Africa. Cheap flight to USA and then overland to the Caribbean. Island hopping, finishing in Central America. Work a passage on a boat down South America. Flight from Argentina to Australia. Boat from Darwin to Bali and then overland through Asia, back to Europe.

- Old whisky barrel from London across the Atlantic, tandem bicycle across America and Canada, stowaway on a cruise liner to Tahiti, coconut raft to Australia, then back to London in a solar powered car. (The great thing about round the world travel is that everything is possible – almost.)

4
Deciding What to Take

If you are travelling for any length of time you will be like a snail for twelve months: everything you need will be on your back so it is important to choose carefully. Your list of equipment will fall into two categories:

- Necessities – clothes, footwear, backpack, sleeping bag, camping equipment and medical supplies.
- Luxuries – anything you can survive without.

CLOTHES

Your wardrobe will depend very much on where you are going. The important thing to remember is to take items relevant to your destination, not your present location – when you are in windswept Britain it is hard to imagine travelling through the scorching Australian outback but you have to ask yourself whether you will really need three pairs of wellies and a golf umbrella?

In both cold and hot climates it is a good idea to have loose-fitting clothing – in cold to help trap body heat and in hot to aid the circulation of cool air.

You will need to pack clothes for two eventualities:

1. Everyday use
Hot climates
Underwear, T-shirts, singlets, cotton trousers (jeans are not the best type of trousers to take because they are heavy, not particularly warm and do not dry quickly), skirts, shorts, one sweater or sweatshirt, loose-fitting cotton shirts, swimwear.

Cold climates
Thermal underwear, fibre-pile jacket, balaclava, mittens, wool socks.

2. Clothes for special occasions
These may be needed for visits to embassies for visas, meeting

dignitaries or simply going to a posh restaurant. They should include –
smart trousers or skirt, tie, sports jacket (optional) and shoes. If your
smart clothes consist of black and whites you could use them if you
happen to find work in a bar or restaurant.

When you are crossing borders it helps to be reasonably smartly
dressed and turned out.

Should you get clothes there?

If you forget something you can usually buy it where you are going –
there is even an illicit Marks and Spencer in northern Pakistan. This has
two advantages:

1. It will probably be cheaper.
2. You will fit into your surroundings more easily if you wear clothes
   bought in the area.

However, this does not mean that you should rush out and kit
yourself out in local dress. This may look glamorous on the locals but it
tends to look pretentious and affected on visitors. Wear what feels
comfortable, and respect the local customs with regard to dress. Many
cultures do not like to see large expanses of bare flesh and you could
cause offence if you wear shorts, singlets and swimwear in certain
Muslim and African countries. Some countries have their own dress
codes which have been made law: Malawi women have to wear long
skirts and it is illegal for them to wear trousers. If in doubt, dress in a
conservative and respectful fashion.

What not to wear

Military-style clothing is not a good idea, particularly in politically
unstable areas (this usually includes countries that have been politically
unstable at any time during the last twenty years). Any khaki green or
camouflaged items should be left at home.

Specialist clothing

Rohan, 30 Maryland Road, Tongwell, Milton Keynes MK14 8HN.
Tel: (01908) 618888. And local stockists.

Berghaus, 34 Dean Street, Newcastle-upon-Tyne NE1 1PG. Tel:
(0191) 232 3561.

FOOTWEAR

These are invariably bulky items so you will have to choose carefully
and frugally. Some of the choices are:

- High quality, leather hiking boots. If you are expecting to do a lot of hillwalking or trekking these would be a good investment. However, they are heavy and difficult to fit into small places. Make sure you break them in first – this means more than just wearing them around the house for a few hours. Thick socks should be worn with them. Available from camping shops and outdoor specialists. £40 upwards.

- Lightweight, canvas walking shoes. Most travellers do a certain amount of walking. In all but the most rugged areas this type of shoe is ideal. They are light, dry quickly and can be squeezed into small spaces. Available from most camping shops and outdoor specialists. £25 upwards.

- Training shoes. Also good for walking in most situations and an asset if someone invites you for a game of squash or to run a marathon.

- Sandals/flip-flips (thongs in Australia). Ideal for the beach and similar situations. They are also good protection when taking showers in dirty bathrooms.

- Slippers. Some people find it comforting to take their own slippers with them. A luxury item.

SLEEPING BAG

Even if you intend travelling in tropical countries a sleeping bag is essential. Geography is no guarantee of temperature – Nairobi, at 6000 feet above sea-level, can get distinctly chilly at night in the winter. Even if you do not use a sleeping bag to sleep in all the time it can double as a ground sheet or even a pillow.

Similarly if you intend to stay in youth hostels or hotels you may think that a sleeping bag is superfluous. But what of the times you may have to sleep on public transport, at an airport, or on the floor of a mud hut?

There are two types of sleeping bag to choose from:

- Down – expensive, but excellent for cold climates. They have the added advantage of crushing down to a very small size. Do not cope well if they get wet though.

- Synthetic – cheaper but not as warm. Worth considering for hotter climates.

The warmest type of bag is the one that is self-contained, while the ones with zips can be used as blankets or groundsheets.

Sheet sleeping bags are useful for hot countries and for strange hotel beds that have dirty or insect-infested sheets.

Suppliers

Some of the best choices for sleeping bags are:

Berghaus, 34 Dean Street, Newcastle-upon-Tyne NE1 1PG. Tel: (0191) 232 3561.

Karrimor, 19 Avenue Parade, Accrington, Lancs BB5 6BR. Tel: (01254) 385911.

Vango, 70 East Hamilton Street, Ladyburn, Greenock PA15 2HB. Tel: (01475) 744122.

BACKPACKS

The method of carrying your life belongings is vital – it could be an exceptionally uncomfortable few months if you and your backpack are incompatible. The old-style, external-framed ruck-sacks are out; the new-style backpack-cum-carry bags are very much in. These are backpacks with conventional padded straps that can be zipped away if necessary, giving the pack the appearance of a soft suitcase. They also have a zip around the entire perimeter of the bag so access is not restricted to the top. The advantages of these are enormous:

- The straps do not flap around and get caught while being transported on planes, trains and automobiles.

- They can be used as carry bags when approaching border posts, thus giving the appearance of greater respectability.

- They can fit into spaces which rigid suitcases would not.

- They can be packed and unpacked with great speed – you do not have to unpack the whole pack to get to something at the bottom.

Buying checklist

When buying this type of pack make sure that you check three things:

1. The strength and quality of the zips. This is imperative because if a zip breaks you have no way of closing the pack.

2. Its waterproofness.

3. The straps. Make sure they are comfortable and that there is a hip strap which fastens around your waist. This will transfer sixty per cent of the weight to your legs.

The one slight disadvantage with this type of pack is that it is marginally less comfortable to carry than the current range of traditional backpacks. However, this is negligible when you consider the advantages.

When you are buying a pack resist the temptation to get the biggest one available – the bigger it is the more you will put in it. Also ensure that you can lock it. If it does not have locks on it then buy half a dozen small combination locks.

Additional bags

To save carrying a backpack around when sightseeing, going to the beach, or shopping, most people take a second, smaller bag with them. This is usually in the form of:

- a daypack – a smaller version of the above type of backpack
- a duffle bag
- a shoulder bag.

As with a backpack make sure you can lock your bag.

Note: Thieves are constantly on the look-out for daypacks and shoulder bags to snatch, so do not carry valuables such as cameras in them.

All good camping shops, or YHA Adventure Shops, will have a wide range of backpacks and daypacks. Some of the top manufacturers are:

Berghaus, 34 Dean Street, Newcastle-upon-Tyne NE1 1PG. Tel: (0191) 232 3561.

Karrimor, 19 Avenue Parade, Accrington, Lancs BB5 6PR. Tel: (01254) 385911.

Vango, 70 East Hamilton Street, Ladyburn, Greenock PA15 2HB. Tel: (01475) 744122.

It is a good investment to pay the money for a quality backpack – it will be your companion for a long time hopefully.

CAMPING EQUIPMENT

For the experienced camper the idea of taking a tent abroad is a good option. For the novice it is a better idea to stick to the proliferation of youth hostels, lodging houses and cheap hotels which you will come across.

If you are going to camp – and bear in mind a tent is a bulky and relatively heavy item to carry around the world – you will have to look at a number of questions:

1. Are there campsites where I am going and if so where are they?

2. Will I be camping at high altitude or sea-level?

3. What type of insects/wild animals are there in the area in which I intend to camp?

4. Will I be camping all the time or only occasionally?

5. Will I be camping on my own or with others?

6. What types of weather can I expect?

The type of tent used will depend on the answers to these questions. Ultimately you will want something that is both strong and light.

Suppliers

Three companies who specialise in a wide range of tents are:

Vango, 70 East Hamilton Street, Ladyburn, Greenock PA15 2HB. Tel: (01475) 744122.

Tent and Tarpaulin Manufacturing Company, 101-103 Brixton Hill, London SW2 1AA. Tel: (0181) 674 0121.

Lichfield, John James Hawley Ltd, Lichfield Road, Walsall WS4 2DH. Tel: (01922) 25641.

They will be able to tell you the nearest stockist in your area.

OTHER NECESSITIES

- Wash bag – soap, shampoo, toothpaste, toothbrush, shaving items (if required), sanitary protection (if required), hair brush.
- Medical bag (see Health).
- Towel – can also double as a pillow, cushion or blanket.
- Travel pillow – one of the most under-estimated travel aids known to man. Surprisingly indispensable for the independent traveller.
- Torch and batteries.
- Compass.
- Whistle.
- Toilet paper.
- Padlock.
- Maps. Make sure you buy these before you go. Some guidebooks have sufficient maps.
- Guidebooks.
- Personal reading. Do not over-load yourself with reading material, but take at least one of your favourite books that you can read over and over again. Books are a good item to swap with fellow travellers.
- Writing material and notebook.
- Swiss Army Knife.

- Candles.
- Small sewing kit.
- Hat – wide-brimmed for hot climates, woollen for cold.
- 'Grippa' bags - small resealable bags for keeping passports and such like dry and clean.
- String and cord.
- Matches.
- Mosquito net.
- Mosquito coils.
- Stock of presents. These can consist of a variety of small items such as postcards, stickers, badges, biros and disposable cigarette lighters.
- Elastic bands.
- Safety pins.

LUXURY ITEMS

Everyone has different ideas about what is a necessity and what is a luxury but if you think you can happily survive without something then it is a luxury. This was illustrated when Colin Smillie from Aberdeen set off on a global trip with one of his friends:

'I looked through his bag and started taking out bottles of aftershave, three ties, a pair of cuff links and his favourite beer tankard. When I asked him why he had packed them he just shrugged and said, 'just in case'. He ended up leaving with about half of what he started with.'

Examples

Some items that can be considered luxuries are:

- Camera – some people cannot travel without one but it is not strictly necessary and it can even be a disadvantage as thieves will be attracted by an expensive camera.
- Waterproofs – may be considered a necessity depending on where you are travelling.
- Hair drier – some people cannot travel without them.
- Adaptor – may be necessary for electrical items.
- Cassette player or Walkman.
- Dental floss – can double as string or thread in an emergency.
- Sleeping roll – can be bulky and it may be better to get used to sleeping on the ground.
- Travel iron.
- Photographs – good for reminding yourself of home and also for showing to people you meet.
- Perfume/Aftershave.

HOW TO PACK WITH MAXIMUM EFFICIENCY

Over-packing is easy to do and you have to be practical and fairly ruthless when you are packing for your travels. Try following these basic steps:

1. Place all items to pack in the middle of the floor.

2. Discard everything that you are taking on the off-chance – will you really need four bottles of aftershave or perfume?

3. Get a friend to go through the pile and see if they can see any superfluous items.

4. See if it will all fit in your pack.

5. If it does not fit – return to 1.

6. If you cannot lift your pack – return to 1.

7. Continue until you have a reasonably weighted pack with which you would feel happy walking long distances if necessary.

8. Do not fill your pack to bursting – you may want to add items as you are travelling.

The schools of thought on the physical process of packing consist of the 'rollers' and the 'folders'. For no particular scientific reason the best method seems to be a combination of the two: some items of clothing are better rolled, while others, such as towels, seem to expand to enormous size with this method and are better lain flat. However you decide to pack, experiment before you leave and find out what is best for you. As with Christmas shopping it is best not to do this at the last minute, but in reality most people do.

CHECKLIST

1. Decide if you will be camping or not.
2. Buy equipment relative to the areas you will be visiting.
3. Make sure your pack is lockable.
4. Make sure you have good quality zips on your pack.
5. Take a sleeping bag.
6. Take one set of smart clothing.
7. Be prepared to buy clothes when you arrive.
8. Pack with your destination in mind.
9. Do not overpack.
10. Take one or two *small* personal luxuries.

Being ill at home is bad enough but it can be a misery if you are travelling. There are a daunting number of weird and not-so-wonderful diseases around the world and in light of this it is sometimes surprising that we go travelling at all. However, many of these illnesses can be guarded against and others can be avoided with a little luck and some careful planning. Being aware of what could happen to you is half the battle of avoiding it.

WHAT TO DO BEFORE YOU GO

There are some vaccinations that you **must** have before going to certain parts of the world and others that are strongly advised:

Required jabs
Yellow Fever
Required under international health regulations for parts of Africa and South America. Valid for ten years and must be received at least ten days before entering the country concerned. Should be given separately from other vaccines. You must obtain an International Certificate for Yellow Fever and it has to be administered at specifically-designated centres.

Cholera
Certain countries in Africa and Asia require a certificate for this but the numbers are declining and you will not be asked for one very often. Nevertheless you should get the vaccination and a certificate. Valid for six months and should be given at least six days before departure. One injection is sufficient although two are sometimes given.

It is a good idea to carry health certificates in your passport, as they are equally important.

Recommended jabs
Hepatitis A
A water-borne virus that occurs mainly in the tropics, particularly in

countries with poor sanitation. Immunisation is with one Gamma Globulin injection and gives up to six months protection. Some people are naturally immune to Hepatitis A so arrange for a blood test first. A Gamma Globulin DOES NOT spread AIDS.

Hepatitis B
Occurs in the tropics and countries bordering the Mediterranean. More serious than Hepatitis A and is transmitted through sexual contact and contaminated blood. Immunisation usually consists of three injections but it can be expensive and is usually used for health workers and such like. If you think you are going to an area where you are likely to be infected, for any reason, then this should be seriously considered.

Japanese B Encephalitis
A rare viral infection that occurs in rural areas of South East Asia and from the Indian sub-continent to Japan, Taiwan and Korea. Two injections give protection for approximately a year. Worth thinking about if you are going to be in these rural areas for prolonged periods of time.

Meningococcal Meningitis
Frequent epidemics in Sub-Sahara Africa, Northern India, Nepal and Saudi Arabia at the time of the Haj Pilgrimage. Epidemics do occur elsewhere, eg Egypt, Sudan and Kenya and if you are travelling to a country where there is an epidemic you would be advised to get this vaccination. It takes the form of one injection that lasts for three years.

Poliomyelitis (polio)
Occurs everywhere in the world and although most people in Britain will have been vaccinated against it you may need a booster. These should be every five years for travellers.

Rabies
Prevalent in rural Africa, Asia and South America. Vaccinations can be given before you go but these are generally reserved for people who will be working with animals. The best bet is to avoid contact with strange animals at all times, even domestic pets. Rabies can be transmitted to man by any contact of saliva with broken skin, the cornea or the lining of the nose or mouth. If you are bitten, or exposed in any other way, by an animal that you think may have rabies it is essential to get professional medical attention as quickly as possible as there is no known cure once the symptoms develop. You will need a course of vaccinations and possibly specific antiserum against rabies. If you have to take a considerable detour to get to suitable medical help then do not hesitate – do it.

Tetanus
Occurs everywhere and travellers should ensure that they have a booster every five years.

Typhoid
Transmitted through contaminated food and water and occurs everywhere except north-west Europe, North America, Australia and New Zealand. Administered in the form of two injections approximately four weeks apart. A booster is recommended every three years. A vaccination that all travellers should have.

Getting help before you go
Always consult your GP when you are travelling abroad, telling him/her all the countries you will be visiting. If you are in any doubt about your vaccination requirements contact:

Hospital for Tropical Diseases, 4 St Pancras Way, London NW1 0PE. Tel: (0171) 387 4411 or (0171) 388 8989/9600 (Travel clinic) or (0839) 337722 (Pre-recorded healthline).

Liverpool School of Tropical Medicine, Pembroke Place, Liverpool L3 5QA. Tel: (0151) 708 9893 (pre-travel advice and medical queries) or (0151) 709 2298 (Travel clinic).

East Birmingham Hospital, Birmingham. Tel: (0121) 766 661.

Ruchill Hospital, Glasgow. Tel: (0141) 946 7120.

Newcastle General Hospital, Newcastle. Tel: (0191) 273 8811.

Lodge Moor Hospital, Sheffield. Tel: (0114) 263 0222.

Southmead Hospital, Bristol. Tel: (0117) 950 5050.

City Hospital, Edinburgh. Tel: (0131) 447 1001.

Seacroft Hospital, Leeds. Tel: (0113) 264 8164.

Monsall Hospital, Manchester. Tel: (0161) 205 2393.

Churchill Hospital, Oxford. Tel: (01865) 741841.

Thomas Cook Vaccination Centre, 45 Berkeley Street, London W1A 1EB. Tel: (0171) 499 4000. Vaccinations and certificates provided.

COPING WITH EVERYDAY HEALTH HAZARDS

Jet lag
A much maligned and misunderstood concept. In medical terms it is called the upset of your circadian (around twenty-four hours) or diurnal (daytime) rhythms. To the layman this means that your body becomes disorientated as you fly through different time zones. It has been estimated that for every time zone you pass through you will need one day to adjust fully. So if you pass through six time zones it will take you six days to adapt. Westwards travel is usually not as bad as eastwards

but it can still have a marked effect.

Jet lag is a very real condition and not a figment of the travel world's imagination. The general symptoms are:

- disorientation
- fatigue
- disrupted sleeping patterns
- disrupted eating patterns
- impaired physical and mental performance.

There is no simple solution for jet lag – except to let your body readjust in its own time. For businessmen and such like this can be a problem but for the traveller with a bit more time on their hands it is worth taking it easy for a few days and coming to terms naturally with the change in your body time. There are weird and wonderful inventions available to combat jet lag, such as Bioclocks which tell you if you should be wearing sunglasses or not, but in this case patience is definitely a virtue.

Seasickness
You may get more serious illnesses while abroad but they will probably not feel worse than seasickness: to some people jumping overboard would be a pleasant alternative. (This type of sickness can also occur in cars and planes – in fact almost any form of motorised transport.) You can try to prevent it by:

- Remaining amidships as much as possible.

- Lying down and keeping your head still.

- Not looking at the sea – if possible keep your vision fixed on the horizon.

- Avoiding fatty foods and excessive alcohol before you travel.

Effective medicines
If all else fails turn to the medicine cabinet. The following have been shown to be effective, particularly if taken at least an hour before travel:

- Cyclizine – Marzine
- Diphenhydramine – Dramamine
- Meclozine – Bonamine, Postafine, Sealegs
- Promethazine – Avomine, Phenergan

If you suffer badly from seasickness, consult your GP before you travel.

Acclimatisation

Thanks to the wonders of air travel we can go from one extreme in climate to another in a matter of hours. This can be exhilarating for the mind – and disturbing for the body, particularly if you are going from a cold climate to a hot one. During acclimatisation three main changes will take place:

1. You will sweat more, at a lower temperature, and for a longer period of time.

2. Changes occur in your blood circulatory system which affect heat loss.

3. Your resting body temperature will fall.

The main result of this will be that you will lose large amounts of body salt and water. Normally this would make you thirsty and develop a taste for salt but since your body thinks it is still back in Britain it will not necessarily send you these signals for the first few days. It is therefore very important that you drink large amounts of water (a minimum of eight pints a day) and eat extra salt. You may not feel like doing this for the first few days but if you do not you will become dehydrated.

Various factors governing how quickly you will acclimatise are:

- Age – the young acclimatise faster.

- Fatigue – do not over-tire yourself.

- Dehydration – if you become dehydrated you will take longer to acclimatise. If your urine is a dark yellow it is a sign you are dehydrating.

- Weight – excess weight slows down acclimatisation.

- Sex – men usually acclimatise quicker than women.

Summary
- Drink at least eight pints of water a day.

- Add extra salt to your food or take salt tablets. This practice should be continued even after acclimatisation.

- Do not try and overdo it on the first few days.

- Wear loose clothing.

- Do not drink excessive amounts of alcohol – this will only hasten dehydration.

- Make sure you acclimatise properly – it can lead to other illnesses if you do not.

COMMON ILLNESSES

Diarrhoea

We have almost as many names for diarrhoea as the Eskimos have for snow (52). Call it what you will, Delhi Belly, Ho Chi Minhs or Tokyo Trots, you will almost certainly get it while you are abroad and it is very different from diarrhoea you may have had in Britain.

Diarrhoea can be caused by contaminated food or water, or it can just be the effect of a new environment, with new germs and bugs, on your system. A mild case will be irritating, with regular trips to the toilet, and a severe case will be totally debilitating – excruciating stomach cramps will be accompanied by an overwhelming, and constant, desire to go to the toilet. If you can, it is best to remain there for as long as it takes. Most cases of diarrhoea only last for three days and if the symptoms persist you may have something more serious so consult a doctor.

It is best to let diarrhoea work its way through your system but if you *have* to travel while you have a serious case it is advisable to take some medication:

- Codeine phosphate – highly effective
- Loperamide – Imodium or Arret
- Diphenoxylate – Lomotil

Most doctors do not recommend taking antibiotics for diarrhoea but if you are going to a very remote area you should enquire about this.

One important side-effect of diarrhoea is that you can become very dehydrated. To remedy this you should carry a sufficient supply of re-hydration powders – Dioralyte or Rehidrat. These can be dissolved in drinking water and will replace lost body fluids and salts.

There are several other diseases that can be caught from contaminated food or water. These include:

Typhoid and paratyphoid
Cholera
Dysentery – bacillary or amoebic
Brucellosis – milk-borne infection

To minimise the chances of catching any of these diseases you should follow a few simple rules:

Don't
Eat in fly infested restaurants.
Buy food or drink from street hawkers. (This is sometimes unavoidable and one of the pleasures of travelling – but you should be aware of the risks.)

Drink anything which contains ice cubes.
Eat food that has been cooked and left on display for a long period of time.

Do
Drink bottled water if possible.
Boil all drinking water or milk.
Use water purification tablets, such as Puritabs.
Peel all fruit.
Be wary of shellfish.
Be wary of ice-cream.

Bilharzia (Schistosomiasis)

One of the most common diseases in many parts of Africa, Asia, the Middle East and South America. It is passed to humans through snails in any contaminated water such as lakes, ponds, reservoirs and even private swimming pools which are supplied by a local stream. Any contact with contaminated water including swimming, wading or paddling can lead to infection. There are two strains of the disease, one of which causes blood in the urine and the other which causes blood-stained diarrhoea. It can take several months for the symptoms to develop and the best way to avoid it is not to swim in contaminated water. Even if the locals say the water is free from bilharzia you should be slight wary and ask the advice of a doctor or local health authority. Treatment of bilharzia has improved greatly over recent years and if you think you may have been infected you should consult a centre for tropical medicine.

Malaria

Malaria is a disease which is transmitted to man by the anopheline mosquito. There are four different varieties of the disease, occurring mainly in tropical regions. There are approximately 250 million cases a year. The disease usually takes the form of a cold stage, a hot stage and a profuse sweating accompanied by a fall in temperature. The cycle takes approximately twenty-four hours and is repeated every other day. It can also recur several days after the initial infection. Two points to remember are:

1. It can be a killer.
2. Steps can be taken to prevent malaria – although in recent years more resilient forms of malaria have been discovered in areas of south-east Asia such as Vietnam.

Effective precautions
The most effective way of preventing malaria is to stop mosquitos biting

you (the anopheline mosquito usually bites between dusk and dawn so this is the important time). This is easier said than done but you can take a few precautions:

- Make sure you are well covered with long trousers, or a long skirt, and a long-sleeved shirt.

- Use an effective insect repellent. Autan is recognised as one of the best, closely followed by Jungle Formula.

- Sleep under insect repellent-impregnated mosquito nets.

- Wear insect repellent-impregnated wristbands and headbands.

- Burning of mosquito coils.

The other way to protect yourself is to take antimalarial drugs while you are travelling. However, due to the different strains of malaria, and the fact that some of them have become resistant to the most common antimalarial drugs it is hard to generalise about the best courses to take.

It is currently agreed that the three most effective antimalarial drugs are:

- Proguanil
- Chloroquine
- Maloprim

These may be used in various combinations, depending on how malarious a certain area is. In many areas the malarious mosquitos have become resistant to chloroquine.

Before you travel to a malarious country it is essential to contact your GP and ask his advice about antimalarial drugs. You will probably be given two types to take – one once a week and the other daily. It may seem an obvious point, but make sure you follow the daily and weekly doses – some travellers save them up for several days and take them all at once, and express surprise when they catch malaria. If your GP is uncertain about the latest malaria guidelines you should consult MASTA (The Medical Advisory Service For Travellers Abroad), London School of Hygiene and Tropical Medicine, Keppel Street, London WC1E 7HI. Tel: (0171) 631 4408.

Other malaria hotlines are provided by PHLS Malaria Reference Laboratory:

- London (0171) 636 7921.
- Birmingham (0121) 772 4311.
- Glasgow (0141) 946 7120.
- Liverpool (0151) 708 9393.
- Oxford (01865) 225570.

Summary
- Find out what type of malaria exists in the area you will be visiting.
- Take expert medical advice with regard to your antimalarial drug requirements. If necessary seek a second opinion.
- Always take these as directed.
- Keep well covered in malarious areas during dusk and night.
- Use an effective insect repellent.
- Use an insecticidal spray in living areas.
- If you develop malaria seek prompt medical attention.

Other insect-borne diseases

Filariasis
Three forms, transmitted by mosquitoes, forest flies and gnats. Most at risk are agricultural workers or people on construction sites.

Kala Azar
A long-term fever which is transmitted by the tiny sandfly. Occurs mainly in areas of the southern Mediterranean. Insect repellente are essential in the battle against sandflies as they can get through mosquito-net mesh.

Sandfly fever and dengue fever
Similar to a severe case of flu. Take precautions as above.

Typanosomiasis (sleeping sickness)
A serious illness but now limited to rural areas of west, east and southern Africa.

SUN, SNOW AND ALTITUDE

Sunburn
Not to be underestimated. In these days of decreasing ozone layers and increasing number of skin cancers it is important to be careful in the sun. Resist the temptation to lie in the sun for hours on end when you first reach a hot country. Fifteen to twenty minutes is more than enough time to expose yourself to the sun if you are not accustomed to it. After this, build up gradually. If you overdo it you may suffer sunstroke, causing blistering of the skin, nausea, vomiting and a severe fever. In extreme cases it can lead to death.

For those who do not like frying in the sun it is advisable to wear a wide-brimmed hat, a shirt and apply a high factor sun cream. Extra care needs to be taken when swimming and if you burn easily it is worth using a sun-block cream which should prevent any burning.

Although it is nice to have a tan the sun should be treated with respect and some people prefer to remain 'pale and interesting'.

Prickly heat

An irritating skin rash which is caused by the blocking of the sweat glands. It is most likely to form on parts of your body where damp clothing presses against the skin, most notably the waist area, the groin, armpit, behind the knees and over the breast bone and the collar bone. You can try and prevent prickly heat by:

- Wearing loose-fitting clothing
- Avoiding man-made fibres and wearing cotton clothing
- Washing regularly with plain water.

If you do contract prickly heat (and it is a very common condition in hot climates) try not to scratch and apply calamine lotion or a dusting powder to the infected area, ensuring it is clean and dry first. To avoid infection of the rash Phisomed is effective as are after-shaves and body lotions.

Hypothermia

For travellers in cold climates this is an important consideration. It occurs when the body temperature falls below 35 degrees centigrade and can be caused by wind, cold and wet. Acute hypothermia victims tend to act in an unpredictable manner – they are listless, surly, shivering and uncoordinated. It is a serious condition and the victims should be given immediate treatment:

- Get them out of any wet clothing.
- Give them shelter.
- Try and warm them as quickly as possible – the best method is body-to-body contact, preferably inside a sleeping bag.
- Give them hot drinks.
- Do not administer alcohol – this only lowers the body temperature.

Altitude sickness

At points over 3,500 metres (11,500 feet) some people suffer from mountain sickness due to the high altitude. This usually takes the form of headaches, fatigue, dizziness, sickness and a rapid heartbeat. If, while climbing, you feel any of these symptoms you should descend to a lower altitude and rest until you make a natural recovery. Conventional pain-killers such as paracetamol can be taken to ease the symptoms.

A more serious form of altitude sickness is Acute Mountain Sickness, which can develop into either potentially fatal High Altitude Pulmonary Oedema or Cerebral Oedema. The symptoms are usually puffiness around the face, blue lips, bubbly breathing and pink sputum. If anyone begins to display these symptoms it is vital that you take them to a lower altitude as quickly as possible.

AIDS AND HIV

The spread of HIV (Human Immunodeficiency Virus) which leads to AIDS (Acquired Immunodeficiency Syndrome) throughout the world is of particular concern to travellers. HIV is contracted through:

- sexual contact – vaginal, anal or oral sex
- blood transfusions with contaminated blood
- injections with contaminated needles.

It is not contracted through:

- hugging or social kissing
- toilet seats
- mosquitoes
- swimming pools
- food
- eating utensils.

People may be infected with HIV for as long as ten years before it develops into full-blown AIDS, and during this period they may not even be aware of their condition. You cannot tell by looking at someone if they are infected as they will appear perfectly healthy.

The greatest chance travellers have of contracting HIV is through casual sexual encounters, particularly with prostitutes. In many countries you will be approached openly by prostitutes, but this group have a high incidence of HIV – it is claimed that all the prostitutes in Mombassa have HIV and it is thought that large numbers of those in Bangkok are infected. Official figures should always be taken with a pinch of salt since some governments, such as Thailand, will deny the existence of AIDS in order to protect their revenue from sex-tourism.

The best way to avoid HIV infection is to steer clear of prostitutes and casual sexual encounters: as yet there is no cure and a one-night stand could lead to a terminal illness.

If you do have casual sex men should always wear a condom and women should insist that their male partners do so. Also, you should have a medical check-up and blood test soon afterwards – if you are infected with HIV you could pass it unknowingly to any sexual partners you have in the future.

The chances of becoming infected with HIV through contaminated blood are decreasing due to improved screening processes around the world, but it is still a potentially dangerous situation. However, if you are in the position where you need a blood transfusion it is unlikely you will be in a fit state to make enquiries about the quality of blood which you are receiving. If you are travelling with other people one of the group should insist that only blood that has been screened is used. It is also important to know your own blood group – you may be needed to give blood for someone with the same as yours.

Reducing the risks

One way to cut down on the possible risks of injections is to take a set of your own sterile needles, syringes and suturing (stitching) equipment. These can be bought from:

MASTA (as above).

British Airways Travel Clinic, 156 Regent Street, London W1. Tel: (0171) 439 9584.

Safety and First Aid (SAFA), 59 Hill Street, Liverpool L8 5SA. Tel: (0151) 708 0397.

Travel Medical Centre Ltd, Charlotte Keel Health Centre, Seymour Road, Easton, Bristol BS5 0UA. Tel: (0117) 935 4447.

Make sure that these items are all clearly marked as First Aid and that you have a covering letter from your doctor stating why you are carrying them.

SNAKES AND SPIDERS

Snakes

As a rule snakes do not attack unless they feel challenged. Although only about twenty-five per cent of snakebites will be poisonous it is important to observe a few basic rules if someone is bitten by a snake:

1. DO NOT apply a tourniquet to the bite area.
2. Clean the infected area and cover it with a clean cloth.
3. Immobilise the limb with a splint.
4. DO NOT cut or suck the wound.
5. Give paracetamol but not aspirin – this may cause bleeding from the stomach.
6. If the snake has been killed place it in a plastic bag to help the doctor administer the correct anti-venom.

One side-effect of a snakebite is that the victim may be suffering from shock.

Sea-snakes are one of the most poisonous varieties of snake but they usually only inhabit deep water. In northern Australia in the summer beaches are provided with netted areas to allow swimmers protection from stingers (poisonous jellyfish) and occasionally sea-snakes.

Spiders

Many of the world's most poisonous spiders inhabit Australia, most notably the redback and the funnel-web. You can lower the risk of a spider (or scorpion) bite by:

- Shaking out shoes and boots first thing in the morning.
- Checking under toilet seats and around the rim of the toilet.
- Having reasonable protection around your ankles when walking in a spider-friendly environment.

If you are bitten by a spider there will be an anti-venom available, but you will have to get to a doctor fast.

SUGGESTED MEDICAL BAG

Selection of plasters and bandages (with a continuous roll)   ____
Elasticated bandages of various sizes   ____
Paracetamol   ____
General antibiotic – tetracycline   ____
Anti-malaria tablets   ____
Diarrhoea treatment – Imodium   ____
Rehydration sachets – Dioralyte, Rehydrat   ____
Anti-AIDS kit – needles, syringes, suturing material   ____
Condoms   ____
Travel sickness tablets – Dramamine, Phenergan   ____
Insect repellent – spray, gel, wipes or roll-on   ____
Insecticidal spray   ____
Anti-fungal cream – Canesten   ____
Anti-histamine cream   ____
Antiseptic cream   ____
Sun block   ____
Good quality sunglasses   ____
Water purification tablets   ____
Oil of cloves (for toothache)   ____
Multi-vitamins   ____
Dusting powder   ____
Indigestion tablets   ____
Throat lozenges   ____
Lip salve   ____
Cotton wool   ____

All medical items should be packed in a clearly marked First Aid box.

TEN GOLDEN RULES FOR STAYING HEALTHY

1. Get all relevant vaccinations before you go.
2. Take time to acclimatise properly.
3. Boil all drinking water and milk.
4. Do not eat uncooked or under-cooked meat or fish.
5. Avoid fly-infested restaurants if possible.
6. Do not have sex with prostitutes or inject drugs with contaminated needles.
7. Find out your anti-malarial requirements and take your pills as directed.
8. Wear several layers of loose-fitting clothing in cold climates – and avoid being in wet clothing for prolonged periods.
9. Only go swimming in bilharzia-free areas.
10. Have a full medical check-up when you return home.

YOUR PERSONAL SAFETY

There are a number of areas which travellers should be wary of when they are abroad. These include:

- black market
- conmen
- theft.

DEALING WITH THE BLACK MARKET

Black markets in foreign currency exist in less-developed countries around the world for two main reasons:

1. The governments set an unrealistically low exchange rate.
2. Locals want foreign currency (usually American dollars or pounds sterling) instead of local currency, which is useless outside their own country.

Some travellers believe it is morally wrong to contribute to the black market but these are greatly out-numbered by those who see it as an acceptable part of life abroad. Most travellers do change at least some of their money in this way and it is a two-way process: the locals are happy with their foreign currency and the traveller has more local currency to spend.

Currency declaration forms

To try and deter black-marketeers some governments, particularly in Africa and South America, insist that all travellers fill in a currency declaration form when they enter the country. This will state how much foreign currency you have, in travellers cheques and cash. Whenever you want to change money into local currency this transaction will be marked on your currency form. Ideally, when you leave the country the amount you have changed and the amount you have left should add up to the original total on your currency form.

Changing money on the black market

If you want to change money on the black market you will have to have some money that has not appeared on your currency declaration form. The easiest way to do this is to keep some aside from the amount you declare. The purist may argue that this is smuggling but as long as you are not greedy and keep it to reasonably small amounts then it may be overlooked by the authorities if they find it. This happened to one traveller as he was leaving Tanzania: 'As I was crossing the border the guards searched my baggage and found $25 that I had not declared. I thought I might be in for an extended stay in a Tanzanian jail but instead the guard just peeled off $5, gave me back the rest and smiled as I entered the country.' How you choose to conceal the money is up to your own imagination but it is rare for body searches to take place. But be warned: some countries, including Ethiopia and Algeria, take currency forms very seriously.

Another way of getting around the question of the currency form is to change it before you cross a border. In some cases this will take considerable skill while there are some countries where the currency form consists of a handwritten piece of paper.

The ethics of the black market

Many countries are lenient towards currency declaration forms and the black market: they know it goes on and as long as it does not get out of hand they turn a blind eye. In respect of this travellers should not abuse the system by trying to change all their money on the black market for the best price possible. Treat it as a privilege and don't be too greedy.

Exchange black market

Apart from money, goods such as clothing, electrical goods and records can be exchanged for large amounts of local currency. This type of market is most common in Eastern Europe. In other parts of the world you may be offered a swap rather than cash.

The dangers of the black market

Since the black market is illegal you have no one to turn to if you get ripped off, robbed or arrested. These things happen regularly (see below) but you can try and avoid this by:

- asking fellow travellers the best places to change money
- never going up a side-street or alley alone
- never displaying large amounts of foreign currency.

CONMEN

It is one of the unwritten laws of travel that where there are tourists there will be people trying to con them out of their money and belongings. As a rule there are two types:

- black market conmen
- all purpose conmen.

Black market conmen
Whenever anyone tries to change money on the black market they run the risk of being conned. One of the favourite techniques is for the conman to work with one or two accomplices who are, or claim to be, policemen. Once you have changed your money you will then be 'arrested' and forced to bribe your way out of trouble. As with most other forms of business in these areas there is a certain amount of haggling involved, as one unfortunate traveller found in Kenya: 'After changing some money with a dealer on the black market I was arrested by a man who looked like a cross between Mike Tyson and Eddie Murphy. He told me that I would go to court in the morning and have to pay a fine of £600. He then offered me an alternative (there is usually an alternative). If I paid him £60 he would let me go. By now I realised it was a scam but since I was technically in the wrong I eventually paid £20 for my release.'

Another favourite trick when changing money is for the conman to show you an envelope with money you are about to receive. Just as he gives it to you there is a commotion and the envelope gets switched. When you look in the one you are given it contains nothing but newspaper.

All purpose conmen
These range from the ingenious to the mundane. Favourite cons:

1. The misplaced student
This will consist of one or two people coming up to you in the street and spinning a long and involved yarn about how they are students who have been forced to flee their own country because of persecution or war. Naturally, they are desperate to get back to see their families so could

you, in the name of humanity, give them some money to help them get back home. Stories like this should be treated with a large fistful of salt and you should not hand over any money.

2. The shoe-shine boy

These occur throughout cities and towns in Third World countries. Some of them are kind, generous and helpful – and they give your shoes an excellent shine. Others are pernicious, spiteful and corrupt. Ignore shoe-shine boys who claim to be able to clean your training shoes with a special fluid – it is only water. More menacing are the shoe-shine boys who work in groups. You will agree a price with one of them before you start and by the time he has finished the price will have risen mysteriously. If you refuse to pay he will turn to his friends who will rally to his defence. You will then be faced by an angry group of shoe-shine boys. If you have the nerve you should pay the original price and walk away.

3. The dissident

In certain African countries there have been incidents when people have been approached by someone in a café. They will tell you they are a dissident and that they are being harassed by the police. They will not ask you for any money though and you leave the café thinking that you have had an insight into the underside of the country. Once you are outside though you will approached by two men who will say that you are under arrest for associating with a known dissident. You may then be taken to a room for interrogation. This is a very unnerving experience but it is a con and you should stick to your guns and not hand over any large amounts of money. Eventually the conmen will get bored with your non-participation, but this may take several hours.

4. The corrupt policeman

This is a simple case of genuine policemen trying to make some extra money by intimidating travellers. They may stop you and ask you to turn out your pockets. If they find anything that they feel is incriminating (this may include an item such as a Swiss Army Knife) they will try to make you pay an instant fine. If you ask to see their superior they will soon get cold feet.

5. The Youth Hostel bus

Be wary of people who pick you up at an airport and offer you a ride to the Youth Hostel or a cheap hotel with their 'courtesy' bus. The chances are that it will appear to run out of petrol almost immediately and the driver will ask you to lend him some money for petrol (it will probably be an inordinately large amount of money for the quantity of fuel involved). He will then drop you at your destination, promise to come back with your money – and disappear into the sunset.

6. *The currency form con*

Some conmen recognise the value of the currency declaration form to the traveller and go to extreme lengths to get them to part with it. This may range from a simple offer to change money for you at a highly lucrative rate, to an involved plan about buying an expensive piece of electrical equipment, which can only be done with the use of your form. If you do hand over your form, the next time you will see your new-found friend will be when he returns with the obligatory phony policeman. Since they have a document which you need when you leave the country, you can expect to do some fairly hard bargaining.

7. *The street-seller*

The sale of 'genuine' artefacts around the world is one that is open to wide-scale abuse. Unless you are an expert in the field though you will be unable to tell a Ming vase from a ceramic dish made a week ago. One way around this is to enlist the help of a local when buying these artefacts. Alternatively, accept the fact that you may have been conned and hope nobody ever tells you.

Dealing with conmen

There is a fine line between openness and gullibility as far as travellers and conmen are concerned. The tricksters will invariably appear very friendly and genuine and may spend hours with you to win your confidence before they make their move. They may even buy you drinks and cups of tea to demonstrate their generosity.

As a rule you should be wary of people who seem over-eager to impress you. A certain amount of cynicism is needed when people first approach you. While you do not want to scare off someone who is genuinely interested in helping you, you should take things slowly – if they are genuine they will respect this and a friendship may develop. If they are conmen they may tire quickly of your wariness and move on to a more unsuspecting victim.

Tips to help you

Other points to consider are:

- Never give someone any important documents such as currency forms or passports – this is a ticket to bribery.

- If you are 'arrested' by the accomplices of a conman insist to be taken to the police station. Even if they are genuine policemen, they will be very reluctant to do this and may prefer to let you go.

- If you lend anyone some money make sure you stay with them until you get it back.

- Always see what you are getting before you pay for it – do not give someone money to buy an item for you.

- Trust your instincts – if something does not feel right then move on.

- Be bold – conmen can be very pushy and if you are as challenging in return they may back down. This does not mean you should get physical, but rather ask them questions that may unease them.

COPING WITH THEFT

This is one of the most unpleasant experiences abroad and one that takes several forms:

- pickpockets
- distractors
- sneak-thieves
- snatchers
- violent theft.

Pickpockets

Even if you are pickpocketed this should not cause a great deal of trauma if you have all your valuables in a money belt. You may lose some loose change but this is not the end of the world. But it underlines the importance of not putting any valuables in pockets.

Pickpockets tend to operate where there are crowds: main streets, local bus stations and sporting events. Be particularly careful in these areas.

Distractors

These are thieves who steal from you while you are concentrating on a diversion. These take several forms. These are some examples from around the world:

- In Brazil, travellers have had a powerful itching agent put down their backs. As they have been scrambling out of their clothes the thieves have ransacked their discarded bags. This is a popular method for stealing cameras.

- In France and Italy, travellers have been accosted by groups of children flapping large pieces of cardboard in their faces. As they try to fend them off their pockets are picked.

- In the former Yugoslavia, women with a baby in their arms approach unsuspecting travellers. Suddenly the baby is thrown to the startled visitor. While he catches the infant and recovers his composure his pockets and bag are plundered. The 'baby' turns out to be a doll.

- In a bus station in Zimbabwe fights have been organised for the benefit of travellers. As they crowd around to see what is happening a number of people set to work on their belongings.

It is hard to recommend a general defence for every instance of this kind which you might come across. The most important thing is to be aware of the dangers and try to recover your composure as quickly as possible if you are subjected to a diversion attack.

Sneak-thieves
Again, these come in all varieties: on local transport, in hotels, even people who have used knives to slit tents and sleeping bags – while people are asleep in them. Some places are more prone to this type of theft than others – beach huts in Thailand for example are a popular target but the golden rule is: Don't leave valuables lying around unattended. For the times you are asleep it is worth taking a few padlocks so you can lock hotel rooms from the inside. Also be careful of the windows: thieves will go to incredible lengths, and heights, to get to your valuables.

Snatchers
The most common example of this is moped drivers in Italy, who drive past tourists, swiping their handbags or daypacks as they go. There are also the unmotorised snatchers who operate on foot. You can minimise the risks of this by:

1. Wearing your daypack around your chest – like a joey in a kangaroo's pouch.

2. Strengthening the belts of moneybelts with thin wire such as piano wire. You should be wary of this if you have a neck-wallet – you do not want to save your money at the expense of your head.

Violent theft
Thankfully this is not as common as the media would like to make out and it should be remembered that it is only the bad news that makes the headlines: there is not much mileage in announcing, 'Thousands of people travelled all over the world today without incident'. Having said

that it does occur and prevention is better than the cure:

- Don't walk along unlit streets, parks or beaches at night.

- Don't flaunt expensive equipment such as cameras.

- Always look positive and if you are lost don't appear too helpless – thieves usually pick on the weakest looking travellers.

- Try and talk your way out of an awkward situation rather than resorting to physical violence.

If you are confronted by someone with a gun or a knife, give them what they want. This does not mean you should hand over your entire belongings. They will probably be most interested in cash so give them this first. If they then ask for your passport and travellers cheques then hand them over too – all these things can be replaced, you cannot.

TEN STEPS TO MAKE YOUR TRIP AS SAFE AS POSSIBLE

1. Never hand over any of your valuable documents – you may become a hostage to fortune.
2. Always carry your valuables in a money-belt.
3. Be wary of people who seem too friendly too quickly.
4. Be extra vigilant in crowded areas.
5. Always find out about the local black market before you think about using it.
6. Keep some cash in your pockets to hand over if you are mugged.
7. Always try and look confident, even if you feel scared out of your wits.
8. Don't show off expensive items such as cameras.
9. Avoid poorly lit areas of towns and cities at night.
10. Be prepared for corrupt officials and stick your ground if you know you are in the right.

6
Facing New Languages and Cultures

HOW TO LEARN A NEW LANGUAGE

Communication is one of the most important aspects of travelling round the world. It is all very well to see stunning sights and majestic views but if you cannot interact with the locals then it will all add up to a rather hollow experience.

It is a fact, and perhaps one that we should not be too proud of, that English is understood, to some degree, on every continent of the world. However, this does not mean that the globetrotter can merely set foot abroad with the 'talk loudly and slowly' attitude. Even if you are understood you will be met with the 'look insulted and unfriendly' approach. A better idea is to try and learn at least some of the local language. This will show people that you are willing to make the effort and a lifelong friendship may then ensue, based on a combination of pidgin English and pidgin Swahili.

When thinking about communicating in another language you should take into consideration how long you intend to spend in a particular country. This will enable you to answer two important questions:

- Do I want to learn a language before I begin my travels?

- Do I want to try and pick languages up as I go along?

Both of these methods have their merits but it depends on your own timetable.

How can I learn a language quickly?
One of the best starting points is local evening classes. Locating these can be done through the invaluable Training Access Points (TAPs), which can be found in most libraries. If you tap in a few simple instructions with your requirements, TAPs will be able to tell you who offers local courses in the relevant subject, where they are and when the courses run from.

Course organisers

There are several organisations who offer language courses and these include:

Accelerated Learning Systems Limited, 50 Aylesbury Road, Aston, Clinton, Aylesbury, Buckinghamshire HP22 5AH. Tel: (01296) 631177. They offer an innovative range of open learning language courses using audio cassettes and suggestopaedia.

The Berlitz Schools of Language Limited, 321 Oxford Street, London W1A 3BZ. Tel: (0171) 408 2474. They offer language courses with a wide range of teaching materials.

BBC Enterprises, Woodlands, 80 Wood Lane, London W12 0TT. Courses are offered using videos, audio cassettes and books.

Centre for Information on Language Teaching and Research, Regent's College, Inner Circle, Regent's Park, London NW1 4NS. Tel: (0171) 486 8221.

Linguaphone, St Giles House, 50 Poland Street, London W1V 4AX. Tel: (0171) 734 0574. One of the best known language-learning companies and they not only offer language courses but also support and specific services for the language learner.

Learning a language in this way can be expensive – well over £200 in some cases. It is probably only worthwhile to undertake this type of language learning if you plan to spend a significant amount of time in a country, or countries, that use this language. For instance if you intend to spend several months in South America it may be an idea to learn some Spanish before you go.

Learning languages as you go

Even for people who do not have a natural gift for languages it is relatively easy to learn a few important phrases in every country you visit. Most guidebooks have a list of phrases and sayings relevant to that country and if you are unsure of the pronunciation then try asking the locals. If you point to the phrase in your guidebook and offer an imploring smile then you will probably meet with a favourable response.

When you have learnt a few words and phrases then do not be afraid to use them. Even if it is just 'hello' or 'thank you' it will show people that you are willing to make the effort and that is the basis of all communication. Try and set yourself a target of learning a certain amount of words a day – say a modest dozen – and you will be surprised how quickly your vocabulary grows.

As with many other aspects of travel, alcohol is a great aid to communication. In bars and pubs around the world locals are made more talkative by the demon drink and it also makes travellers more loquacious. Apart from periods of fluent gibberish you will find that you are more willing to try and get your tongue around the local language and this can be an effective way to increase your linguistic knowledge.

Practical tips
When learning a language abroad there are a few points that should be considered:

- Be patient – you will not become a native speaker overnight.

- Be prepared to accept advice from the people who know what they are talking about *ie* the locals.

- Be prepared to practise – no-one will mind if you make a few mistakes.

- Try and persevere and resist the temptation to lapse into English.

The benefits of communicating in local languages

Grant Cairncross, an experienced traveller, is convinced that it is vital to try and communicate with people in their own language and always makes the effort to learn at least a few phrases relevant to the country in which he is travelling – even if it is just to ask directions to the nearest pub:

'While I was travelling through eastern Africa I found that most people had a knowledge of English but I felt it would be insulting to presume that they would understand me, so I did my best to learn a few words of their language, even if I was only in a country for a few days.

'This paid dividends and I found people frequently took the trouble to correct my faltering pronunciation. In Kenya you only had to say "Jambo" (Hello in Swahili) to someone and they would greet you with a dazzling smile. I encountered some people who refused to learn even the basics of a language and they were invariably met with an indifference that sometimes bordered on disdain.

'On one occasion my limited knowledge of a language helped me hitch a lift that took me 300 kilometres. I was stuck in Karonga in northern Malawi trying to get south. In one of the drinking halls I struck up a conversation with a truck driver and managed to ask him in Bantu (the local language) if he wanted a beer. As a result of this he offered me a lift to the capital Lilongwe. I would say that a willingness to learn languages is one of the most important items a traveller can take with them.'

The ten most important phrases to learn in another language

1. Hello – basic, but of invaluable use.

2. Thank you – good manners and also a simple way to show you are willing to try and use the local language.
3. That's good – if you utter this with a wide smile then you will be able to negotiate a variety of situations.
4. Where is the airport/train station/coach station/local overcrowded minibus? – this does depend on you being able to follow the reply you are given!
5. Stop this deathtrap, I would like to get off – applicable if the local transport gets a bit too much for your nerves.
6. Two beers, please – it is always a good idea to learn how to ask for two of anything, so you can sustain yourself and also have the means to befriend a local truck driver etc.
7. Where is the post office/bank/hospital/local embassy? – useful for all official matters.
8. Is the water safe to drink? – whatever the response it is best to presume that the answer is 'No'.
9. A dog ate my currency declaration form – invaluable when you are going through customs having changed all your money on the black market.
10. I'm sorry, but I think you are looking for my twin sister/brother – only to be used in emergencies such as arrest/deportation etc.

Communicating with hand signals

One popular way of communicating with someone who does not speak your language is through hand gestures. While this can be a very effective method you should be wary of hand signals that have an accepted meaning in your own country. For instance many countries accept the thumbs-up sign to signify something that is good or okay. However, in parts of the Middle East it is used as an insult.

If in doubt keep your hands in your pockets or use them to point at particular objects.

Dos and dont's of communicating abroad

Do
- Accept that you are the pupil and not the teacher.
- Be prepared to listen, and learn from what you hear.
- Communicate through methods other than speech – body language and hand signals can be particularly effective.
- Try and learn a few words and phrases before you visit a country.
- Be prepared to practise at every opportunity.

Don't
- Try and make people understand you by shouting.

- Presume that everyone will have a knowledge of English.
- Intersperse English with local languages – it will only create an embarrassing crossbreed.
- Use any words if you are unsure about their meaning.
- Respond to a question if you do not know what you have been asked.

HOW TO LEARN LOCAL SOCIAL ETIQUETTE

An important talent for global travellers is an ability to adapt to new cultures and the different ways in which they operate. The first step to take is to realise things that we take for granted at home may be totally opposite in different parts of the world. For instance, in some countries it is an offence for women to show their faces in public; some cultures think it is unhygienic to use toilet paper; eating with hands is considered perfectly normal in many parts of the world; in some areas people get upset at outward displays of anger; and in Muslim countries people take great offence if they are asked for their Christian names.

What the traveller needs to do is leave preconceptions at home and be prepared to re-educate themselves as to the ways of the world. One of the best ways to do this is to watch the locals: what do they wear; how do they greet each other; how do they buy things; how do they eat their meals; and how do they deal with officials.

Although it is not necessary for travellers to 'go native' and try and act exactly like the locals, a certain amount of sensitivity to their ways is needed – if only to avoid giving offence and getting yourself into trouble.

Customs relating to barter

In many parts of the world barter is the most common way of doing business. At its best it can be something of an art form and a satisfying, sociable way of doing business. The usual barter scenario consists of the seller and the buyer both setting their preferred prices and after much head-shaking, muttering, mock incredulity and, frequently, laughter, a compromise is reached.

But barter has its own rules and etiquette as Karen Swanson explains: 'While I was travelling in China I went to a local market in Nanjing to buy my breakfast. I spent about ten minutes bartering for a few pieces of fruit and when the transaction was completed the stall owner looked very downcast. I later learnt that it is customary for the first sale of the morning to set the standard for the rest of the day. Because I had haggled to get a particularly low price the vendor had to use that as a benchmark for the rest of the day and he lost money. The next day I went back and offered a higher price and the man beamed enthusiastically at me.

'In Zimbabwe I came across a similar problem. I was buying a statue of an elephant in Harare and I could tell that the salesman was not properly involved in the whole barter process. It was a very bright day and I was wearing my sunglasses. After a few minutes he asked me if I would take them off. I then realised that one of the integral parts of barter is eye contact and without that the seller feels like a fish out of water. When we could both look at each other the haggling went ahead in its normal animated fashion.'

Bartering tips

When engaged in bartering travellers should try and follow a few basic rules:

- Be prepared to take your time – it is not the same as popping into Marks and Spencer to buy a pair of socks.

- Do not get annoyed – barter is as much about social interaction as it is about buying something.

- Do not try and force the seller into anything – the Barter Union is a powerful thing and you will soon be surrounded by a crowd of angry sellers.

- Be flexible – give and take is the motto of all good bartering.

The moral side of barter

One point to remember about barter is that while you want to get the best possible price you are probably significantly wealthier than the person with whom you are bartering. It does no harm to settle on a price slightly higher than that which you would prefer to pay. You will almost undoubtedly still end up with a bargain and the seller will be satisfied. However, try not to pay too much over the odds as this will just bump up the price for the people who come after you.

The giving of presents

Every traveller should be aware of the importance of presents. These can be given in a variety of circumstances:

- As a 'Thank you' when you have been staying with people you have met.
- As an introduction when you first reach a new destination.
- As a bribe to ease your way through official channels.

The first instance is similar to how you may act at home. If you have been put up by friends or relations you may buy them a small gift as a sign of your gratitude. Exactly the same approach should be adopted when you are abroad. If you are invited into someone's home or taken out for a meal it is polite to offer a small gift in return. This may be something as simple as a bunch of flowers or a present from your home town. This type of present not only acts as a thank you but it may also ingratiate you to your hosts if you ever return.

In many remote parts of the world presents can act as ice-breakers and help you achieve acceptance. Pens, pencils and postcards from home are good items for children, while adults could be offered cigarette lighters or playing cards. If you have a Polaroid camera this can also be useful but be careful and make sure it is okay for you to take photographs. Also, it can be an expensive way to make friends if you get a bit snap-happy.

Some travellers distribute sweets to children that they meet on their way. This is a slightly dubious habit – do we really want to spread Western tooth decay around the world? – and a better idea is to hand out something small and constructive.

Bribery is a way of life for officials in many countries and you have to accept that you will have to give a certain number of 'presents' on your travels. These will usually take the form of money but sometimes customs officials will take a shine to something in your luggage, perhaps a torch or a pocket knife. Try not to give up items like this but if the officials are insistent then you might not have any choice.

Customs relating to clothing

While you may think that your Hawaiian shirt is the definitive fashion statement, people in other countries may not agree. Some countries are very conscious of the way people dress and you should be careful not to breach any local customs.

Muslim countries are the most sensitive as far as dress codes are concerned. Efforts should be made to avoid showing large areas of naked flesh, particularly legs and arms, and wearing provocative clothing. In many hot countries it makes sense to keep your body well covered anyway as it will protect you against the pain of sunburn. Loose-fitting, moderate clothing is the best bet for both comfort and keeping on the right side of the locals.

In general if your appearance is smart – clean clothes and tidy hair – then the chances are that you will encounter fewer problems, particularly with official figures such as police and customs officers. Always make a special effort to look smart when you are crossing borders between countries.

The taking of photographs

The majority of travellers carry a camera with them and gathering pictures of far flung corners of the world is one of the great pleasures of travelling. But to make sure that it remains a pleasure and does not turn into a nightmare, there are certain rules that should be observed by any travelling David Baileys:

- Never photograph any military installations.

- Never photograph bridges in militarily sensitive countries.

- Be careful when photographing industrial complexes or areas that make a country look primitive.

- Always find out whether the locals object to being photographed.

- Be prepared to pay people to take their photograph.

- If in doubt – Don't Take The Picture.

Some areas are more photographer sensitive than others, as Michael Gourlay discovered when he was travelling in Kenya:

'Most of the time I was photographing wildlife and they turned out to be some of the more docile subjects I encountered. Most of the tribesmen are very tuned into the idea of tourists with cameras and most of them charge fees for standing in front of the lens. Sometimes this can be quite a large amount. However, if you decide to ignore their requests for payment you can get into a lot of trouble.

'In some of the more remote areas the local tribes will not allow photography under any circumstances. And they mean it. I heard one story of a man in northern Kenya who ignored this warning and he ended up with a spear in his chest.'

TEN RULES FOR COPING WITH LOCAL CULTURES

1. Approach everything with an open mind.
2. Always try and learn at least a little of someone else's language.
3. Do not use hand signals if you do not know their local meaning.
4. Treat barter as a commercial form of communication.
5. Do not always try and get the lowest possible price for something.
6. Take a plentiful supply of small, cheap and constructive presents.
7. Take a small supply of luxury presents.
8. Accept that some people and cultures treat cameras as weapons.
9. Be prepared to show people how their cultures contrast to your own.
10. Accept that you have a lot to learn.

7
Earning Money on Your Travels

If you have your heart set on a period of uninterrupted travel then the idea of working may not be at the top of the agenda. However, since not everyone has a bank account that resembles Richard Branson's the notion of working at some point on your travels is one that should be considered. There are a number of instances where working may be the preferred option to lying on a beach or visiting another stunning temple:

- Complete lack of money. This is a situation that, hopefully, should not occur, but if you do find yourself penniless then a period of paid employment may be the only option.

- You want to stay somewhere for an extended period. If this happens then you may want to work not only to earn money but also to get to know the area and the people better – employment is one of the best ways to become integrated somewhere.

- You change your original plans. This happens all the time when you are travelling and if you suddenly decide that you want to take an unplanned side trip somewhere then you may need to work to earn the additional funds.

For an in-depth look into the world of temporary employment abroad take a look at my own book *How to Find Temporary Work Abroad* (How To Books Ltd).

What are the opportunities?

WORKING IN TOURISM

Wherever there are tourists there will be employment openings and all travellers should at least give this some consideration as a means of earning money. There are a variety of opportunities within the general heading of tourism: hotels, restaurants, pubs, clubs and ski resorts. As a traveller you will have the advantage of frequenting these types of places already so keep your eyes open when you are in bars and restaurants to see if there are any signs for staff wanted. Also, bars are usually good places to extract information from the locals and they may know about available jobs.

How do I find a job?

If you are interested in bar or nightclub work then the 'being-in-the-right-place-at-the-right-time' method is the best. Since this area of the employment market tends to be extremely fluid, opportunism is sometimes more important then experience.

Try nightclubs and pubs in the morning (but not too early!) since the manager may have more time to see you then and even if you are applying on spec make sure you are smart and respectable. Treat every door you knock on as a prospective job interview. The secret to this method is to knock, knock and knock again.

Another possible source of casual employment in the catering industry is in the fast-food outlets that have sprouted in almost every city in the world. Due to the nature of the work staff get fed-up with great regularity and there are often openings of some description. Fluency in a foreign language is not always necessary: if you can master 'cheeseburger', 'French fries' and 'large coke' in a different language then you may be perfectly qualified.

Points to consider

- Are you prepared to work long unsociable hours and do all the dirty jobs going?
- Do you have a set of suitable clothes for work in the hospitality industry?
- Do you know a foreign language – or are you prepared to learn one?
- Are you prepared to put up with numerous rejections if necessary?
- Be prepared to use your wits – large festivals and sporting events provide excellent opportunities for short-term employment in tourism.

FRUIT PICKING

Although mechanisation is becoming increasingly common in the world of agriculture there are still fruit growers around the globe who are looking for pickers. Whether it is grapes, oranges, apples or tomatoes there are numerous chances for casual employment in this agricultural area. The drawbacks of the job are clear:

- Back-breaking work.
- Long hours.
- Low pay in most cases.
- Basic living conditions.

For this reason locals in fruit picking areas, from the cherry orchards of the Okanagon in western Canada to the vineyards of the Barossa valley in Australia, are somewhat reluctant to throw themselves wholeheartedly into the task of picking these produces. In some cases workers come from several hundred miles away.

The best areas for prospective fruit pickers are southern Europe, Australia, New Zealand, South Africa and North America. Since many fruit growers are not over-concerned with employment regulations, persistence is sometimes more productive than having the right papers. Local employment agencies (such as the Commonwealth Employment Service in Australia) can direct you to the fruit growing areas of a country and tell the current employment requirements. If you go to these areas you may be approached on the street and asked if you want a picking job.

Try these exercises to discover the most productive fruit growing areas in the world:

- Check the labels of wine bottles to see which regions of a country they come from.
- Look at the labels of origin of fruits in your local supermarket.
- Check packets of raisins and other dried fruit and see where they came from – dried fruit was once ripe fruit waiting to be picked.

LABOURING

If you like fresh air, hard work and working in a team then labouring could be an avenue for casual work. If you have a qualification in a trade, such as a carpenter or an electrician, then you could be in great demand in various parts of the world – there is usually work in Australia for qualified tradesmen. Make sure you take any relevant certificates and references with you.

Even if you do not have a qualification it could be possible to pick up work as a labourer. Wherever there is any sort of construction, be it a new motorway or a holiday resort, there will be various vacancies for casual labourers. These are sometimes on a day-to-day basis and so they are not advertised in newspapers. You can either turn up to the site and ask the foreman if there is any work or in some cases employment centres recruit casual labourers on a daily basis. The most important thing to note here is that you have to turn up *early*: recruitment is done by taking the first ten or twenty or thirty people who have arrived that morning so being ready by 6am is not an unrealistic target.

Spoken from experience
Brendan Coyle used this method to great effect in Australia:

'When I was in Sydney I had a couple of weeks to kill before I was due to travel up to the Great Barrier Reef. I was told that there might be some labouring work around so I got up at the crack of dawn and went to the local CES (employment office) before six o'clock. There was a group of about fifteen of us and after twenty minutes a pick-up truck appeared. The driver wanted four people to dig a swimming pool so I jumped in. This was hard work in blazing heat but I earned £400 for a week's work. This meant that I was able to spend an extra two weeks up on the Barrier Reef.'

It is possible for women to find labouring jobs but you will have to be prepared for the usual discrimination and chauvinism – give as good as you get and you will probably be accepted more readily.

Practical tips

If you are trying to find labouring work remember:

- Try to find the areas with the most intensive construction.
- Look up building contractors in the *Yellow Pages* and contact them personally.
- Turn up at sites first thing in the morning to see if there is any work.
- Be enthusiastic and willing to do a variety of strenuous and back-breaking jobs.

FACTORY WORK

One of the most boring forms of work you are likely to come across but for that reason it tends to be well paid. A good way to find this type of work is from local newspapers or else approach the factories directly. The best qualifications are the ability to start early in the morning (or work the night shift) and be able to sit through hours of tedium. Countries such as Australia, New Zealand and North America offer the best opportunities for this type of work.

TEACHING ENGLISH AS A FOREIGN LANGUAGE (TEFL)

Although this can be a career in itself it is also a type of work that can be used for short periods. The great advantage of teaching English is that it can be done in virtually all corners of the world, including some where more conventional employment opportunities are limited.

If you are seriously considering earning money from teaching English abroad then there are two questions you should ask yourself before you go:

1. Do I want a recognised qualification?
2. Do I want to adopt the freelance approach?

The official line on TEFL

In recent years there has been a marked increase in the number of organisations offering TEFL qualifications. These vary greatly in intensity, quality and price. The standard recognised qualification is the Royal Society of Arts (RSA)/University of Cambridge Local Examinations Syndicate (UCLES) Certificate for Teaching English as a Foreign Language to Adults. This is an intensive, practical course (four weeks if you undertake it on a full-time basis) and competition for places is stiff. You will have to attend an interview, at which you may be given a short written test dealing with common grammatical and semantic problems that may occur while you are teaching. With this in mind it would be a good idea to take a look at either *Rediscover Grammar* by D Crystal (Longman) or *Discover English* by R Bolitho and B Tomlinson (Heinemann).

How much will it cost to train?

Most RSA Certificate courses cost in the region of £700-£800. Although this is a large lump sum to pay out it is worth remembering that the Certificate is highly thought of around the world and once you have it you will be able to virtually pick a job in the country of your choosing. Look at it as a valuable investment.

Where can I do the course?

RSA Certificate courses are held at centres all over Britain. Four of the major ones are:

International House, 106 Piccadilly, London W1V 9FL. Tel: (0171) 491 2598.

International Languages Centres Limited, White Rock, Hastings, East Sussex TN34 1JY. Sister centre of International House and they have a computerised database which matches applicants with TEFL qualifications to jobs primarily in the Middle or Far East.

Bell School of Languages, 1 Redcross Lane, Cambridge CB2 2QX. They run courses in Cambridge, Norwich, Saffron Walden, Bath and London.

Basil Paterson Tutorial College, 22 Abercromby Place, Edinburgh EH3. Tel: (0131) 556 7695. Run a one month full-time TEFL course for £850 or it can be undertaken as a six month part-time course.

Other centres

For a list of other centres offering RSA Certificates contact:

UCLES, 1 Hill Road, Cambridge CB1 2EU.
RSA, 8 John Adam Street, London WC2N 8EY.

British Council, English Language Information Unit, 10 Spring Gardens, London SW1A 2BN.

Other TEFL qualifications

In addition to the RSA Certificate there are numerous other introductory TEFL courses around the country. Some of these have the advantage of being taught by organisations who have language schools abroad, so once you have gained your qualification you are very likely to be given a job with them.

Trinity College, 16 Park Crescent, London W1N 4AH. Offer courses in Teaching Language to Speakers of Other Languages (TESOL) at their centres around the country. As intensive as the RSA Certificate but generally slightly cheaper. A well thought of alternative which allows you to teach children too.

Inlingua Cheltenham, Rodney Lodge, Rodney Road, Cheltenham GL50 1JF. Tel: (01242) 253171. Offer a variety of courses including a five week TESOL course for £725 and a two-week TEFL introduction course for £285.

Linguarama, New Oxford House, 16 Waterloo Street, Birmingham B2 5UG. Tel: (0121) 632 5295. Courses in Alton, Bath, Birmingham, London, Manchester and Stratford-upon-Avon. Run a five day introductory TEFL course for £205. Linguarama also run over 35 schools worldwide.

Primary House, 300 Gloucester Road, Horfield, Bristol BS7 9PD. Tel: (0117) 931 1119. Jobs in Greece virtually guaranteed for those who pass the weekend course for £120 and then a home-study course for £55.

Surrey Language Centre, Sandford House, 39 West Street, Farnham, Surrey GU9 7DR. Tel: (01252) 723494. One week introductory TEFL course for £175. There is also a four week, full-time TEFL course for £275.

Any type of TEFL qualification is an asset and one the independent traveller will probably use while on the road rather than organising a job before they go. If this is the case then take with you any certificates and references and remember to make copies of them and leave these at home.

Freelance English teaching

Not everyone likes to follow the official method and TEFL is an area where the one overriding requirement is to be able to speak English. If you can do this then, with a little initiative and determination, you will be able to find work abroad. If you have a degree, of any kind, or any similar qualifications then it is a good idea to take this with you. Prospective employers are sometimes just as impressed with this as a TEFL qualification.

Spoken from experience

While Sally Abrahams was travelling through Africa and Asia she found that teaching English was not only a way of making a bit of extra money but also a good way of meeting people:

'In Zimbabwe I went on a wildlife safari and while I was talking to the guide he told me that a lot of the children in his village had great problems with learning English. I offered to go there and give them some basic English lessons and he happily took up my offer. The children were wonderfully enthusiastic and I spent a week there, teaching them songs, poems and nursery rhymes. I was only paid a small amount but the generosity of the villagers was overwhelming and I wished I could have stayed longer.

'In Bangkok I was a bit more confident about my teaching abilities and so I answered an advertisement for a private English teacher. The employer was a Thai businessman whose son was going to America and he wanted to make sure that his English was of a good quality. I spent four weeks of fairly intensive tutoring but the boy was a very diligent pupil and I was well paid for my effort. The businessman was well pleased at the end of the month and when the boy went to America I received a postcard from him – written in excellent English.'

However, not all employers are as fair as those that Sally encountered and TEFL teachers should always try and steer clear of unscrupulous operators. If in doubt walk away.

Further reading

- *EFL Careers Guide*, EFL Limited, 64 Ormley Road, Ramsey, Isle of Man. A comprehensive directory of Introductory, Certificate, Diploma and MA courses. Also addresses for job-hunting overseas.
- *Teaching English Abroad*, by Susan Griffith. Vacation Work, 9 Park End Street, Oxford.

Points to consider about TEFL

1. You do not need a TEFL qualification to teach English abroad but it would definitely increase your chances of getting a good job.
2. If you only want to use teaching English as a stop-gap method for earning some extra money then adequate education qualifications may be enough for you to pick up some part-time teaching.
3. Be prepared for anything. Teaching English is not all grammar and spelling. You find yourself singing nursery rhymes to four-year-olds in Zimbabwe or composing shopping lists for Japanese housewives. Flexibility and an active imagination will be your most valuable tools.
4. If you come across an employer who is unscrupulous to the students

then you will probably be treated in the same fashion.
5. Keep an open mind – teaching English abroad will not be the same as what goes on in the classrooms of Britain.

MISCELLANEOUS WORK OPPORTUNITIES

There are as many types of miscellaneous casual work as there are addresses in a traveller's notebook. Some of the possibilities are:

- Baby sitting – proof of responsibility is useful for this.
- Deck-hand on a prawn trawler.
- Door-to-door salesperson – companies are always looking for thick-skinned individuals to sell anything from encyclopaedias, to double-glazing.
- Film extra – particularly in Asia where countries such as India have a massive film industry.
- Jackaroo on an Australian sheep station.
- Selling time-share in Thailand.

Freelance opportunities

You do not have to be an employee to make money while you are travelling. Many people adopt a freelance approach, relying on their own initiative rather than the vagaries of the job market.

Busking

If you can sing, play the guitar, juggle chain-saws or tap dance in green wellies then you could turn to busking to earn some extra money. Make sure you know the local laws regarding this before you start and be prepared to be moved along by the police. Stick to areas where there are large crowds, such as shopping areas or outside large sporting events. Try and make your act original and do not encroach too near to other buskers. Always check the situation with the police and also the local busking community – buskers have their own code of conduct and become irate if their rules are breached.

When busking it pays to make the effort to be original and stand out, as Mike Paterson discovered in New Zealand: 'I usually travel with my kilt and when I was in Christchurch I met an ex-pat who was willing to lend me his bagpipes so I jumped at the chance to do a bit of busking. As well as a few odd stares I also made a fair bit of money – a lot of it from people who were willing to pay to have their photograph taken next to me.'

Gambling

Perhaps not the safest way to make some extra cash but worth thinking about if you are an expert poker player or can do a few card tricks such as 'Spot the Lady'. Whenever you win money gambling there is always the risk that the loser will turn nasty, so a quick tongue and an even quicker pair of legs are invaluable when you are engaged in this type of activity.

Selling
If you make jewellery, design T-shirts or paint watercolours you could set up a small stall. Again, there may be local regulations regarding this so you should enquire as to whether you need a permit. Otherwise make sure you keep one step ahead of the authorities.

One potentially lucrative area for selling is food. You can do this yourself by setting up a stall selling cold drinks, sandwiches or chocolate but this might not ingratiate you with the local traders. Alternatively you could sell items for someone else and take a commission on each sale. This is popular among ice-cream companies in Australia – you are given a tray full of ice-cream, pointed towards the nearest beach and told to sell, sell, sell. Even working on a commission basis you can make a lot of money this way: John Shinner from Surrey did this in Sydney and earned $A100 a day – plus all the ice-cream he could eat.

Street painting
In tourist areas it is increasingly common to see areas of pavement covered in large pastel paintings of anything from the Beatles to Van Gogh's *Sunflowers*. If you have a knack for drawing, a good set of pastel crayons and an ability to stop people walking on the designated piece of pavement then this could be a lucrative side-line.

SELLING YOURSELF

When it comes to casual employment it is not necessarily true that everything comes to he who waits. In reality it does not always even come to he who searches the newspapers and goes knocking on doors. Sometimes you have to take the initiative and sell yourself and your employment skills. This can be done in a variety of ways:

1. Placing advertisements in local newspapers. State what you are looking for and what you have to offer. For example: 'Experienced dishwasher seeks dirt and grease to clean in any city hotel or restaurant', or 'Do your lawns need mowing? Your leaves need raking? Or your hedges need trimming? All odd jobs around the garden undertaken. Previously employed by Kew Gardens, London.'
2. Placing similar advertisements in shop windows.
3. Handing out leaflets extolling your virtues as a labourer/babysitter/

barman.

4. Promoting yourself verbally. This should not be done in an over-bearing fashion: if you hear of an opening then subtly suggest that you could be the person to fill it.

Key qualities you need

The most important qualities when looking for casual work abroad are:

- flexibility
- initiative
- opportunism
- persistence
- sense of humour.

THE BEST COUNTRIES FOR CASUAL WORK

The determined traveller will be able to find a way of earning a few pennies wherever they are but there are some countries that offer better opportunities than others.

Australia

An excellent place for travellers to supplement their funds – despite the recent recession there are casual jobs and the wages tend to be good. The best openings are in tourism, fruit picking and labouring. Despite their 'whinging Pom' tag the Brits are usually considered good workers and you should never be short of work for too long here.

The best way to qualify for employment in Australia is to apply for a Working Holiday visa. This is valid for a maximum of a year and you are eligible if:

1. You are aged between eighteen and twenty-five.
2. You want to travel in Australia and supplement your income with periods of employment for a maximum of three months in one place.
3. You hold a valid UK, Irish, Canadian, Dutch or Japanese passport.
4. You have enough money for a return ticket and to support yourself for the first few months of your stay. (This is approximately £2,000, but if you need proof of this you can borrow the money, obtain a bank statement and then pay it back.)

There is a charge of $A100 for a Working Holiday Visa and you should not apply more than four weeks prior to your proposed departure date. You can only have a Working Holiday Visa once so make sure that you are going to take full advantage of it.

Once you are in Australia you may want to use the Commonwealth

Employment Service (CES) in your job search. This is the Australian equivalent of the Jobcentre.

Australian visas can be obtained from:
Australian High Commission, Australia House, The Strand, London WC2B 4LA *or:*
Australian Consulate, Chatsworth House, Lever Street, Manchester M1 2DL.

New Zealand
Work permits are harder to obtain than in Australia but it is possible to get one for casual work if you write to the nearest Immigration Service. However, this can be costly ($NZ117) and tiresome. An easier way is to obtain a tax number (this can be done by going to the nearest Inland Revenue Department and asking for one) and show this to potential employers.

As a rule it should be possible to find casual work in New Zealand, but do not abuse the system. For further information:
New Zealand Immigration Service, 5th Floor, New Zealand House, 80 Haymarket, London SW1Y 4TE.

United States of America
It is notoriously difficult to legally find casual work in America: unless you can arrange an H-1B Temporary Worker Visa (which has to be done through an American employer before you enter the country and can take up to eight months), a B-1 Voluntary Work Visa or a Q Visa (an International Cultural Exchange Visa which is valid for up to 15 months) you can only work illegally. Due to the range of job opportunities – from barman in Disney World to ski instructor in Colorado – a lot of people do this. However, there are a few points to consider:

1. Make sure you have adequate funds when you enter the country: at least $500 for every month of your proposed stay and credit cards.

2. Due to new laws social security cards now need to be physically inspected by employers so you cannot just think up a number. Some people may be willing to take your word for it though.

3. Be on the look-out for immigration officials, particularly if you are in an area where there are large number of illegal workers – such as Florida and Texas.

4. If employers are unscrupulous enough to take on illegal labour they may be unscrupulous in other ways too.

Africa, Asia and Latin America

Due to a number of reasons, such as large local work forces, local regulations and unstable economies, the chance of getting casual work in these countries is little better than zero. You may find a few days work as a film extra or a model but you should not rely on employment if you are travelling in these areas. In many ways it is not necessary because the cost of living and travelling is invariably so cheap that you would not achieve any great financial gain by working.

If you want to work in Third World countries then your best bets are:

• Teaching English as a Foreign Language.
• Working for a voluntary organisation.

Go for the unusual

Whatever type of casual work you do, try on at least one occasion to do something that you would not have the chance to do at home. Working in a bar in Sydney may be enjoyable and financially rewarding but will it be so different from working in a bar in London or Glasgow? Instead of spending three months as a waiter do it for six weeks and then spend the rest of the time on a prawn trawler or scrabbling about picking grapes. Seeing a different side of life is one of the great joys of a year abroad.

CHECKLIST

1. Do you need a work permit for the countries in which you are intending to look for casual work?
2. Do you know the consequences of working illegally in various countries?
3. Do you know where to locate the official centres for finding casual work?
4. Have you gained any relevant experience at home?
5. If not, can you convince employers that you would be an asset to their business?
6. Will you be treating casual work as a financial necessity or as a means to earn some extra cash while you put down roots for a while?
7. Do you want to do something that is out of the ordinary?
8. Are you prepared to take numerous rejections before finding a job?
9. Will you take the initiative in the job search?
10. Are you prepared to turn your hand to anything?

8
Trouble-shooting

No-one likes to think of doom and disaster befalling them when they are travelling but it should be considered and sometimes it is a case of 'forwarned is forearmed'. There are a number of things that can go wrong when you are abroad, from losing all your money to becoming seriously ill. While people should be aware of what might happen to them, and how best to combat it, this does not mean they should become paranoid whenever they read a newspaper report about travellers being attacked or having to be flown home due to illness. Problems do occur when people are travelling but serious ones are rare.

LOSING SOME OF YOUR MONEY

Travellers should carry their money in a combination of:

- cash
- travellers cheques
- credit cards.

If you lose notes and coins there is little you can do about it apart from reporting it to the local police and then hope you can claim it on your insurance.

If you lose your travellers cheques this be a bit more serious since you will probably be carrying more money in this form than in cash. Contact the police immediately and, if possible, get in touch with the nearest agent dealing with the relevant travellers cheques. The two most common types of travellers cheques are American Express and Thomas Cook. Both companies, particularly the former, are very good at refunding stolen or lost travellers cheques and replacements usually arrive within a couple of days.

If your credit cards are stolen then try and contact your bank or building society as quickly as possible, before someone goes on an international spending spree. It is a good idea to have your cards protected by a company such as Card Protection Plan (CPP), 198 King's Road, London SW3 5XX, who will do all the work for you. In the case of your cards being stolen CPP will cancel all of the relevant items and arrange for replacements to be issued. If you contact them from outside the UK there is a reverse charge number in case you do not even have the price of a phone call.

LOSING ALL OF YOUR MONEY

If you lose your cash, travellers cheques and credit cards in one go then your first reaction may be to throw yourself off the nearest tall building. While this is understandable, do not despair – all is not lost.

The first reaction of someone who has been made penniless may be to go to their nearest embassy or consulate and plead for mercy. Unfortunately this may not be met with much sympathy – embassies encounter hundreds of people who land destitute on their doorsteps asking for repatriation due to lack of funds. Very few of these cases are successful and if they do manage to be put on the next plane home they will have to pay for the privilege once they get back. Embassies are more concerned with people who have got themselves in trouble with the law or have serious medical problems.

A better idea for the penniless traveller is:

- Try and find some emergency work.
- Have some money wired to you from home.

The best type of work may be of the freelance type as detailed in Chapter 7 – basically something that provides you with money as quickly as possible.

Wiring money abroad

The issue of wiring money abroad is a contentious one. Although it sounds like a simple operation, getting one bank to telex another, it is rarely that straightforward. There are two ways to have money wired to you in another country:

1. Contact a family member or friend and give them the details of the bank at which you require the money to arrive. Depending on where you are in the world this could take anything from a couple of days to a week. Also, you may have to pay exorbitant bank charges.

2. Before you leave you can arrange with your bank to wire money as required to their affiliated banks around the world. Again you will be charged for this and it should really be used to pick up money as you travel rather than relying on it if you lose everything.

FALLING ILL

If you become seriously ill, or even think you may have contracted a serious illness, then medical attention should be sought as quickly as possible. If you are not in a fit condition to do this yourself then you should hope you have good medical insurance and an able travelling companion. If you are in a large city then it should be possible to get to a hospital reasonably quickly. If in doubt ask at a large hotel for information about hospitals and doctors.

It can be an unnerving experience to be treated in a foreign country but the most important thing to remember is to insist that any injections are made with sterile needles.

If you are in a remote area the best bet will be to find the nearest mission hospital. Not only will this be able to provide important medical attention but there is a good chance that there will be an English-speaking doctor available.

If in doubt about an illness then it is best to come home rather than risk a life-threatening condition. You can always carry on with your trip once you have recovered.

Helpful organisations

One organisation that offers emergency medical services abroad is Europ-Assistance, 252 High Street, Croydon, Surrey CR0 1NF. They have a network of doctors, vehicle rescue services and other related services in over 200 countries. The Red Cross also have representatives in most countries of the world.

WHAT IF YOU ARE ATTACKED?

In addition to the physical effect of being attacked or mugged the psychological effects can be longer lasting. It must be said that attacks on travellers are the exception rather than the rule but if it does happen then a few steps should be taken:

- Inform the local police – they may not be able to do too much but they will want to know what happened.

- If the attack is a serious one then inform your local embassy – they like to know if there is a pattern of attacks on certain nationalities.

- Give yourself time to recover from the shock of the attack – this may be in the form of a delayed reaction.

- Surround yourself by as many friendly faces as possible – safety in numbers is comforting after a disconcerting attack.

- Try and take something positive from the incident and think how a repeat incident can be avoided.

KEEPING IN TOUCH WITH HOME

One of the best ways to overcome any problems that occur is to stay in contact with family and friends at home. This is also a necessity when things go wrong and you need to contact someone quickly. The best ways of doing this are:

- Telephone and telegrams
- Fax
- Letters

Using the telephone and telegrams

Telephone calls can be made most easily from central post offices and large hotels. Telegrams are usually sent from central post offices. In some countries it can be a frustrating experience trying to make an international telephone call – a general rule is the smaller the town, the more erratic the service.

Sending a fax

If you have someone at home who has a fax machine, or access to one, then this can be a good way of contacting people quickly. Faxes can be sent from some post offices (the bigger the better) and the larger hotels.

Writing a letter

This method is not the quickest for getting in touch with people but it can be incredibly comforting to get a letter from home. Poste Restante (having letters sent to a specific post office abroad, for the addressee to collect) can be used as a way to collect mail, and American Express and Thomas Cook customers (you qualify as a customer if you buy their travellers cheques) offer a mail receiving service at their offices around the world. When sending and receiving letters, times of delivery should be thought of in terms of weeks rather than days.

ENSURING YOU DO NOT HAVE TO RETURN HOME

When things go badly wrong the immediate temptation is sometimes to pack your bags and head home. While in some cases (serious illness or prolonged financial destitution) this may be the preferred option, there are instances where you should try and battle through the bad times:

Homesickness

Every traveller suffers from this from time to time and the best way to get over it is to ask yourself whether you would rather give up your travels for the sake of seeing family and friends. The answer is frequently 'no' and it is surprising how unchanged things are when you do eventually get home. A telephone call home is an effective way to alleviate the symptoms – and cheaper than a plane ticket home.

Illness

Even a bout of diarrhoea can be very upsetting while you are travelling but unless you think that it is developing into something worse then you should try and grit your teeth and wait until you recover. Make sure you give yourself plenty of time to recuperate. Once you have recovered you will feel invigorated and better for the experience.

Shortage of money

This is different from a complete lack of money. If you are running short of the readies then instead of returning home (which may not be an option of course) a better idea is to try and earn some cash (see Chapter 7) and cut back on your expenditure.

Action to take if you do have to return home

If you have to curtail your travels prematurely for any reason your aim should be to get back on the road as quickly as possible. The longer you spend at home then the harder it will be to get back into travel mode. In cases such as this you will probably have to be even more positive than when you first set off and there are a few steps to take:

- Don't try and rush to get back – make sure you are fully fit and have sufficient funds.

- Assess what you have already done. This will undoubtedly inspire you to greater feats.

- Compare your experience abroad with your home environment, Whatever the comforts at home you have to ask yourself whether it is worth giving up your future travels for the security of what you already know about.

- Try and keep your mind in travel mode – it is all to easy to slip back into the old routine.

- If necessary find work at home in order to finance your return abroad.

CHECKLIST FOR DEALING WITH PROBLEMS ABROAD

1. Do not keep your money/travellers cheques/credit cards all in the same place.
2. Leave details of travellers cheques and credit cards with a responsible person at home.
3. Only contact embassies if it is a genuine emergency.
4. Make sure that you have adequate medical insurance – always plan for the worst.
5. Keep a note of your blood type with you and also a set of sterile needles.
6. Seek local advice about areas of a city/country that are considered unsafe.
7. If you are attacked the mental effects could be as damaging as the physical ones, so deal with both of them.
8. Leave a list of addresses where you can be contacted in each area you are planning to visit.
9. If it is a genuine emergency then do not hesitate to return home.
10. If you do have to return home you will need to make a determined effort to get back on the road.

BACK AT LIFE'S CROSSROADS

Coping with being back home

One of the hardest aspects of long term travel is adjusting to life at home when you finally decide to return. The concept of culture shock is often mentioned in relation to visiting different countries but after a period of weird, wayout and wonderful experiences abroad it can be even more of a shock to come back to the everyday realities of life at home. The first thing you will notice is how similar everything seems in comparison to what you have done while travelling.

Readjusting

When you get back home you should take a few steps to overcome your 'returning home shock'. You can do this by:

1. Putting things in perspective

It can be very depressing to come home and either return to the same old way of life or, worse, face the prospect of unemployment and an uncertain future. But if you look at these situations in terms of what you have done with your time abroad then they will not look so bleak. It can be very comforting to know that you have done something unique: with this knowledge it is a lot easier to confront any uncertainties that face you in the future.

2. Preserving what you have done

The memory of even the most exhilarating experiences fades with time so when you get home you should produce a concrete record of your time abroad:

- Put your photographs in an album rather than letting them gather dust in a drawer.

- Transfer your photographs onto a video tape.

- If you kept a diary then write this up and add your thoughts once you have the chance to look at the experience with hindsight.

- Produce an overall project of your year abroad – this will not only delight family and friends but it will also bring a glazed look to your eyes when you read it in years to come.

- Try writing articles for newspapers or magazines about your experiences.

- Keep in touch with people you meet during your time abroad – having visitors from overseas is one of the best ways to relive your own experiences.

3. Looking to the future

If after a period of time (at least two or three months) you still feel unsettled then you should think seriously about travelling again. One year often expands to two or three and you should not feel guilty if this is what you really want to do. After spending time travelling between school and university, students frequently repeat the exercise once they have graduated. Some even make a full-time career of it.

Returning to the job market

This is one of the great grey areas about travelling for an extended period. Personnel officers generally say they are in favour of people who have travelled, citing benefits such as personal growth and greater experiences. However, there are a couple of drawbacks to this:

- Travellers are sometimes seen as being eccentric.
- There is always the fear that a reformed traveller may throw it all in and take to the road again.

With increasing unemployment (particularly graduate unemployment which, according the Association of Graduate Careers Advisory Services' Central Services Unit, is approaching the ten per cent mark), people contemplating a period of travel will have to consider how it will affect their employment prospects once they return. There is one school of thought that argues it is not worth working for an employer who does not recognise the benefits of travelling. If people have the confidence to travel round the world then they will probably have the ability to find a good job when they return. The public sector are very open-minded when it comes to employing people who have invested some of their time in travelling.

Show employers your experiences in the best possible way
When trying to re-enter the job market you should be proud of your experiences and show them in the best possible light. Instead of writing on your CV 'I spent six months in Peru working with local tribes', say 'I spent six months organising the local tribes in the construction of a new irrigation system. I was in charge of a group of ten people, which involved management skills, inter-personal skills, flexibility, initiative and stamina. The system was completed on time and has doubled the village's agricultural output.' Do not be afraid to sell yourself.

- Explain what you did, with the emphasis on the positive contributions you made.
- What you learnt from the experience.
- How you have benefited personally.
- The benefits that you will be able to bring your employer.

Seeking alternative employment
If you do not want to go back on the treadmill of conventional employment you could consider alternative means of earning a living. This could be anything from an independent travel consultant to setting up your own voluntary organisation. People have even been known to write books based on their experiences abroad.

Questions to ask yourself when you return
1. Am I happy with what I have done?
2. Am I happy with being back home?
3. Have I spent enough time getting used to being back home?
4. Do I want to go travelling again?
5. If so, what do I want to do?
6. Do I have a good record of what I have done?
7. Can I show employers that I have benefited from travelling?
8. Have I learnt things that could lead to a new career?
9. Can I pass on my experiences to others?
10. Will life ever be the same again?

SECTION TWO

The purpose of this section is to give an overview of the countries of the world. It is not intended to be a definitive guide to each country, space precludes this, but it is hoped it will give a taste of each country and give prospective travellers some hints. One of the best aspects of travel is anticipation and if people know something about the countries of the world this can be used to fire the imagination.

For countries that travellers think they will be spending any length of time in it is recommended that specific guide books are consulted. The *Lonely Planet* and the *Rough Guides* are two of the best series available.

In this section Europe has been treated as a stepping-off point for a round the world trip and therefore it has not been dealt with in any great detail. In many ways a tour of Europe can be regarded as a separate event and many travellers decide to do this and then embark on a round the world adventure.

At the time of writing there are a number of countries that it is inadvisable to visit, usually for reasons of civil war or unrest. These countries have been noted but these facts can change rapidly. If you are in any doubt about a country you are planning to visit then get in touch with the Foreign Office or the relevant embassy to check out the current situation.

9
North Africa

ALGERIA

Capital: Algiers
Type of Government: Republic
Official languages: Arabic and French
Population: 25 million

Currency: Dinar
Size: 2,381,745 square km
Climate: Generally hot, dry and
humid
National Airline: Air Algerie

General information
Foreign occupation of Algeria dates back to when it was a province of the
Roman Empire. Following occupation by the Turks in the 16th century the
region became a pirate state, from where ships in the Mediterranean were
attacked. In the 19th century Algeria was annexed by the French and this
situation was maintained until 1962 when France granted Algeria its
independence. Since then the country has been troubled by political and social
unrest, despite multi-party reforms being introduced in 1989.

Food and drink
Both Arab and French influences are to be found in the local cuisine. Cous-cous
(semolina, usually served with a meat stew) is the staple diet and chicken,
seafood casse-croûte (stuffed French bread), brochettes and salad are widely
available.

Internal transport
In the north of the country there is a reliable and efficient bus service but
hitching is generally a more popular way to get around, although this is not
recommended for single women. Much of southern Algeria consists of the
Sahara Desert. There are three main routes through the desert and they can be
tackled with your own vehicle (careful planning is needed) or you can try and
hitch a ride on the trucks which travel south.

Things to see
Algiers, north Algeria. Useful for official matters.
    Beni Abbes, west Algeria. An oasis town in the desert, with magnificent dunes
nearby.
    Constantine, north Algeria. Stunning views of the nearby Rhumel Gorge.

El Oued, northeast Algeria. Known as the 'Town of 1000 Cupolas' in recognition of the domed buildings in the town.

Tamanrasset, south Algeria. The destination of most people heading across the Sahara.

Grand Erg Occidental and grand Erg Oriental, west and east Algeria respectively. Two areas of the Sahara, with villages, dunes and oases.

Useful addresses
Algerian Embassy, 54 Holland Park, London W11 3RS. Tel: (0171) 221 7800.
Algerian Tourist Office, 6 Hyde Park Gate, London SW7. Tel (0171) 584 5152.
British Embassy, Residence Cassiopee, Batiment B, Chemin des Glycines, Algiers.
British Council, 6 Avenue Souidani Boudjemaa, Algiers.

EGYPT

Capital: Cairo	Currency: Egyptian pound
Type of Government: Republic	Size: 1,000,000 square km
Official language: Arabic	Population: 58 million
Climate: Generally hot and dry	National airline: EgyptAir

General information
The site of one of the world's oldest civilisations: the recorded history of the areas dates back at least 6000 years. The ancient history of Egypt is usually divided into 30 dynasties, beginning in 3100 BC and ending in 343 BC with the death of the last pharaoh, Nectanebo II.In 1798 Napoleon conquered Egypt and established it as a French protectorate. This lasted until 1801 when he was defeated by the British and the Ottomans. In 1914 Egypt became a British protectorate and by 1922 the country was independent. Following independence, Egypt has had a number of conflicts with its Arab neighbours and, although the situation began to improve in the 1980s, there are still some factions within the country who use terrorism to try and achieve their goals. Some of these groups have targeted tourists in recent years and this should be kept in mind when travelling in Egypt.

Food and drink
The Arab culinary influence is predominant in Egypt and there is a great variety to choose from. Some cheap and tasty dishes include *fuul* (fava beans), *ta'amiyya* (fried chickpea balls), *tahina* (sesame spread), *kufta* (skewered meat), *kushari* (lentils, rice, noodles and onions). Chinese, Korean, Indian and Western cuisine can also be found throughout Egypt.

Internal transport
Cairo has a good selection of transport ranging from buses, the metro, trams and taxis. Local buses and deluxe versions travel to most places in the country and they are frequent and cheap. Taxis go from city to city and this is quicker and more expensive than buses. Bicycles are readily available for hire and this is

a good cheap way to see the country. Rail is one of the best ways to travel in the Nile Valley and the 1st class and the air-conditioned 2nd class offer reasonable comfort at a good price. For people who want to sail along the Nile there are *feluccas* (traditional sailboats) that operate up and down the river.

Things to see
Cairo, northeast Egypt. One of the great cities of the world and one that is steeped in history and culture. One of the highlights of Cairo is the Tutankhamen artefacts in the Egyptian Museum.

Giza Pyramids and the Sphinx, northeast Egypt. One of the Seven Wonders of the World and a sight that rivals Victoria Falls for surpassing all expectations.

Alexandria, north Egypt. A fascinating city with a long history and a former capital of Egypt.

Aswan, southeast Egypt. At a point where the Nile is stunning, this city has a fine collection of ancient temples and ruins.

Luxor, central east Egypt. The site of ancient Thebes and an area that is rich in historical significance. Most notable is the Valley of the Kings, where the tomb of Tutankhamen was discovered.

Useful addresses
Egyptian Embassy, 26 South Street, London W1Y 8EL. Tel: (0171) 499 2401.
Egyptian Tourist Office, 168 Piccadilly, London W1Y 9DE. Tel: (0171) 493 5282.
British Embassy, Ahmed Ragheb Street, Garden City, Cairo
British Council, 192 Sharia el Nil, Agouza, Cairo.

LIBYA

Capital: Tripoli   Currency: Libyan dinar
Type of Government: People's Republic   Official language: Arabic
Population: 4.6 million   Size: 1,759,540 square km
Climate: Hot and humid

General information
The Italians annexed the area in 1912 and during the Second World War the area was the scene of several important battles. In 1951 the United Kingdom of Libya was created. In 1969 Colonel Gaddafi took control following a military coup. Since then relations with the West have been strained. Be cautious.

Food and drink
A mixture of north African and Arab cuisines.

Internal transport
Hitching is a good way to get around, but not for single women, and there are buses but these are erratic and infrequent.

Things to see
Tripoli (Tarabulus), northwest Libya. Some attractive buildings can be seen.

The Ancient Cities, northwest Libya. Various Greek, Roman and Byzantine ruins, the most well known being Leptis-Magna, 120 km east of Tripoli.

MALI

Capital: Bamako
Type of Government: Republic
Official language: French
Size: 1,204,021 square km
National airline: Malitas Air

Currency: CFA (Communaute financière africaine) franc
Population: 8.5 million
Climate: Generally hot and dry

General information
In the 19th century the French occupied the country and named it French Sudan. Although it became a part of French West Africa it gained independence as Mali in 1960. In 1969 there was a military coup and in 1985 Mali went to war with Burkina Faso. In 1991 the military regime was overthrown and the new leaders promised a multi-party democracy. Travellers should be aware of people being over-friendly, talking politics or trying to sell something.

Food and drink
There are several French restaurants and street stalls sell a good selection of foods: brochettes, ragoût, fish, rice, fried plantains, sweet potatoes and couscous.

Internal transport
The roads are poor but the bus service is reasonable, if a little slow. Taxis and pick-ups also operate. One of the best ways of getting around is the riverboats on the Niger River.

Things to see
Bamako, southwest Mali. Useful mainly for administrative matters.
  Timbuktu, central Mali. Somewhere you have to visit, just to say you have been there.
  Djenne, south Mali. An old trading town oozing with history and folklore.
  Dogon Country, south Mali. A collection of villages that are of great historical, anthropological and archaeological interest.

Useful address
Mali Embassy, 89 Rue du Cherche-Midi, 75006 Paris.

MOROCCO

Capital: Rabat
Type of Government: Kingdom
Official languages: Arabic, French and Spanish
National Airline: Royal Air Maroc

Population: 27.5 million
Currency: Dirham
Size: 458,730 square km
Climate: Warm and dry – over 300 days of sunshine a year

General information
In the 5th century Mauritania fell to the Vandals. For centuries afterwards the Arabs and the Berbers were in virtual continuous conflict. In the 15th century Morocco was attacked by the Spanish and the Portuguese and until the 19th century it enjoyed the dubious privilege of being a base for the Barbary pirates.

The Europeans began taking an interest in Morocco in the 19th century and the French were the first to assert their dominance but this was challenged by the Germans. In 1912 the country was partitioned into French and Spanish protectorates and in 1923 Tangier was also partitioned.

In 1956 France and Spain agreed to give up the protectorates and they became a sultanate. A year later Morocco was declared a kingdom. In 1975 the Spanish Sahara was divided between Morocco and Mauritania. The withdrawal by Mauritania from the Western Sahara four years later led to several skirmishes and the UN were required to try and bring peace to the area in 1991.

Food and drink
An exotic blend of African, French, Spanish and Arabian cooking. Some of the local dishes include: Harira – a rich peppery soup. Bstilla – chicken or pigeon in pastry and flavoured with delicate herbs and spices. Couscous – steamed semolina served with vegetables, lamb or chicken. Tajine – a slow-cooked stew. Mshoui – local roast lamb. Djaja Maamra – steamed stuffed chicken. There is also French, Spanish, Italian and Chinese cuisine available. Local beer and wine is of a consistently good standard. Mint tea is drunk widely.

Internal transport
All the major centres are linked by an economical rail system that offers modern, air-conditioned trains. There are also two national coachlines and the road network is one of the most extensive and well kept in Africa. There are also internal flights between all the major towns.

Things to see
Tangier, northern Morocco. At the northern tip of the country this is a fascinating mix of cultures and includes spacious beaches and sea caves.

Marrakesh, southwest Morocco. The former imperial capital of Morocco and a city of architectural beauty and historical significance.

Agadir, southern Morocco. One of the country's most popular resorts.

Casablanca, west Morocco. A must for all film buffs – and everyone else.

Rabat, northwest Morocco. One of the imperial cities and the present capital.

South Morocco. From the towering Atlas Mountains to the edge of the Sahara Desert this is an area that combines remarkable scenery with local culture and historical significance.

Useful addresses
Moroccan Embassy, 49 Queen's Gate Gardens, London SW7 5NE. Tel: (0171) 581 5001.
Moroccan Tourist Office, 205 Regent Street, London W1R 7DE. Tel: (0171) 437 0073.

British Embassy, 17 Boulevard de la Tour, Rabat.
British Council (BP 427), 22 Avenue Moulay Youssef, Rabat.

TUNISIA

Capital: Tunis
Type of Government: Republic
Official languages: Arabic and French
Climate: Mild winters and hot and dry
summers

Currency: Tunisian dinar
Size: 164,150 square km
Population: 8.5 million
National Airline: Tunis Air

General information
The empire of Carthage grew up here from the 7th century but this did not last and the Roman conquered the area and it became known as 'the granary of Rome'. The Ottoman Turks conquered Tunisia in 1574 and it was in the 18th century that European powers began to take an interest in the area.

In 1883 Tunisia became a French protectorate, causing an upsurge of nationalist interest. During the Second World War there was a period of brief occupation by the Germans and in 1956 the nationalist movement secured independence. Although there was a coup in 1987 it was a peaceful one and Tunisia remains a stable and moderate country.

Food and drink
The French and Arabic culinary influence is strong in Tunisia. Chicken, chips, pizzas and a wide variety of cakes are also freely available.

Internal transport
Budget buses, air-conditioned coaches and taxis ensure that road transport is efficient and cheap. Hitching is possible but in some areas this can be slow. The rail network is generally slow and inefficient. Daily ferries operate between Sfax and Kerkennah Islands.

Things to see
Tunis, north Tunisia. A fascinating city and justifiably called the gateway to Africa. Also the site of the Roman ruins of Carthage.

Dougga, north Tunisia. The site of notable Roman ruins.

Douz, central Tunisia. A Sahara town that holds the popular oasis festival in December.

Kairouan, north central Tunisia. One of the most important cities in the Islamic culture.

Kerkennah Islands, east coast. Good for exploring rather than lying on a beach.

Tozeur, west Tunisia. A relaxed oasis town.

Useful addresses
Tunisia Embassy, 29 Prince's Gate,London SW7 1QG. Tel: (0171) 584 8117.
British Embassy, 5 Place de la Victoire, Tunis.

10
West Africa

BENIN

Capital: Porto Novo
Type of Government: Republic
Official language: French
Size: 112,600 square km

Population: 4.8 million
Currency: CFA (Communauté
financière africaine) franc
Climate: equatorial

General information
In the 17th century the Aja kingdom of Dahomey was a centre for the slave trade but this ended in 1893 when the country was occupied by the French. It became part of French West Africa and in 1960 Dahomey was declared an independent republic within the French Community. Several military coups followed and when Dahomey changed its name to Benin in 1975 the country was being run as a Marxist-Leninist state. In 1990 there was a move towards a more democratic form of government.

Food and drink
Seafood is the best of the local cuisine and western food from hamburgers to pizzas is fairly common.

Internal transport
Ageing taxis and bush taxis operate on the country's limited road network and there are two main railway lines.

Things to see
Cotonou, south Benin. The country's administrative capital.
    Abomey, south Benin. The historical capital of Dahomey – the palace is well worth a visit.
    Ganvie, south Benin. A village built on stilts in the middle of a lagoon.
    Porto Novo, south Benin. A capital that is more like a large, colonial town.

Useful address
France: Benin Embassy, 87 Avenue Victor-Hugo, 75116 Paris.

BURKINA FASO

Capital: Ouagadougou
Type of Government: Republic:
Official language: French
Size: 274,000 square km
National Airline: Air Burkina (internal)

Population: 9 million
Currency: CFA (Communauté
    financière africaine) franc
Climate: Dry and hot

General information
In 1898 the country became part of the French protectorate of Soudan and in 1919 it became the protectorate of Upper Volta in its own right. In 1932 it was divided between Niger, Côte d'Ivoire and Soudan but this experiment was abandoned in 1946. This led to a call for independence, which was achieved in 1960 when Upper Volta gained its freedom from France. Since then there have been various military coups and in the last ten years there have been territorial disputes with neighbouring Mali.

Food and drink
The cuisine is generally uninspiring but average steaks and beer are widely available. Food stalls are good for cheap meals.

Internal transport
Road transport can be an erratic business as the roads are of a poor quality. There are trains between the main cities and you can choose between the normal service or the more expensive Express. Taxis can be used over long distances.

Things to see
Ouagadougou, central Burkina Faso. A former colonial centre that is fragmented but has a good museum and a game reserve nearby.
    Banfora, western Burkina Faso. A peaceful area where canoeing is popular.
    Koudougou, central Burkina Faso. An area with hospitable people and interesting villages.

Useful address
Burkina Faso Embassy, 150 Buckingham Palace Road, London SW1W 9SA. Tel: (0171) 730 8141.

COTE D'IVOIRE

Capital: Yamoussoukro – Abidjan is the
    commercial and diplomatic capital
Official language: French
Climate: Tropical
National Airline: Air Ivoire

Population: 12 million
Type of Government: Republic
Currency: CFA (Communauté
    financière africaine) franc

General information
Before becoming a French colony in 1893 the Ivory Coast was sought after by

several European trading nations. In 1904 it became part of French West Africa and independence from France was achieved in 1960. Recently there was a potential leadership crisis, but this was averted and a multi-party democracy was introduced in 1990.

Food and drink
There are several types of international cuisine available and Lebanese is one of the most common. Local food stalls offer rice with sauce, brochettes and barbecue sauce, all at very low prices.

Internal transport
Buses and taxis are the most popular way of getting around although taxis are more expensive. There is a rail network but this has a limited number of services.

Things to see
Abidjan, south Côte d'Ivoire, the main city in the country and considered the New York of West Africa.

Ile Boulay and Adobo-Doume, south coast. Two popular areas for a break from the city.

Bondoukou, east Côte d'Ivoire. An Islamic centre that has over 40 mosques.

Useful addresses
Côte d'Ivoire Embassy, 2 Upper Belgrave Street, London SW1X 8BJ. Tel: (0171) 235 6991.
British Embassy (BP 2581), 5th Floor, Immeuble Shell, Avenue Lamblin, Abidjan.

EQUATORIAL GUINEA

Capital: Malabo:
Type of Government: Republic
Official language: Spanish
Population: 348,000

Currency: CFA (Communauté financière africaine) franc
Size: 28,051 square km
Climate: Equatorial

General information
Formerly a Spanish colony, Equatorial Guinea was the last African colonial territory to become independent, in 1968. In 1979 the president was overthrown by a military coup.

Food and drink
Choice of foods is erratic since there are frequent shortages. The markets and food stalls offer meals from seafood to pizzas.

Internal transport
Many roads are unsealed but hitching is a good way to get around. There are ferries that connect the mainland, but they are old and have a tendency to sink.

Things to see
Malabo, west coast. Situated on an island off the coast this is a charismatic colonial town with a distinctly Spanish identity.

Bata, west Equatorial Guinea. The principal town on the mainland.

GAMBIA

Capital: Banjul
Type of Government: Republic
Official language: English
Population: 861,000

Currency: Dalasi
Size: 10,689 square km
Climate: Sub-tropical
National Airline: Gambia Airways

General information
The Portuguese were the first Europeans to establish trading posts in the 15th century and the following century the English followed their example. The British administered the area from Sierra Leone, and in 1843 it became a crown colony. It was separated from Sierra Leone in 1888 and in 1965 Gambia gained independence. In 1981 Senegal intervened to thwart an attempted coup and the two countries have continued to have close ties.

Food and drink
International food including Chinese, Vietnamese and French can be found, as can hamburgers and fish and chips. Local seafood is excellent and the local beer, Julbrew, is worth a try.

Internal transport
The road system is good and there are numerous taxis, pick-ups and government buses. Hitching is also a reasonable possibility. Ferries can be taken to cross the country's main river.

Things to see
Bakau/Fajara, west Gambia. More facilities than the capital and plenty of nightlife. A major resort area in the country.

Georgetown, central Gambia. A tranquil town that has a reggae feel to it.

Juffre, Albreda and James Island, west Gambia. Made famous by Alex Haley as the starting point for his novel *Roots*.

Abuko Nature Reserve, west Gambia. Home of vervet monkeys, bush buck and crocodiles.

Useful addresses
Gambia High Commission, 57 Kensington Court, London W8 5DG. Tel: (0171) 937 6316.
British High Commission (PO Box 507), 48 Atlantic Road, Banjul.

GHANA

Capital: Accra

Currency: Cedi

Type of Government: Republic
Official language: English
Population: 15 million

Size: 238,305 square km
Climate: Sub-tropical
National Airline: Ghana Airways

General information
In 1472 the Portuguese set up trading posts in what was the Gold Coast. Slavery was one of the main trades of the area and the British and Dutch had a number of skirmishes over this issue. In 1874 the Gold Coast became a British colony. In 1957 Ghana became an independent state. In the years that followed independence there were several military coups and it was only in 1992 that there were multi-party elections. Despite this the opposition parties have refused to accept the result of these elections.

Food and drink
Street stalls and chop houses are the best places to get cheap, local food. Meat in a spicy sauce is common, as is *fufu* (yam dumplings). Other delicacies include akrantie, snail soup, kebabs and crab. The most popular drink is ice-cold beer.

Internal transport
Both the road and the rail system are only just recovering from years of neglect. Private buses and taxis can be used to get around the major centres but in more isolated spots minibuses and Mammy Wagons are most common. These are basically anything with four wheels and an engine than can propel it in a straight line. The trains are slow and the network is limited to the south.

Things to see
Accra, south Ghana. A lively and bustling capital.
    Kumasi, central Ghana. A major cultural centre and the old Ashanti capital.
    Mole Game Reserve, northern Ghana. Various wildlife can be seen here including lions, leopards and monkeys.
    Nakpanduri, northeast Ghana. With magnificent views this village is perfect for quiet relaxation.

Useful addresses
Ghana High Commission, 13 Belgrave Square, London SW1X 8PR. Tel: (0171) 235 4142.
British High Commission (PO Box 296), Barclays Bank Building, High Street, Accra.
British Council, PO Box 771, Liberia Road, Accra.

GUINEA

Capital: Conakry
Type of Government: Republic
Official language: French and eight
    local languages
National Airline: Air Guinea

Currency: Guinea franc
Size: 245,857 square km
Climate: Humid on the coast and
    cooler inland
Population: 7 million

General information
From the 15th century European traders were operating in this area. Part of Guinea became a French colony in 1891 and four years later it became part of French West Africa. In 1958 French Guinea became independent and since then it has been run as a single-party state, with the army taking control in 1984.

Food and drink
Meat and seafood make up most of the local dishes and street stalls offer barbecued corn and brochettes (kebabs). Lebanese, Portuguese and Italian cuisine is also available.

Internal transport
Buses, minibuses, taxis, pick-ups and trucks are available but the road system is limited and in a poor state of repair. There are also internal flights for getting around.

Things to see
Conakry, west Guinea. Useful mainly for administration matters.
   Cap Verga, west Guinea. A popular beach area.
   Dabola, central Guinea. Old French colonial town in pleasant surroundings.
   Nzerekore, south Guinea. A town in the mountains and a good spot for walking.

Useful address
Guinea Embassy, 24 Rue Emile-Meunier, 75016 Paris.

GUINEA-BISSAU

Capital: Bissau   Population: 1 million
Type of Government: Republic   Currency: Peso
Official languages: Portuguese and   Size: 36,125 square km
   Crioulo   Climate: Sub-tropical

General information
Under the influence of the Portuguese the area was targeted by slave traders from the 15th century onwards. It became a Portuguese colony in 1879 and an independent republic in 1974. After a military coup in 1980 democratic rule was reintroduced in 1984. In 1994 there were democratic elections.

Food and drink
Barbecued corn, meat and cous-cous make up the majority of the local cuisine. Barbecued pigeon and fresh prawns are also local favourites. Beer and wine are readily available.

Internal transport
Ferries are used to get to some of the country's numerous islands. On the

mainland the road system is improving but erratic.

Things to see
Bissau, west Guinea-Bissau. A very pleasant, relaxed capital.
   The Bijagos Archipelago, west Guinea-Bissau. A group of islands that retain much of the local history and culture. Bubaque and Caravela are the most popular.

Useful address
Guinea-Bissau Embassy, 8 Palace Gate, London W8 4RP. Tel: (0171) 589 5253.

LIBERIA

Liberia has suffered various bitter civil wars in recent years and it is not recommended that travellers venture into this area.

MAURITANIA

Due to political unrest in recent years and a general lack of opportunities for visitors this is a place for the seasoned traveller only.

NIGERIA

Capital: Abuja
Type of Government: Federal Republic
Official language: English
Population: 110 million
National Airline: Nigerian Airways

Currency: Naira
Size: 923,773 square km
Climate: Hot and dry (north)
   hot and wet (south)

General information
The Portuguese were the first Europeans to arrive here, in the 15th century, and they used the territory as a centre for slavery. By 1906 Britain was in control of Northern and Southern Nigeria, which were united in 1914. Following a rise in nationalist concerns Nigeria became a federation in 1954 and six years later the country became independent. With frequent changes in the military regimes coupled with economic problems Nigeria suffered several years of instability. In 1993 it seemed that some order might be restored when democratic rule was introduced. Travellers should still exercise great caution when travelling in parts of the country. Abuja is a new capital and Lagos remains the capital in all but name.

Food and drink
Much of the food in Nigeria is of the curry, rice, stew, beans, omelettes and chips variety. There is also a smattering of Chinese and Korean food on offer. The local palm wine should be sampled, but treated with respect.

Internal transport
Some of the roads are potholed and dangerous, as is the condition of a large

proportion of the buses and taxis on the road. Unfortunately the rail system has suffered from years of neglect so road travel is the most common method of getting around. Try to choose a mode of transport that looks at least moderately roadworthy.

Things to see
Not Lagos if you can help it.
Yankari Game Reserve, central Nigeria. A moderate selection of wildlife.
Calabar, southwest Nigeria. An old colonial town that is more peaceful than other parts of the country.
Jos, central Nigeria. Set in lush hills this town offers a cool climate and a selection of local culture.
Kano, north Nigeria. A town with a history dating back 1000 years.

Useful address
Nigerian Embassy, 9 Northumberland Avenue, London WC2. Tel: (0171) 839 1244.
British High Commission, 11 Eleke Crescent, Victoria Island.

SENEGAL

Capital: Dakar
Type of Government: Republic
Official language: French
Population: 8 million
National Airline: Air Senegal

Currency: CFA (Communauté financière africaine) franc
Size: 197,722 sq km
Climate: Generally hot and dry (cooler December to May)

General information
During the 14th and 15th centuries the area was part of the Mali empire but then the French began to take control. By the 20th century political moves towards independence were initiated. This process was largely peaceful and independence was achieved in 1960. In 1982 it formed the Senegambia Confederation with Gambia and since then its progress has been stable and steady.

Food and drink
Street barbecues offer grilled meat and hot sandwiches at very reasonable prices. Restaurants sell Western and African food, including the local *maffe*, rice and groundnut sauce with meat and potatoes.

Internal transport
Taxis, minibuses and pick-ups operate on most of the main routes throughout the country. Even for taxis the prices are very moderate. There is a local rail service but most people prefer to travel by road. There are also ferries operating from Dakar.

Things to see
Dakar, west Senegal. The most expensive city in west Africa but it is very modern and very large. The nearby Ile de Goree, an old slaving station, is the main tourist attraction.

M'Bour, west Senegal. A tourist town with a good beach.

Touba, central west Senegal. The main pilgrimage centre in the country.

Basse Casamance, southwest Senegal. A small national park with monkeys, duikers and numerous birds.

Useful addresses
Senegal Embassy, 11 Phillimore Gardens, London W8 7QG. Tel: (0171) 937 0925.

British Embassy and British Council (BP 6025), 20 Rue du Docteur Guillet, Dakar.

SIERRA LEONE

Capital: Freetown
Type of Government: Republic
Official language: English (Krio widely spoken)

Currency: Leone
Size: 73,326 square km
Climate: Hot and humid
Population: 4.5 million

General information
In the 18th century part of the country was ceded to Britain and in 1896 it became a British protectorate. In 1961 Sierra Leone became independent within the Commonwealth. During the 1960s there were several military coups: in 1971 the country became a republic and six years later a one-party government was introduced. In 1992 there was another military coup.

Food and drink
Sandwiches, stew and rice are the most common types of food. Lebanese and Indian food can also be found.

Internal transport
There is no national airline and the roads are the only way to get around. However, the roads are potholed and petrol is at a premium. Hitching is possible and taxis and minibuses are the most common forms of public transport. Expect overcrowding and keep an eye on your luggage.

Things to see
Freetown, west Sierra Leone. A languid and colonial style capital.

Outamba-Kilimi National Park, northwest Sierra Leone. A good place to see elephants, hippos, monkeys and crocodiles.

Tiwai Island Wildlife Sanctuary, southwest Sierra Leone. Monkeys, butterflies and birds abound here.

Useful addresses
Sierra Leone High Commission, 33 Portland Place, London W1N 3AG. Tel:
(0171) 636 6483.
British High Commission, Standard Bank of Sierra Leone Building, Lightboot
Boston Street, Freetown.

TOGO

Capital: Lome
Type of Government: Republic
Official language: French
Size: 56,000 square km

Currency: CFA (Communauté
financière africaine) franc
Population: 3.5 million
Climate: Sub-tropical

General information
Between the 17th and 19th centuries the area was frequently raided by European
powers in search of slaves. After the First World War Togoland was divided
between France and Britain. In 1960 Togo became independent from France,
with the British section joining Ghana. From 1967 to 1991 General Eyadema
was in power and following his fall from grace a multi-party constitution was
approved.

Food and drink
Local fish is plentiful and street stalls sell a variety of local food including rice,
fufu (yam dumplings), brochettes and barbecued corn. Senegalese, Vietnamese
and Continental cuisine is also available, as is local beer.

Internal transport
Roads are generally good in the country and one of the best ways to travel is by
minibus or pick-up truck. Taxis are a little more expensive but can take you long
distances. The rail network is limited and only reaches to the most populated
areas.

Things to see
Lome, south Togo. A stopping off point for the Sahara. There are also beaches
nearby.
    Aneho, south Togo. The old colonial capital.
    K'Palime, south Togo. A resort town near Togo's highest mountain.
    Parc National de la Keran, north Togo. The country's most important game
park, famous for antelopes and baboons.

Useful addresses
Togo Embassy, 30 Sloane Street, London SW1. Tel: (0171) 235 0147.
British Embassy (PO Box 80607), Rue Miramar, Lome.

11
Central Africa

BURUNDI

Capital: Bujumbura
Type of Government: Republic
Official languages: French and Kirundi
Population: 5.5 million

Currency: Burundi franc
Size: 27,834 square km
Climate: Hot and humid around
Lake Tanganyika, cooler in
mountains

General information
Due to the current unsettled situation in neighbouring Rwanda travellers should exercise caution when considering visiting Burundi.

Useful address
Burundi Embassy, 46 Square Marie Louise, 1040 Brussels.

CAMEROON

Capital: Yaoundé
Type of Government: Republic
Official languages: French and English
Population: 12 million
National Airline: Air Cameroun

Currency: CFA (Communauté
financière africaine) franc
Size: 475,422 square km
Climate: Hot deserts to tropical
forests

General information
The Portuguese first visited this area in the 15th century. In 1884 the Germans established the protectorate of Kamerun, which lasted until after the First World War, when the area was split into the French and British Cameroons. In 1960 the French section was declared independent and the British section followed a year later. In 1972 a united republic was created. In 1992 free elections were held but these were boycotted by opposition parties. Riots ensued and a state of emergency was declared. Travellers should be careful if visiting here.

Useful addresses
Cameroon Embassy, 84 Holland Park, London W11 3SB. Tel: (0171) 727 0771.
British Embassy (BP 547), Le Concorde, avenue Winston Churchill, Yaoundé.
British Council (BP 818), avenue J. F. Kennedy, Yaoundé.

CENTRAL AFRICAN REPUBLIC

General information
General unrest in recent years has caused problems for travellers and various hassles have been reported, ranging from theft to killer bees. If possible, travellers should try and steer clear of this troubled republic.

CHAD

General information
Following colonisation by the French, Chad became independent in 1960. However, since 1963 there has been considerable unrest in the country and the situation is currently unstable for travellers. If possible, a route avoiding Chad should be chosen.

CONGO

Capital: Brazzaville
Type of Government: Popular Republic
Official language: French
Size: 342,000 square km

Currency: CFA (Communauté financière africaine) franc
Population: 2.3 million
Climate: Equatorial north, drier and hotter coast

General information
The Portuguese were the first Europeans to arrive here but they were superseded by the French in the 19th century and in 1910 Middle Congo became one of the four territories of French Equatorial Africa. In 1960 the Congo gained its independence from France. For 30 years the country was ruled by various military leaders but in 1992 the people of the Congo voted in a referendum for a multi-party system, which is currently finding its feet.

Food and drink
Cheap food is available in the markets and this is usually of a good, basic nature. A small selection of international restaurants can be found in the capital.

Internal transport
The roads are generally in poor condition and the train is the best way to get around. Ferries are in operation for people wishing to travel to neighbouring Zaire.

Things to see
Brazzaville, south Congo. The main point of interest for the traveller – an enjoyable capital, with a cathedral, a mosque and several markets.

Useful address
Congo Embassy, 37 bis, rue Paul Valéry, 75016 Paris.

GABON

Capital: Libreville
Type of Government: Republic
Official language: French (Bantu languages widely spoken)
Climate: Tropical

Currency: CFA (Communauté financière africaine) franc
Size: 267,000 square km
Population 1.2 million
National Airline: Air Gabon

General information
A former centre for the slave trade, the country was settled by the French in the 19th century and in 1910 it became one of the four territories of French Equatorial Africa. In 1960 independence was achieved but despite rich reserves of oil the country's economic prosperity was brief. Due to a one-party system of government an underground movement was formed to try and achieve a democracy. This seemed to have happened in 1990 when multi-party elections were held. However, this was later declared void after accusations of vote rigging.

Food and drink
Meat features in many local dishes and it can be as exotic as gazelle and crocodile. The French influence is noticeable in much of the cooking.

Internal transport
Buses and bush taxis operate between the main cities but they tend to be rather expensive and the state of the local roads is poor. The rail system is a better bet – it is punctual and offers first and second class carriages. There are also boats that can be used to get around the country and although they are cheap they can get quite crowded.

Things to see
Libreville, west Gabon. The capital and main port which still retains much of its French influence.

Coco Beach, northwest Gabon. An unspoilt beach with an interesting fishing village nearby.

There are also three national parks where elephants, gorillas, leopards, mandrills, monkeys and antelope can be seen: Parc National de l'Okanda and Parc National du Petit Loango.

Useful addresses
Gabon Embassy, 48 Kensington Court, London W8 5DB. Tel: (0171) 937 5285.
British Embassy (BP476), Batiment Sogame, Blvd de l'Independence, Libreville.

NIGER

Capital: Niamey
Type of Government: Republic
Official language: French
Population: 8 million

Currency: (Communauté financière africaine) franc
Size: 1,267,000 square km
Climate: hot and dry (largely Sahara)

General information
After being occupied by the French in 1883 the area became part of French West Africa in 1904. In 1960 the country achieved independence and in 1974 the government was overthrown by a military coup. Military rule continued until 1991 and in 1993 the country's first democratic elections were held.

Food and drink
Basic food consisting of rice, beans, chicken, brochettes, omelettes and spaghetti can be bought from street stalls and restaurants.

Internal transport
There are good bus links between the major towns although the government-run SNTN buses are more expensive, and more comfortable, than the local taxis which ply the same routes. Boats can be used to travel up and down the Niger River.

Things to see
Niamey, west Niger. Its main interest is in its administrative functions.
    Agadez, central Niger. A traditional town that offers a break from the desert.
    Arlit, northwest Niger. Surrounded by dramatic mountains.

Useful address
Niger Embassy, 154 Rue de Longchamp, 75116 Paris.

RWANDA

At the time of writing there is a bitter civil war being waged in Rwanda. Due to this the country should be considered off-limits by travellers.

SUDAN

Since 1985 Sudan has been engulfed in famine and civil war. From 1991-1993 the situation worsened due to fighting between tribal factions. The future looks very uncertain and travellers should leave Sudan off their itinerary.

UGANDA

Capital: Kampala
Type of Government: Republic
Official language: English (Swahili
    and Luganda widely spoken)

Currency: Ugandan shilling
Size: 236,860 square km
Population: 19 million
Climate: Generally warm but cooler
    in the mountains

General information
The Buganda tribe were the dominant force during the 18th and 19th centuries. This was put to an end in 1894 when Uganda became a British protectorate. In the 1950s Milton Obote began a movement that was to lead to independence in 1962. Obote made himself president but he abused his powers and was overthrown by Idi

Amin in a military coup in 1971. Amin administered a brutal regime and an estimated 300,000 of his opponents were tortured and murdered. In 1979 Amin was ousted and Obote returned to power. He again tried to rule the country in a corrupt fashion and was overthrown in 1985. National instability followed and the situation continues to be very uncertain and there is still some fighting in the north of the country – so this area should be avoided if possible.

Useful addresses
Uganda High Commission, 58-59 Trafalgar Square, London WC2N 5DX. Tel: (0171) 839 5783.
British High Commission and British Council (PO Box 7070), 10-12 Parliament Avenue, Kampala.

ZAIRE

Capital: Kinshasa
Type of Government: Democratic Republic
Climate: Sub-tropical
National Airline: Air Zaire

Currency: Zaire
Size: 2,345,409 square km
Official language: French (African languages also spoken)
Population: 37 million

General information
The Portuguese arrived in the kingdom of Kongo in the 15th century and exploited the locals for use in the slave trade. It was not until the 19th century that the interior of the country began to be properly explored, first by David Livingstone and then by Henry Morton Stanley. The latter was sponsored by the Belgian government and this resulted in the country becoming the Belgian colony of the Belgian Congo in 1908. During the 1950s the Belgians allowed the emergence of various African political parties and this resulted in independence for the Republic of the Congo in 1960. A period of civil war followed and in 1971 the Congo was renamed Zaire. In 1978 the country's leader Mobutu announced a one-party state but unrest in the country erupted in 1990 when there was widespread rioting and looting. Mobutu then announced that he was going to introduce a new democratic regime but the current situation is uncertain.

Food and drink
There can be food shortages throughout the country but in Kinshasa basic fare of fish, rice, beans and hamburgers is cheap. Local delicacies of eels, caterpillars, grasshoppers and termites are also on offer.

Internal transport
Travelling through Zaire is different to most other African countries due to the large areas of jungle. It is very much a case of using your initiative and preparing yourself for an adventure whenever you are going any great distance. Be prepared to take any form of transport that is on offer, be it truck, land cruiser, ferry or beaten-up van.

Things to see

Kinshasa, west Zaire. A bustling city that contrasts with the rest of the country. Keep your wits about you at all times.

National parks are the main attraction in Zaire and two of the best are Parc National De Kahuzi-Biega (famous for gorillas) and Parc National Des Virunga.

Useful address

Zaire Embassy, 26 Chesham Place, London SW1X 8HH. Tel: (0171) 235 6137. British Embassy (BP 8094), 9 Avenue de l'Equateur, 5th Floor, Kinshasa.

Working Abroad

Essential Financial Planning for Expatriates and their Employees
Jonathan Golding

With the expansion of European and other overseas workplaces, more people than ever are going to work abroad. This book has been specially written to help the prospective expatriate and his/her employer understand the financial implications of working abroad. Using a systematic step-by-step approach, it gives important guidance on every stage of going abroad and returning home from structuring the contract of employment properly, to making up unpaid national insurance contributions on return to the UK. With its helpful case histories, flowcharts, checklists and question and answer sessions, the book will be essential for all employed and self-employed expatriates, personnel managers, recruiters, professional advisers and others concerned with overseas postings. Jonathan Golding brings 18 years' professional experience to this book. An author and lecturer in the field of taxation he has worked for Price Waterhouse (UK Expatriate Consulting Services), Ernst & Young, KPMG Peat Marwick, as well as the Inland Revenue, and is now an independent Tax Consultant.

International Venture Handbooks – £14.99hb. 159pp illus. 1 85876 007 0.
Please add postage & packing (UK £2 per copy. Europe £3 per copy.
World £5 per copy airmail).

Plymbridge Distributors Ltd, Estover Road, Plymouth PL6 7PZ,
United Kingdom. Tel: (01752) 695745. Fax: (01752) 695699. Telex: 45635.

12
East Africa

DJIBOUTI

Capital: Djibouti
Type of Government: Republic
Official languages: French and Arabic
Population: 520,000

Currency: Djibouti franc
Size: 21,783 square km
Climate: Hot and dry
National Airline: Air Djibouti

General information
The French arrived here in the 19th century and in 1896 the area was declared a French colony. In 1977 Djibouti became an independent country but suffered as a result of war between Ethiopia and Somalia. In 1988 the country needed aid from the West after a locust plague.

Food and drink
Cheap, local meals consist mostly of stew and maize meal. Some western cuisine can be found in the larger restaurants.

Internal transport
The rail network is the most common way to get around. Dhows operate off the coast.

Things to see
The capital Djibouti is the main point of interest for the traveller, although it is not a great tourist attraction.

Useful address
Djibouti Embassy, 26 Rue Emile-Menier, 75166 Paris, France.

ETHIOPIA

Capital: Addis Ababa
Type of Government: Republic
Official language: Amharic (English, French, Italian also widely spoken)
Size: 1,000,000 square km
National Airline: Ethiopian Airlines

Currency: Birr
Population: 50 million
Climate: Hot and dry in the southern regions and more temperate in the mountains and the central plateau

General information
It is claimed that the original rulers of this land were descended from Solomon and the Queen of Sheba. In 1935 the country was occupied by the Italians. In 1941 the Allies drove out the Italians and the Ethiopian emperor, Haile Selassie, returned to the country. In 1974 Selassie was deposed and replaced with a military regime. Since then severe droughts and bitter independence battles in Eritrea, Ogaden and Tigre have resulted in over a million deaths. Since 1991 there has been a change of direction and relative peace has come to the country.

Food and drink
Outside the main population centres the staple diet is *wat*, a spicy sauce with meat, beans and lentils. This is supplemented by *injera*, a local bread that is spicy and cheap. In the larger towns there are a variety of *wat*, made with chicken, eggs, lamb, fish and chick peas. The locals also eat raw meat but this is not recommended. The local beer has a distinctive taste as does the powerful *arakie*, a local firewater.

Internal transport
During the long period of military rule it was very difficult to travel around Ethiopia. This has now changed and there is a good internal air network. Road travel is the other way to get around but buses are erratic and the roads are generally in a poor condition.

Things to see
Addis Ababa, central Ethiopia. A large sprawling city that contains all the pros and cons of this country.
    Lalibela, north Ethiopia. Famous for its 11 rock-hewn churches.
    The Rift Valley Lakes, southern Ethiopia. A lush area where some of the lakes are national parks.
    Simien Mountains, north Ethiopia. A national park with a variety of wildlife and magnificent views.

Useful addresses
Ethiopian Embassy, 17 Princes Gate, London SW7 1PZ. Tel: (0171) 589 7212.
British Embassy (PO Box 858) Dessie Road, Addis Ababa.
British Council (PO Box 1043), Artistic Building, Adwa Avenue, Addis Ababa.

KENYA

Capital: Nairobi
Type of Government: Republic
Official language: Swahili, English
National Airline: Kenya Airways

Population: 25 million
Currency: Kenyan shilling
Size: 582,644 square km

Climate:
Tropical on the coast and sub-tropical inland. Snow can be seen on Mount Kenya. The Long Rains occur between March and June and the short rains take

place between November and December.

General information
The coastal areas of Kenya were occupied by the Arabs from as early as the 7th century. In the 16th and 17th centuries the Portuguese settled in the country but they were driven out of Mombasa by the Arabs in 1698. In 1895 the country was declared a British protectorate (East Africa Protectorate).

After the Second World War there was a growing feeling of discontent in the country. This was focused on Jomo Kenyatta, a member of the majority Kikuyu tribe who had studied in London. He returned to Kenya to lead the active Kenya African Union. In 1952 the nationalist movement erupted into violence with the bloody Mau Mau uprising. This led to the irrevocable path to independence and in 1963 this goal was achieved. Kenyatta became Kenya's first president and he ruled with a moderate and diplomatic style, even though he controlled a one-party state.

Kenyatta died in 1978 and he was replaced by Daniel arap Moi. In 1992 multi-party elections were held after several years of protest for greater democracy in the country. Although Moi was elected President his party did not win a majority and the county assumed an uneasy stand–off.

Food and drink
There is a wide variety of culinary influences in Kenya: Kenyan, Indian, European and Asian. Travellers can therefore dine on anything from hamburgers to curry. Fresh fruit is exotic and plentiful and the standard local fare is *ugali* – maize meal boiled into a white paste or solid lump. Kenya beer is good and there is also local wine produced in the Naivasha region.

Internal transport
Rail and road links are both good in Kenya. The train from Nairobi to Mombasa is luxurious while coaches and mini-buses (*matatus*) are cheap but the traveller is likely to discover religion in a hurry. There are also good air links in Kenya.

Things to see
Wildlife is one of the principal reasons for visiting Kenya and some of the most popular safari parks include Masai Mara Reserve; Tsavo East National Park; Meru Park; Mount Kenya National Park; Samburu Reserve; Turkana Reserve; and Losai Reserve.

Mombasa. Kenya's largest port and a fascinating mixture of African, Asian and Arab cultures.

Malindi. A coastal town and an ideal place for snorkeling, diving and deep sea fishing.

Gedi National Park, near Malindi. Home of the Gedi Ruins.

Useful addresses
Kenyan High Commission, 45 Portland Place, London W1N 4AS. Tel: (0171) 636 2371.

British High Commission, 13th Floor, Bruce House, Standard Street (PO Box
   30465), Nairobi.
British Council, ICEA Building, Kenyatta Avenue (PO Box 40751), Nairobi.
Kenya Airways, 5th and 6th Floor, Barclays Plaza, Loita Street (PO Box 41010),
   Nairobi.

MADAGASCAR

Capital: Antananarivo   Currency: Malagasy franc
Type of Government: Republic   Size: 587,041 square km
Official languages: Malagasy and French   Population: 12.5 million
Climate: tropical   National Airline: Air Madagascar

General information
This island was occupied by Muslim traders in the 8th century and the
Portuguese were the first European visitors when they landed in the 16th
century. In 1896 the French established the island as a protectorate and in 1946
it became a French overseas territory. Independence was achieved in 1960 and
this was followed by a military coup in 1972 which lasted only three years. A
socialist regime then took over but this resulted in economic disaster and multi-
party elections were held in 1993.

Food and drink
The French influence can be found in much of the cuisine and good Vietnamese
food is also available.

Internal transport
The internal air system is good if you are prepared to pay the expensive prices.
The roads are poor although there are three types of transport that can be used:
big taxi; bush taxi; pick-up trucks; and regular buses. There are also a few train
routes and although the prices are reasonable the trains are slow.

Things to see
Antananarivo, central Madagascar. An atmospheric capital which is situated on
a steep hillside.
   Ambalavao, southern Madagascar. An important spiritual centre and known
as 'the home of the departed'.
   Antsirabe, central Madagascar. Known for its volcanic lakes and the hot
springs.
   Nosy Boraha, off the east coast of Madagascar. A picturesque, tranquil
island.

Useful address
Madagascar Consulate, 16 Lanark Mansions, Pennard Road, London W12
   8DT. Tel: (0181) 746 0133.

MALAWI

Capital: Lilongwe
Type of Government: Republic
Official languages: Chichewa
and English
National Airline: Air Malawi

Currency: Kwacha
Size: 94,079 square km
Population: 8.3 million
Climate: Tropical and hot at sea
level. Temperate in the mountains

General information
Some of the first Europeans to visit Malawi were the Portuguese in the 17th century and their influence is still visible today. During the 1850s David Livingstone entered Malawi while travelling to Botswana. He remained there for a number of years and carried out missionary work.

Following Livingstone's influence the country became a British protectorate in 1891. In 1953, despite opposition from other African nations, it joined with Northern and Southern Rhodesia to form the Federation of Rhodesia and Nyasaland. In 1963 the Federation was dissolved and Nyasaland gained internal self-government. In 1964 independence was achieved and two years later Malawi became a republic within the British Commonwealth. It has been a one-party state since, with President for Life Dr Hastings Banda as its only leader. Opposition to his authoritarian, hard-line style grew in the 1990s and in 1994 Banda was ousted in democratic elections.

Food and drink
In some parts of the country, particularly the north, food can be quite scarce and it is a case of eating what is on offer. Fish from Lake Malawi is one of the local staples and chicken and meat stew is eaten regularly. Fruits such as mangoes are plentiful. Malawi has its own Carlsberg brewery and so the beer is excellent and cheap. The local brew is milky, full of 'floaters' and smells like sweaty socks!

Internal transport
Since Lake Malawi is one of the principal features of the country, ferries play a large part in the local transport infrastructure. Boats sail the length of the Lake and this takes approximately three days. Accommodation can be basic and the tables in the dining area are used frequently as beds. Local coaches are cheap but usually crowded and slightly hair-raising. There is also a luxury coach service between the two main centres, Lilongwe and Blantyre.

Things to see
Malawi is an excellent place for wildlife safaris and the outdoors.

Kasungu National Park, Central Region. A wilderness area that can be explored on foot and which has the highest concentration of elephants in the country.

Lake Malawi National Park, southern Malawi. An area of Lake Malawi that is renowned for its proliferation of exotic tropical fish.

Liwonde National Park, southern Malawi. Lakes and woodlands offer opportunities for game viewing, bird-watching and photography.

Nyika National Park, northern Malawi. Situated in the northern mountains this is the largest and the highest national park in the country.

There are also a number of excellent game reserves: Majete, southern Malawi; Mwabvi, southern Malawi; Nkhotakota, central Malawi; and Vwaza Marsh, northern Malawi.

Useful addresses
Malawi High Commission, 33 Grosvenor Street, London W1X 0DE. Tel: (0171) 491 4172.
British High Commission (PO Box 30042), Longadzi House, Lilongwe 3.
British Council (PO Box 30222), Plot No. 13/20, City Centre, Lilongwe 3.
Department of National Parks and Wildlife, PO Box 30131, Lilongwe 3.

MAURITIUS

Capital: Port Louis	Currency: Mauritius rupee
Type of Government: Republic	Size: 1843 square km
Official languages: English and French	Climate: Tropical
Population: 1.2 million	National Airline: Air Mauritius

General information
This island was visited by the Arabs in the 10th century and the Portuguese in the 16th century but it was finally the Dutch who settled the area in 1598. In 1715 the French took control of the island and in 1814 it shifted to British rule. In 1968 Mauritius became independent within the British Commonwealth. Political unrest followed and the Prime Minister was overthrown in 1982. In 1992 Mauritius became an independent republic.

Food and drink
Local food is mostly curries, served with rice noodles or roti (Indian bread). Curries are made of local produce which vary from chicken to octopus.

Internal transport
The local roads are good and the bus services are of a high standard. Passenger boats operate to neighbouring islands.

Things to see
Port Louis, northwest Mauritius. A small capital with some interesting buildings and a good natural history museum.
    Mahebourg, southeast Mauritius. The old French colonial town.
    Northern Beaches, north Mauritius. Sunbathing, snorkeling and swimming in beautiful surroundings.
    Rodrigues Island, east of Mauritius. A quiet, volcanic island.

Useful addresses
Mauritius High Commission, 32-33 Elvaston Place, London SW7. Tel: (0171) 581 0294.
British High Commission, King George V Avenue, Floreal.

British Council (PO Box 111), Royal Road, Rose Hill.

MOZAMBIQUE

Capital: Maputo
Type of Government: Republic
Official languages: Portuguese, Makua
is the most common African language
Population: 15.7 million

Currency: Metical
Size: 784,961 square km
Climate: Hot all year, with greater
humidity during the wet season
National Airline: LAM

General information
The country became a Portuguese colony in the 16th century and in 1951 it was designated as an overseas province of Portugal. This ignited a nationalist movement that was led by FRELIMO. They conducted a fierce terrorist campaign and in 1975 independence was granted. However, the fighting continued as FRELIMO and the South African-backed Renamo fought for control of the country. In 1992 a peace treaty was signed which brought an end to this bitter civil war.

Food and drink
International cuisine, particularly Portuguese, is available in the capital but in the country it is a question of eating what you can get – usually stew with boiled maize meal.

Internal transport
The civil war has left its mark and it is not always safe to travel by road or rail. If you do so you will find the roads are in poor condition but truck drivers will be pleased to give you a lift. There are internal flights but cancelled timetables and overbooking are common.

Things to see
Maputo, southeast Mozambique. Worth a look around if only to see the scars of the civil war.
   Beira, east Mozambique. Impressive, and quiet, beaches nearby.

Useful addresses
Mozambique Embassy, 21 Fitzroy Square, London W1P 5HJ. Tel: (0171) 283 3800.
British Embassy (CP 55), A. Vladimir I Lenine 319, Maputo.

SEYCHELLES

Capital: Victoria
Type of Government: Republic
Official languages: English and French;
Creole is widely spoken

Currency: Seychelles rupee
Size: 444 square km
Population: 70,000
National Airline: Air Seychelles

Climate
Equatorial but variable. May to October is cool and dry, December to March is hotter and wetter.

General information
The French were first attracted here in the 18th century by the spices on the islands. In 1794 the British occupied the islands and 1903 they became a British crown colony. In 1976 the Seychelles became an independent republic within the Commonwealth. During the 1980s there were several South African sponsored attempts to seize power by force but these were defeated. In 1992 the first multi-party elections were held.

Food and drink
Local food is a mixture of French, Indian and Chinese cuisine. Fish, curry, octopus, sausage with green pumpkin, fruit bat curry and pork stew can all be found in local restaurants. *Calou* is the local tipple.

Internal transport
There are internal flights between half a dozen of the islands but this is not the cheapest way to get around. Only the two main islands, Mahé and Praslin, have sealed roads and buses to run on them. Ferries are the cheapest way to undertake a bit of island hopping.

Things to see
Mahé. The main island and where the capital Victoria is located.
   Cousin, Bird and Aride Islands. Three islands that are a must for bird lovers.
   Praslin. Secluded beaches and 4000 palms that are reputed to be over 800 years old.

Useful addresses
Seychelles High Commission, 50 Conduit Street, London W1A 4PE. Tel: (0171) 439 0405.
British High Commission, Victoria House, 3rd Floor, 161, Mahé.

SOMALIA

In recent years Somalia has suffered greatly from famine and civil war. Although a ceasefire was declared in 1993 the situation is still volatile and travellers would be advised to avoid this area if at all possible.

TANZANIA

Capital: Dodoma – Dar-es-Salaam is still the accepted capital
Type of Government: Federal Republic
Official languages: Swahili and English
Population: 27 million

Currency: Tanzanian shilling
Size: 945,087 square km
Climate: Cool in the mountains and hotter on the semi-desert plains
National Airline: Air Tanzania

General information
Arab traders and slavers were the first to exploit the strategic trading position of Tanzania and they had many skirmishes when the Portuguese arrived in the 16th century. The island of Zanzibar was of great importance and it was used by the Omani Sultan, Seyyid Said, who established his capital there in 1832. At about the same time the British began to take an interest in the area, particularly when Tanganyika became a German protectorate in 1891. After the First World War Britain took control of the country and it remained this way until Julius Nyerere negotiated independence for Tanganyika in 1961. Shortly afterwards Zanzibar and Pemba merged with the mainland to create Tanzania. Nyerere pursued a distinctly socialist agenda and although the political situation has remained stable the country has suffered great economic hardship. Despite this Nyerere is considered one of the great African elder statesmen.

Food and drink
Tanzania is not renowned for its culinary delights – shortages often mean that it is a case of taking what you can get. Stews, curry and maize meal are the most common types of food available. Hamburgers, steaks and pizzas can also be found periodically. Local beer would not win any awards.

Internal transport
There are two rail systems and the TAZARA line (built with the help of the Chinese) is cheap but there are very few services. The Central Line goes to more destinations and although it can be slow it is an enjoyable way to travel. There are 1st, 2nd and 3rd class compartments on trains and it is best to travel 1st or 2nd if possible. Travel by road ·is slow and uncomfortable – the buses and minibuses (*matatus*) are badly maintained and hopelessly overcrowded. Motorised dhows and hydrofoils operate between the mainland and Zanzibar.

Things to see
Dar-es-Salaam, west Tanzania. Not an inspiring capital but more relaxed and safer than some others.

Arusha, northeast Tanzania. A pleasant town, surrounded by local tribes and wildlife parks.

Zanzibar Island, east coast. Known as the 'Spice Island' this exotic location is where cultures and nationalities mix in exuberant fashion.

Wildlife: Tanzania is one of the best locations in Africa for viewing a wide variety of wildlife.

Arusha National Park, east Tanzania. Home of the majestic Mount Kilimanjaro, the highest mountain in Africa. It takes a trek of five days to reach the summit and climbers should make sure they are properly prepared.

Ngorongoro Conservation Area, east Tanzania. One of the most famous wildlife areas in the world – and it lives up to its reputation, particularly the renowned Crater.

Serengeti National Park, northwest Tanzania. Owes much of its considerable fame to the annual wildebeest migration.

Selous Game Reserve, southeast Tanzania. The world's largest game reserve.

Elephant, buffalo, hippo and lion are plentiful here.

Useful addresses
Tanzanian High Commission, 43 Hertford Street, London W1Y 7TF. Tel:
(0171) 499 8951.
Tanzanian Tourist office, 77 South Audley Street, London W1Y 5TA. Tel:
(0171) 499 7727.
British High Commission (PO Box 9200), Permanent House, corner Azikiew
St/Independence Avenue, Dar-es-Salaam.
British Council (PO Box 9100), Samora Avenue, Dar-es-Salaam.

HOW TO GET A JOB IN
TRAVEL & TOURISM

Mark Hempshell

Would you enjoy working in travel and tourism? Do you already
have a local position, but want to venture overseas? Whatever your
age, background or qualifications, this book will open doors for
you. With lots of examples, it shows how and where to obtain
really great jobs as couriers, holiday reps, coach drivers, tour guides,
entertainers, sports instructors or airline staff. Or how about
working on cruise ships, in top hotels and restaurants, on safaris,
summer camps, winter sports or other exotic assignments? The
book tells you what each job involves, the skills, qualifications,
experience, language, training, permits, pay and conditions – plus
where to find the vacancies and how to apply. Someone has to do
all these glamorous jobs – use this book, and it could be you! Mark
Hempshell's other books include *How to Get a Job in Hotels &
Catering* in this series.

£8.99, 176pp illus. 1 85703 113 X.
Please add postage & packing (UK £1 per copy.
Europe £2 per copy. World £3 per copy airmail).

How To Books Ltd, Plymbridge House, Estover Road,
Plymouth PL6 7PZ, United Kingdom.
Tel: (01752) 695745. Fax: (01752) 695699. Telex: 45635.

13
Southern Africa

ANGOLA

Angola has suffered from one of the longest and bloodiest civil wars in recent African history. At the time of writing the situation is still unstable and so travellers should consider leaving Angola off their agenda.

BOTSWANA

Capital: Gaborone
Type of Government: Republic
Official languages: English. Tswana is also widely spoken

Currency: Pula
Size: 582,000 square km
Population: 1.3 million
National Airline: Air Botswana

Climate
Mixed: rainy season November to March; dry and hot, but with cold nights, May to August. June and July can be very cold at night in the desert regions.

General information
In 1852 the Boers tried to amalgamate the area into the South African Republic but the Botswana people stood firm and Britain had to intervene.

In 1885, following further conflicts with the Boers, the area to the south of the Molopo River became the British crown colony of Bechuanaland and the area to the north became the British Protectorate of Bechuanaland. Following agricultural and economic difficulties South Africa again, in 1924, tried to gain control of Bechuanaland but were rebuffed once more.

The first stirrings of nationalism occurred in the 1940s. The nationalists succeeded in their aims when, in 1966, the Republic of Botswana was declared independent. The following year large quantities of diamonds were discovered and this has ensured the country's economic prosperity for the last 30 years. This has been matched by a stable government that has managed to work amicably with its neighbours and create a peaceful and successful country.

Food and drink
Botswana has a variety of international cuisine ranging from Chinese and Indian to American burger bars. Local dishes include stew and mealies (maize meal), pickled spinach, goat and mopane worms. This type of fare can be found at the

local food markets. As with other countries in the region the local beer is the pungent, milky *chibuku*.

Internal transport
Buses and minibuses can be taken to most parts of the country but the services tend to be erratic and when they do run they are overcrowded. Hitchhiking is a popular alternative and there is also a reasonable rail service. Although this tends to be slow it is more punctual than the buses. There are also domestic flights available but these tend to be expensive.

Things to see
Okavango Delta and Moremi Wildlife Reserve, northwestern Botswana. The largest inland delta in the world and rich in wildlife and birdlife. Also rich in mosquitoes unfortunately.

Chobe National Park, northern Botswana. One of the best places in the country to view elephants, for which it is famous.

The Kalahari Desert, central Botswana. One of the longest unbroken stretches of sand in the world. Home to the Kalahari Bushmen and the Tswana pastoralists.

Makgadikgai Pans Game Reserve, central Botswana. Unpronounceable but a dazzling sight of naturally created white floors of the desert. Gemsbok, springbok, wildebeest and zebra can be viewed here.

The Tuli Block, eastern Botswana. A collection of massive eroded rocks, sandrivers and woodlands.

Useful addresses
Botswana High Commission, 6 Stratford Place, London W19 9AE. Tel: (0171) 499 0031.
British High Commission, Queen's Road, The Mall, Gaborone (Private Bag 0023).
Botswana Tourism Development Unit, Private Bag 0046, Gaborone.
Department of Wildlife and National Parks, PO Box 131, Gaborone.

LESOTHO

Capital: Maseru   Currency: Loti
Type of Government: Kingdom   Size: 30,340 square km
Official languages: Sesotho and English Population: 1.8 million
National Airline: Lesotho Airways

Climate
Since all of Lesotho is over 1000 metres in altitude the winters are cold and fresh in the mountains, while the summers are hot and dry, with violent thunderstorms.

General information
Formerly called Basutoland, the country came under British protection in 1868,

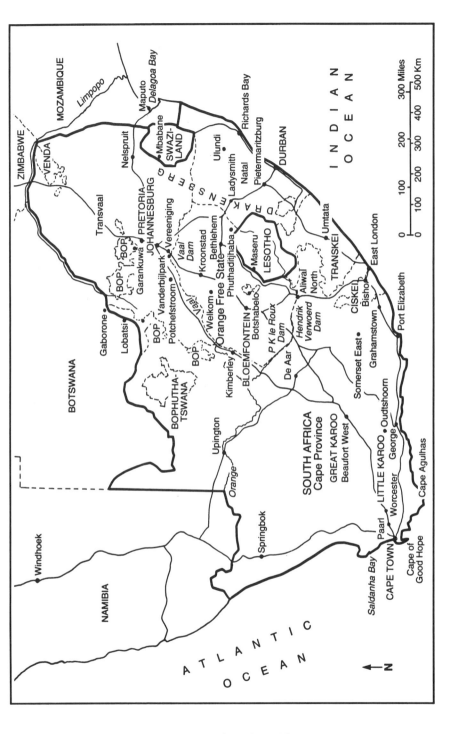

Fig. 2. Map of Southern Africa.

129

following clashes with the Orange Free State. Three years later it was annexed by the Cape Colony but in 1884 it came under direct British administration. This continued until 1966 when Lesotho became independent. Freedom brought its own problems: there was a state of emergency from 1970 to 1973 and a military coup in 1986. Military rule lasted until 1993.

Food and drink
Due to its proximity to South Africa there is a reasonably cosmopolitan selection of foods. Stews and curries are popular standbys and French, Italian and Chinese food is also available.

Internal transport
Bus and minibus taxis are the best ways of getting around. The main roads are in good condition and the minibus taxis are quicker than the buses but they travel shorter distances. There is no rail network for travellers.

Things to see
Maseru, northwest Lesotho. A capital which is steeped in African history.
　　Butha Buthe, north Lesotho. Famous for the nearby dinosaur prints in the ground.
　　Sehlabathebe National Park, east Lesotho. A remote and attractive wildlife park.
　　The southeast border region is one of the best places in Africa for trekking.

Useful addresses
Lesotho High Commission, 7 Chesham Place, London SW1X 8HN. Tel: (0171) 235 5686.
British High Commission, PO Box 521, Maseru.
British Council (PO Box 429), Hobson's Square, Maseru 100.

NAMIBIA

Capital: Windhoek	Currency: South African rand
Type of Government: Mandated Territory	Size: 824,269 square km
Official languages: Afrikaans and English	Climate: Hot and dry – much arid desert
National Airline: Namib Air	Population: 1.8 million

General information
In 1884 the area became a German protectorate but during the First World War it surrendered to South Africa, which was given a mandate to run the country, then called South West Africa, but not to occupy it. This constriction was generally ignored and in 1966 South Africa tightened its control on its neighbour despite international protests. In respect of this the South West Africa People's Organisation (SWAPO) mounted an intense guerrilla war against the occupying nation. After years of fighting SWAPO's demands were granted and in 1990 South Africa granted Namibia its independence. In the same year the

country joined the Commonwealth.

Food and drink
German style food is common as is traditional western type cuisine such as steaks, pizzas and all-you-can-eat buffets. South African beer is readily available. For beer lovers Windhoek has its own Oktoberfest.

Internal transport
Although the bus network is not particularly extensive the buses are good value and usually stick fairly closely to the timetable. Hitching is possible but there is not always a lot of traffic and truck drivers sometimes expect to be paid for lifts. There is a moderate rail system but trains are slower than the comparative buses.

Things to see
Windhoek, central Namibia. A modern capital that still retains some of its historical features.

Daan Viljoen Game Park, central Namibia. Near Windhoek and a popular place for viewing game.

Luderitz, southwest Namibia. A throwback to German colonisation.

Walvis Bay, west Namibia. A harbour ringed by some of the world's largest sand dunes.

Etosha National Park, north Namibia. One of the most unique wildlife parks in Africa.

Namib-Naukluft Park, west Namibia. The country's largest wildlife park.

Fish River Canyon and Ai-Ais, south Namibia. The confluence of two rivers create one of the most spectacular sights on the continent.

SOUTH AFRICA

Capitals: Pretoria (administrative)
　　Bloemfontein (judicial)
　　Cape Town (legislative)
Type of Government: Republic
Population: 38 million

Currency: Rand
Size: 1,221,042 square km
Official languages: Afrikaans and
　English
National Airline: South African
　Airways (SAA)

Climate
Ranging from cool and wet in the southwest in winter (June to August), to very hot in Natal and the north in summer.

General information
Between 1000 and 1500 various Bantu-speaking tribes moved from central Africa to the south. The Dutch were the first Europeans to take a serious interest in the country and in 1652 the Dutch East India Company settlement in the south of the country moved further into the interior. At the end of the 17th century the white settlers were joined by a significant number of Huguenot refugees.

In 1814 Britain took control of the country, angering many of the Dutch (or Boer as they were to become) farmers in the process. Tension erupted during the 1880s when the Boers tried to reassert their authority during the Boer Wars. Both sides realised that this was counter-productive and in 1910 they combined with the Union of South Africa. In 1947 the system of apartheid – the racially discriminatory system that aimed to segregate whites, blacks and coloureds – was introduced.

Apartheid led to bitter conflicts between the blacks (led primarily by Nelson Mandela and the African National Congress (ANC)) and the white minority. South Africa became an international outcast as the racist policies led to discrimination and the deaths of thousands of people.

In 1989, F W de Klerk became the president of South Africa and he began to break down the system of apartheid. In 1990 Mandela was released from prison and in 1994, despite periods of fierce fighting between the ANC and the rival Zulu Inkatha movement, multi-racial elections were held for the first time in South Africa. In May 1994 Nelson Mandela was inaugurated as the first truly democratically elected president.

Food and drink

South Africa produces high quality meat, vegetables and seafood but the standard of cuisine is moderate rather than exceptional. Large steaks are very popular, as are pizzas, hamburgers and chips. In some areas, most notably around the Cape, there is a mixture of Malay and Dutch cuisine which is more inspired than the traditional Western type fare. African beer and wine are cheap and very good.

Internal transport

There are good road and rail links for travellers throughout the country. Autonet runs many of the long distance buses and they have three types of service – Translux (luxury), Trancity (economy) and Transtate (general). Minibus taxis operate over shorter distances but in the past they have been attacked by warring factions – check with the locals to see what the current situation is. Driving is good way to get around if you want to buy or hire a car. There is a rail system that connects all the major cities and these are reasonably priced.

Things to see

Johannesburg, northeast South Africa. The country's capital in all but name and a precocious city.

Cape Town, southwest South Africa. Said by many to be the most beautiful city in the world.

Durban, southeast South Africa. A holiday town with good beaches and surf.

Kimberley, central South Africa. The location of gold and diamond mines.

South Africa has some superb wildlife parks and some of the best include De Hoop Nature Reserve, The Drakensberg, Kalahari Gemsbok National Park, Karo National Park, Mountain Zebra National Park, Mkambati Nature Reserve and the world famous Kruger National Park.

Useful addresses
South African Embassy, Trafalgar Square, London WC2N 5DP. Tel: (0171) 930 4488.
South African Tourist Board, 5 & 6 Alt Grove, London SW19 4DZ. Tel: (0181) 944 6646.
British Embassy, 6 Hill Street, Arcadia, Pretoria 0002.

SWAZILAND

Capital: Mbabane
Type of Government: Kingdom
Official language: Siswati and English
Population: 770,000
Climate: Cool in mountains, very hot in plains

Currency: Lilangeni – the South African rand is also legal tender
Size: 17,4000 square km
National Airline: Royal Swazi Airways

General information
Although the Swazi people occupied this land in the 18th century it became a South African protectorate in 1894. After the Boer War Swaziland came under British rule, until 1968 when it became an independent kingdom within the Commonwealth. Although political parties were banned in 1978 the country's administration is based on traditional tribal democracy and is one of the few remaining monarchies in Africa.

Food and drink
Stew and rice, hamburgers, steaks, pizzas, curries and seafood indicate that the South African influence is strong in Swaziland. South African beer is also readily available.

Internal transport
The road system is good and it is cheap and easy to get around by buses, express buses and minibuses. Hitching is possible but there is not always a lot of traffic.

Things to see
Mbabane, west Swaziland. The main attractions are the Why Not? disco and the nearby Cuddle Puddle.
   Ezulwini Valley, west Swaziland. The royal valley complete with a museum, waterfalls and the Royal Village.
   There are a number of national parks and reserves in Swaziland and these include Hlane Game Reserve (white rhino and antelopes), Malolotja Nature Reserve (antelope), Mlawula Nature Reserve (rhino and crocodiles) and Mlilwane Wildlife Reserve (hippos, rhino, giraffe and zebra).

Useful addresses
Swaziland Embassy, 58 Pont Street, London SW1X 0AE. Tel: (0171) 581 4976.
British Embassy, Allister Miller Street, Mbabane.

ZAMBIA

Capital: Lusaka
Type of Government: Republic
Official language: English
National Airline: Zambia Airways

Currency: Kwacha
Size: 752,262 square km
Population: 8.5 million

Climate
Cool and dry from May to August, hot and dry from September to October, and wet from November to April.

General information
After suffering at the hands of Arab slave traders in the 18th century the area was then visited by British missionaries in the 19th century. This led to Cecil Rhodes, who appreciated the worth of the mineral wealth in the land, incorporating the area into Rhodesia and in 1924 it became a British protectorate as Northern Rhodesia. From 1953-1963 it was a member of the Federation of Rhodesia and Nyasaland before becoming the independent Republic of Zambia in 1964. For nearly 30 years Kenneth Kaunda ran the country as a one-party state and he contributed to its economic decline. In 1990 there were protests against Kaunda and in 1991 he was defeated in democratic elections.

Food and drink
Apart from stew with boiled maize meal much of the food consists of steaks, hamburgers and curries.

Internal transport
Most of the country's roads are in a poor state of repair. Trucks and buses are the order of the day and there is also a luxury bus service that operates between Lusaka and Livingstone. On the TAZARA railway line there are two trains a day to the major centres.

Things to see
Lusaka, south Zambia. An administration capital and a place to be cautious, particularly at night.
   Victoria Falls (see Zimbabwe).
   Livingstone, southwest Zambia. The nearest town in Zambia to Victoria Falls.
   Mbala, north Zambia. The site of an interesting tribal museum.
   Kafue National Park, southwest Zambia. Plenty of wildlife and accommodation on offer.

Useful addresses
Zambian High Commission, 2 Palace Gate, London W8 5NG. Tel: (0171) 589 6343.
British High Commission (PO Box 50050), Independence Avenue, Lusaka.
British Council (PO Box 34571), Heroes Place, Cairo Road, Lusaka.

ZIMBABWE

Capital: Harare
Type of Government: Republic
Official language: English (Shona and
  Ndebele also spoken)

Currency: Zimbabwe dollar
Size: 390,245 square km
National Airline: Air Zimbabwe
Population: 9 million

Climate
Dry and hot. Winter runs from May to August but it is still warm. The rainy season is from November to March.

General information
In the early 19th century a number of Zulus, in what is now South Africa, came into conflict with the great Zulu leader, Shaka Zulu. They settled in what is now southwest Zimbabwe and were the ancestors of the country's Ndebele people. This did not go down well with the local Shona tribe and this ignited what was to be over 100 years of tribal conflict.

Towards the end of the 19th century Cecil John Rhodes visited southern Africa and began mining gold and diamonds and colonising the area for Britain. Rhodesia was subsequently named after Rhodes and for much of the 20th century it remained under a repressive white regime. Efforts to create a more democratic society backfired in 1965 when the Prime Minister, Ian Smith, announced a Unilateral Declaration of Independence. There then followed a bitter internal conflict as the Ndebele and the Shona fought against their white rulers for independence. After much inter-tribal rivalry and bloodshed this was eventually achieved in 1980 when the name of the country was changed from Rhodesia to Zimbabwe. Since independence Zimbabwe has enjoyed a period of stability and moderate economic growth.

Food and drink
Fresh meat is one of the most popular choices and barbecues are plentiful. One of the local dishes is powdered maize meal that is boiled into a solid pulp. It is usually eaten with meat stew. Beer brewed in South Africa is plentiful and the local brew, *chibuku*, should be tried, if only once. It is milky, pungent and has pieces of fibre floating in it. It should be approached with extreme care.

Internal transport
Rail transport varies from good to luxurious and most major centres are served. Roads are good although local buses tend to be overcrowded and standards of driving are erratic. Minibuses and taxis are cheap ways to get around cities.

Things to see
Victoria Falls. One of the great tourist attractions in the world and a sight that actually surpasses its reputation.

Great Zimbabwe Ruins. Impressive ruins which indicate a thriving civilisation as early as AD 1200.

Bulawayo and the Matopos National Park. Zimbabwe's second city, situated in close proximity to the atmospheric national park where Cecil Rhodes is buried.

Hwange National Park. Zimbabwe's premier wildlife park. 14,000 square kilometres is home for over 100 species of animal and 400 species of birds.

The Eastern Highlands. Lush, mountainous area that offers respite from the hotter, drier lowlands.

Lake Kariba. A man-made lake that offers game viewing, sailing and fishing.

Harare. A manageable and relaxed capital city.

Useful addresses

Zimbabwe High Commission, Zimbabwe House, 429 The Strand, London WC2R 0SA. Tel: (0171) 836 7755.

Zimbabwe Tourist Office, c/o Zimbabwe High Commission as above.

British High Commission, Stanley House, Stanley Avenue, Harare (PO Box 4490).

British Council, 23 Stanley Avenue, Harare (PO Box 664).

Air Zimbabwe, PO Box AP 1, Harare Airport, Harare.

Zimbabwe Council for Tourism, 9th Floor Travel Centre, Jason Moyo Avenue, Harare.

HOW TO GET A JOB IN AUSTRALIA

Nick Vandome's complete guide to all aspects of job-finding in Australia, looking for work, what pay and conditions to expect, and the current economic climate is explained alongside key information about tax, contracts, your rights at work and more: all you need to know to earn your Aussie dollars. 'Indispensable.' *TNT Magazine.* 'Packed with information which is well presented and easily accessible.' *Bulletin/National Association of Careers & Guidance Teachers.* 'A complete step-by-step guide.' *Australian Outlook.*

£8.99, 176pp. illus. 1 85703 048 6
Please add postage & packing
(UK £1 per copy. Europe £2 per copy.
World £3 per copy airmail).

How To Books Ltd, Plymbridge House, Estover Road,
Plymouth PL6 7PZ, United Kingdom.
Tel: (01752) 695745. Fax: (01752) 695699. Telex: 45635.

14
Northern Asia

CHINA

Capital: Beijing
Type of Government: Republic
Official language: Mandarin Chinese
National Airline: Air China

Population: 1.3 billion
Currency: Yuan
Size: 9,597,000 square km

Climate
Generally temperate. Some areas in the south are sub-tropical and tropical and the northern areas are significantly colder.

General information
In the 21st century BC the first Chinese Dynasty, the Xia, came into being and heralded the beginning of the slave society in China. This lasted until approximately 221 BC when a move was made towards a more feudal society. At this time the Qin Dynasty came to power and this led to the first unified, multi-national state in Chinese history. Several other feudal dynasties followed including the famous Ming Dynasty (1368-1644).

By the 17th and 18th centuries European powers were beginning to exploit the trading potential of China. There was internal opposition to this which came to a head in 1846 when Britain declared war on China. The resulting Opium War led to the Treaty of Nanking which left China as little more than a semi-colonial country.

In 1911 there was a revolution against the ruling Qing and China's last Dynasty was defeated and the country became a republic. Despite this there was still unrest and in 1921 the Communist Party of China was founded. Following occupation by the Japanese until the end of the Second World War the communists wrested power from the ruling Guomindang (National People's Party). In 1949 the People's Republic of China was created. This also marked the rise of Mao Tse-tung.

In 1966 Mao launched the great proletarian Cultural Revolution. It was claimed that this was to eradicate 'revisionism' but in reality it was a method to dispose of Mao's opponents and strengthen his grip over the country. Mao died in 1976 and this man who was once regarded as a national hero has since been discredited.

During the 1980s the Chinese rulers tried to introduce some democratic reforms but this backfired when students began demanding ever greater freedom. This culminated in the Tiananmen Square massacre when thousands of students were killed by government forces. This led to China being roundly condemned around the world and although they claim they have improved human rights in the country rumours to the contrary persist.

Food and drink
Ordering a portion of Chinese fried rice or sweet and sour chicken from your local Chinese take-away will not really prepare you for the culinary delights of China itself. There are eight major schools of Chinese cuisine, each named after the area where they are most popular: Shandong, Sichuan, Jiangsu, Zhejiang, Guandong, Hunan, Fujian and Anhui. The variety of dishes is staggering but some of the ones you may encounter are: Roast Beijing Duck, Beggar's Chicken, Dongpo Pork, West Lake Fish with vinegar, Shrimp and Longjing Tea Leaves, 'Squirrel' Mandarin Fish, Stir Fried Eels in Hot Oil, Roast Suckling Pig, 'Leopard Cat' braised with Three Kinds of Snake, Camphor-Leaf Smoked Duck, Gongbao Chicken Cubes, Fish Fragrant Pork Slivers, Mapo Beancurd and Rice Noodle Soup. In the more remote areas it may be the case of stir-fried vegetables with rice or noodles. Chinese leaf tea is drunk everywhere and the national tipple is the fiery Mao Tai.

Internal transport
There is a good system of internal air flights in China but the safety record of some of the airlines means that you take your life in your hands to some extent. Rail travel is a better bet if you are not in too much of a hurry and it is a fascinating way to see this vast and varied country. Tickets are usually for hard or soft class and ticket prices are more expensive for travellers than for locals. If possible try and get some local help when buying a rail ticket because the process is crowded and tortuous. The cities usually have good bus services but it is worth following the local example and going by bicycle.

Things to see
Beijing, Hebei Province, northeast China. A wealth of treasures including the Great Wall of China, the Ming Tombs, the Palace Museum, the Summer Palace, the Temple of Heaven and the Beijing Zoo.
    Chengde, Hebei Province, northeast China. One of the ten most scenic areas in the country.
    Hangzou, Zhejiang Province, southeast China. Beautiful lakes and an area famous for its silk.
    Kunming, Yunnan Province, south China. A popular area for travellers, known as the 'Ever Spring City'.
    Lhasa, Tibet, southwest China. It is easy to believe that time has stood still in this fascinating country where Buddhism is the main forces in people's lives. The Potala Palace is the main attraction.
    Qufu, Shjandong Province, east China. Birthplace of the philosopher Confucius.
    Shanghai, Jiangsu Province, east China. China's most westernized city and a

vibrant place with sights and nightlife in equal measures.

Urumqi, Zinjiang Uygur, northwest China. A remote area of the country with dramatic, sparse scenery, a lake at 1830 metres above sea level and an underground water system.

Xian, Shaanxi Province, central China. The location of famous archaeological remains including the world famous Qin Terracotta Warriors.

Useful addresses
Chinese Embassy, 31 Portland Place, London W1N 3AG. Tel: (0171) 636 5726.
China National Tourist Office, 4 Glentworth Street, London NW1. Tel: (0171) 935 9427.
British Embassy, 11 Guang Hua Lu, Beijing.
China Travel Service, 8 Dongjiaominggziang, Beijing 100005.
China Youth Travel Service, 23-B Dongjiaominggxiang, Beijing, 100006.

HONG KONG

Capital: Hong Kong
Type of Government: British colony
  with Governor
Official languages: Chinese and English

Currency: Hong Kong dollar
Size: 1,070 square km
Climate: Sub-tropical

General information
The British flag was first planted on Hong Kong in 1841. It became a Crown Colony and soon established itself as an important trading post and a stepping-off point for entry into China. By the end of the 19th century the rest of Hong Kong had been ceded to Britain, who took a 99 year lease on the colony. That lease expires on 1 July 1997, when sovereignty of Hong Kong will revert to China and the colony will become a Special Administrative Region of China. The existing legal, fiscal and administrative systems are guaranteed to remain in place for a minimum of 50 years after the handover.

Food and drink
Hong Kong has an international sweep of excellent cuisine. All styles of Chinese cooking, Vietnamese, Indian, Japanese, Korean, Thai, Indonesian, Singaporean, Malaysian, Filipino and Western. Seafood is a speciality, cooked in any of the above styles. Drinks range from Chinese tea, to local beer, to Chinese wine.

Internal transport
Most of Hong Kong's transport is efficient and cheap. You can choose between double-decker buses, minibuses, maxicabs, trains (high speed and underground), ferries, trams and rickshaws.

Things to see
Star Ferry. Operates between Hong Kong and Kowloon Islands and is one of the world's great ferry rides.

Hong Kong Park. A place to go for a tranquil break.

Victoria Park. 554 metres above sea level and affording a superb view of most of Hong Kong.

Hollywood Road. The heart of Hong Kong's antique trade.

Man Mo Temple. One of the oldest and largest temples in the territory.

Lantau Island. Home of the world's largest outdoor bronze Buddha.

Ocean Park. Southeast Asia's largest leisure complex.

Stanley. An ideal spot for shoppers on the south of Hong Kong Island. Also walks and beaches.

Kowloon Mosque. The prayer centre for Hong Kong's 50,000 Muslims.

Temple Street Night Market. A spot for some lively night shopping.

Sung Dynasty Village. An example of life in China 1,000 years ago.

Lamma Island. The closest of the outlying islands.

Useful addresses

Hong Kong Government Office, 6 Grafton Street, London W1X 3LB. Tel: (0171) 499 9821.

Hong Kong Tourist Association, 4th & 5th Floors, 125 Pall Mall, London SW1Y 5EA.Tel: (0171) 930 4775.

British Council, Easey Commercial Building, 255 Hennessy Road, Wanchai.

Hong Kong Tourist Association, 35th Floor, Jardine House, 1 Connaught Place, Central, Hong Kong. Tel: 852 801 7111.

JAPAN

Capital: Tokyo	Currency: Yen
Type of Government: Constitutional monarchy	Size: 372,480 square km
	Population: 123 million
Official language: Japanese	National Airline: Japan Airlines

Climate

General mild, but ranging from sub-arctic in the north to sub-tropical in the south.

General information

Although Japanese emperors were historically thought of as divine descendants of the sun goddess, from 1186 AD the real power was held by the military shoguns. This ended in 1867 when Emperor Mutsuhito gained power and four years later the feudal system was ended in the country. In the 19th and 20th centuries Japan occupied several Asian countries and in the Second World War it fought against the Allies, resulting in the dropping of atomic bombs on Hiroshima and Nagasaki.

Since the Second World War Japan has made rapid economic progress but in recent years it has received international criticism for some of its economic policies. The country has also been shaken by a series of corruption scandals which have resulted in a rapid succession of premiers.

Food and drink
There is a wide range of international cuisine in Japan but the local food is exceptional. There are several types of Japanese cuisine and they include *Kaiseki* (fish and vegetables cooked to preserve their natural flavour), *Sukiyaki* (beef and vegetables cooked in special iron pans), *Shabu-shabu* (beef and vegetables cooked into a special broth), *Tempura* (food deep-fried in vegetable oil), *Sashami* (raw seafood and fish), *Sushi* (seafood and fish arranged on a bed of rice, and served with soy sauce and pickled ginger), *Nabe Cuisine* (food boiled at the table in an earthenware pot), *Soba* and *Udon* (two types of noodles, which can be used with a main meal or eaten as a snack). Japanese green tea is a popular drink and Japanese beer and whisky are excellent.

Internal transport
Japan has arguably the best internal transport system in the world. The rail network is fast, reasonably priced and remarkably efficient. Japan Rail Passes are a good way to use the network but they must be bought before you go to Japan. There are two types – Ordinary for regular fares and Green for superior class. Just for the experience it is worth taking a commuter train during the Tokyo rush-hour – it is a whole new concept in being crowded. The bus network is equally impressive. The air network is expansive but also more expensive than buses or trains.

Things to see
Tokyo, southeast Japan, a thoroughly modern city that has temples, palaces, parks, markets, nightlife, shops and everything else you could want.

Hakone, southeast Japan. One of the most popular tourist resorts in Japan.

Mount Fuji and Five Lakes, central Japan. The highest mountain in the country but its picturesque setting and symmetrical appearance are its main attractions.

Kyoto, central Japan. Rich in the past culture and heritage of Japan's ancient rulers. The centre of traditional crafts such as silk weaving and lacquer ware.

Japan also has over thirty national parks and there are numerous small islands to visit.

Useful addresses
Embassy of Japan, 101-104 Piccadilly, London W1V 9FN. Tel: (0171) 465 6500.
Japan National Tourist Organisation, 167 Regent Street, London W1R 7FD. Tel: (0171) 734 9638/9.
British Embassy, 1 Ichibancho, Chiyoda-ku, Tokyo 102.
British Council, 2-Kagurazaka 1-Chome, Shinjuku-ku, Tokyo 162.
Japan National Tourist Organisation Center, Kotani Building, 1-6-6 Yuraku-cho, Chiyoda-ku, Tokyo.

NORTH KOREA

At the time of writing travel in North Korea is not recommended due to the political situation.

SOUTH KOREA

Capital: Seoul
Type of Government: Republic
Official language: Korean
Population: 43 million

Currency: Won
Size: 98,447 square km
Climate: Temperate
National Airline: Korean Air

General information
Following division into north and south after the Second World War, South Korea has had an uneasy relationship with its northern neighbours. Despite the fact that the countries signed an economic pact in 1992, tensions remain.

Food and drink
Rice, noodles, beancurd, bean sprouts and lentils are the basics of Korean cuisine. Main meals, usually three a day, often consist of communal hotpots and grilled meat. Chilli and garlic are used freely in most types of cooking. The most popular local drink is *soju*, a fierce concoction made from sweet potatoes.

Internal transport
There are good bus, rail and air networks for travellers. Travel in the cities is quick and easy.

Things to see
Seoul, north South Korea. A vibrant city that has benefited greatly from hosting the 1988 Olympic Games.
    Han River Lake, north South Korea. An area with the country's most scenic lakes.
    Mount Sorak, north South Korea. A delightful mountain that provides excellent trekking and climbing.
    Kyongju, east South Korea. An area rich in Korean history, dating back 2000 years.

Useful addresses
South Korea Embassy, 4 Palace Gate, London W8 5NF. Tel: (0171) 581 0247. British Embassy, 4 Chong-dong, Chung-ku, Seoul.

TAIWAN

Capital: Taipei
Type of Government: Republic
Official language: Mandarin Chinese

Currency: New Taiwan dollar
Climate: Sub-tropical
Population: 21 million

General information
The island was discovered by the Portuguese and ceded to Japan in 1897. For a number of years the USA offered Taiwan protection against mainland China but these ties were severed in 1979. Since then Taiwan has improved its relationship

with mainland China and the two countries are closely linked.

Food and drink
Chinese cuisine predominates in the country.

Internal transport
The bus system is well developed and there are two main types of service: cheap and standard. There are also illegal bus companies running 'wild chicken' buses which are cheap but erratic. The rail network is also good. Ferries also operate to the islands dotted around Taiwan.

Things to see
Taipei, north Taiwan. A boom city that has plenty to see and do but also the problems associated with a large city.

North Taiwan. Mountains, beaches and hot springs ensure this is a place to 'get away from it all'.

Southeast Taiwan. An easy paced area that has some of the country's finest beaches and temples.

Southwest Taiwan. The banana growing area and there are also some interesting islands, Hsiao Liuchio and Penghu, off the coast.

Useful address
Taiwan Embassy, 50 Grosvenor Gardens, London SW1V 0EB. Tel: (0171) 396 9152.

15
Southeast Asia

BRUNEI

Capital: Bandar Seri Begawan
Type of Government: Sultanate
Official language: Malay – Chinese and
    English widely spoken

Population: 280,000
Currency: Brunei dollar
Size: 5,800 square km
Climate: Tropical

General information
In the 16th century Brunei controlled all of Borneo and also parts of the Philippines. However, by 1888 its power had dwindled and it became a British protectorate. Since 1962 the sultan has ruled by decree and the country achieved full independence in 1983. In 1929 large deposits of oil were discovered and this has had a dramatic impact on the country in terms of economic well-being and self-sufficiency.

Food and drink
Western influences dominate many of the capital's restaurants and the best bet for local food is the foodstalls at the riverfront.

Internal transport
Many people seem to have their own cars so public transport is somewhat lacking. However, buses and taxis can be found.

Things to see
Bandar Seri Begawan, north Brunei. Of interest if only to see the wealth that oil has brought to the country. The Omar Ali Saifuddin Mosque is magnificent and the museum is interesting. There are several beaches just out of town and also a village on stilts – Kampong Ayer.

Useful addresses
Brunei High Commission, 19 Belgrave Square, London SW1X 8PG. Tel: (0171) 581 0521.
British High Commission (PO Box 2197), 5th Floor, Hong Kong Bank Chambers, Jalan Pemancha, Bandar Seri Begawan.

CAMBODIA

General information
Although the murderous regime of the Khmer Rouge was supposed to have been blunted by a peace agreement in 1991, fighting has continued in some areas and it is not generally recommended that travellers visit here. If you do then make sure you check out the current situation before you go.

INDONESIA

Capital: Jakarta
Type of Government: Republic
Official language: Bahasa Indonesia
Population: 179 million

Currency: Rupiah
Size: 1,903,650 square km
Climate: Tropical
National Airline: Garuda Indonesia

General information
In 1292 Marco Polo was one of the first Europeans to set foot on the island archipelago that is now Indonesia. Two hundred years later, in 1509, the Portuguese arrived in search of spices. They in turn were defeated by the Dutch. There was a brief period of British rule between 1811-16 but the area remained a Dutch colony until Japanese occupation during the Second World War.

Following the end of the Second World War the push for independence became unstoppable and in 1945 Indonesia declared itself a republic under the leadership of Dr Sukarno. In 1949-50 the country was formally granted independence. In 1966 Sukarno's government was overthrown by a military coup led by General Suharto. Suharto introduced a harsh military regime which has been tested by a variety of crises, including separatist movements in East Timor and Irian Jaya.

Food and drink
There are Chinese, Western, Japanese and Korean cuisines throughout the country but the local methods of cooking predominate. Rice and noodles are the staple diet and these have been gaining in popularity as other traditional foods such as corn, sago, cassava and sweet potatoes have lost some of their appeal. Fish is used frequently in cooking and spices and hot chilli peppers give the food a distinctive kick. Tropical fruits such as mangoes, papayas and pineapples are plentiful. Some common dishes are *sate, nasi goreng* (fried rice) and *bakmi goreng* (fried noodles). Local beer is produced as is *brem*, a powerful rice wine.

Internal transport
There is a well developed air service between many of the islands and there are also numerous ferries if you are looking for a cheaper option. On land there are trains and coaches and in the cities there are taxis, motorcycles to rent, minibuses (mikrolet, oplet/bemo and colt), tricycles and horse carts.

Things to see
When visiting Indonesia it is a question of picking certain islands to visit.

Sumatra, western Indonesia. Places to visit – Riau, Padang, Palembang and Lampung.

Java, central Indonesia. Places to visit – Jakarta, Yogyakarta, Bandung, Krakatoa Volcano, Ujong Kulon wildlife reserve, Semarang, Malang and Baluran.

Bali, central Indonesia. The premier tourist destination in Indonesia.

Sulawesi, western Indonesia. Places to visit – Ujung Pandang, Pulau Kayangan, Watampone, Manado, Airmadidi and Tora-tora.

Useful addresses
Indonesian Embassy, 38 Grosvenor Square, London W1X 9AD. Tel: (0171) 499 7661.
British Embassy, 75 Jl. M. H. Thamrin, Jakarta Pusat. Tel: 021 330904.
British Council, S. Widjojo Centre, 57 Jalan Jendral Sudirman, Jakarta.
Garuda Indonesia, Jl. Merdeka Selatan 13, Jakarta. Tel: 021 3801901.

LAOS

Capital: Vientiane

Type of Government: Democratic Republic

Official language: Laotian – French is widely spoken

Currency: Kip

Size: 235,700 square km

Climate: Tropical

Population 4.5 million

General information
Europeans first visited this country in the 17th century and in 1893 it became a French protectorate. During the Second World War the Japanese occupied the country and in 1949 Laos became independent within the French Union. In 1953 there was a civil war that lasted 20 years and in 1975 the communist Pathet Lao movement grabbed power. Recent years have been notable for border clashes with Thailand.

Food and drink
Moderate Chinese and Vietnamese cuisine is available and the street stalls offer sticky rice, barbecued chicken and *paddek* (fermented fish). *Lao lao* is the local tipple and it is like a stronger version of sake.

Internal transport
Local transport is basic and buses are the best bet but this does not mean that they are recommended.

Things to see
Vientiane, north Laos. Not one of the most stimulating of capital cities but there are some interesting socialist monuments and good local handicrafts. It is sometimes hard to get too far out of the capital for sightseeing.

Useful address
Laotian Embassy, 74 Avenue Raymond-Poincaré, 75116 Paris.

MALAYSIA

Capital: Kuala Lumpur	Currency: Ringgit
Type of Government: Federation	Size: 330,000 sq km
Official language: Bahasa Malaysia	Climate: Tropical
Population: 18 million	National Airline: Malaysia Airlines

General information
Consisting of 11 separate states, much of Malaysia's early history was influenced strongly by Hindu-Buddhists. However, by 1400, when the Malacca Sultanate was at the height of its power, Malacca was dominated by Islam. A hundred years later, in 1511, the area had been captured by the Portuguese. In 1641 the Portuguese were in turn defeated by the Dutch.

Due to its strategic trading location Britain began to take an interest in the Malay states. The East India Company established several trading stations and in 1815 Malacca was under British control. This was extended to the rest of the Malaysian states in 1909.

The first stirrings of Malaysian nationalism began in the 1930s and the momentum was maintained until 1957 when independence was granted to the Federation of Malaya. In 1963 Malaysia came into being.

In recent years there has been considerable unrest from the Chinese community in Malaysia, who believe they are not fairly represented in the government. This included communist guerrilla activities which resulted in stern retaliatory measures. However, the situation has stabilised recently.

Food and drink
Malaysian cuisine is of a spicy, oriental nature. Rice and noodles are the basis for many meals and chicken and fish are used liberally in several dishes. From the intriguingly named *chicken chop* to traditional *satay* (meat cooked on skewers) there are a variety of local dishes that can be found in restaurants and also roadside stalls and food bazaars. In addition to local food there is also the choice of Chinese, Indian, Nyonya, Portuguese and European cuisine. Fresh tropical fruit is one of the delights of Malaysia, with mangosteen, rambutan, guavas and papayas in abundance. There is also the controversial durian – a pineapple shaped fruit that inspires powerful opinions.

Internal transport
Rail travel is one of the most efficient and inexpensive ways to get around, particularly if the local Railpass scheme is utilised to its full potential. Taxis and air-conditioned buses connect all the major centres and there are numerous ferries to the Malaysian islands.

Things to see
Perlis, northwest Malaysia. The country's smallest state, but there are beaches, shopping, the caves of Kaki Bukit and a snake farm.

Kedah, northwest Malaysia. The beaches of Langkawi Island and the capital, Alor Setar, are the main attractions.

Malacca (Melaka), southwest Malaysia. The country's most historic city which has experienced a variety of influences.

Pahang, central Malaysia. The largest state on Peninsular Malaysia which has large areas of rainforests, part of which forms the exotic National Park.

Sarawak, eastern Malaysia. Rich in wildlife, local culture, mosques and temples. Wildlife highlights include barking deer, wild boar, honey bears and the protected Orang Utan.

Sabah, eastern Malaysia. A mountainous region that has lush tropical rainforests.

Kuala Lumpur, western Malaysia. Attractions in this cosmopolitan capital include Chinatown, the National Monument, Lake Gardens, the National Mosque, the National Museum and the Central Market.

Useful addresses

Malaysian Embassy, 45 Belgrave Square, London SW1X 8QT. Tel: (0171) 235 8033.

Malaysian Tourism Promotion Board, Malaysia House, 57 Trafalgar Square, London WC2N 5DU. Tel: (0171) 930 7932.

British High Commission, PO Box 11030, 13th Floor, Wosma Damansara, Jalan Semantan, 50732 Kuala Lumpur.

British Council, PO Box 10539, Jalan Bukit Aman, 50480 Kuala Lumpur.

National Tourism Council Malaysia (NTCM), c/o Malaysia Tourist Information Complex, 109 Jalan Ampang, 50450 Kuala Lumpur.

MYANMAR (BURMA)

Capital: Rangoon
Type of Government: Republic
Official language: Burmese
Population: 43 million

Currency: Kyat
Size: 678,000 square km
Climate: Tropical

General information

From the 13th century the country was ruled by the Mongols, the Shans, the Mons and the Burmese Alaungpaya. By 1885 the country was under British control as part of British India. This lasted until 1937 when it was separated from India. During the Second World War the Burmese first fought with the Japanese and then against them, in support of the British. In 1948 Burma became independent.

Burma's modern history has been dogged by periods of military rule and human rights violation. In 1988 there was a widespread call for a more democratic system but this was met with severe and violent reprisals. Strict martial law was enforced and although elections were held in 1990 the result was ignored by the military rulers. Today the situation is still very unsettled and, as the situation stands, travellers should think carefully before visiting Myanmar.

Food and drink

Curry and rice are available everywhere but be careful – the local's idea of hot may not match your own! Local delicacies also include grasshopper kebabs. Burmese beer is reasonable, if a little expensive.

Internal transport
When travelling anywhere in Myanmar visitors should always take great care as all types of transport can be targets for guerrilla attacks. Always ask local advice before undertaking any type of journey.

Things to see
As with transport you will be well advised to seek local opinion before venturing too far from Rangoon. The capital itself has a good selection of temples including the revered Shwedagon Pagoda. Other places to consider are Mandalay, Pegu, Pagan and Inle.

Useful addresses
Myanmar Embassy, 19A Charles Street, London W1X 8ER. Tel: (0171) 629 6966.
British Embassy and British Council, 80 Strand Road, Rangoon.

PAPUA NEW GUINEA

Capital: Port Moresby
Type of Government: State
Official language: English plus 700 local dialects
Population: 4 million
National Airline: Air Niugini

Currency: Kina
Size: 462,840 square km
Climate: Lush and fertile in the mountains, humid in the swampy plains

General information
The southeast and the northeast sections of the country were under the control of Britain and Australia respectively at the beginning of the 20th century. In 1921 the two territories merged and in 1971 they were renamed Papua New Guinea, achieving full independence four years later. In 1990 there was a rebel uprising and although this fizzled out in 1992 there is still considerable tension between various tribes in the country. Travellers should be careful in the Highlands and also in Port Moresby where there have been a number of muggings and burglaries in recent years.

Food and drink
The food is generally poor – an unimpressive clone of Australian meat pie and chips cuisine.

Internal transport
Poor – roads are infrequent and of a poor quality. Flying is one of the best ways of getting around although it can be expensive – as can most things in Papua New Guinea. Ships also operate along the coast and rides can be negotiated if you are prepared to wait around the ports.

Things to see
Port Moresby, south Papua New Guinea. The nearby beaches are the highlight of PNG's capital.

Highland area, central Papua New Guinea. Local villages, mountainous scenery and an annual Highland Games are the highlights of this region.

Others points of interest in Papua New Guinea are the opportunities for hillwalking and the islands that are dotted around the main coast.

Useful address
Papua New Guinea Embassy, 14 Waterloo Place, London SW1R 4AR. Tel: (0171) 930 0922.

PHILIPPINES

Capital: Manila
Type of Government: Republic
Official language: Filipino
Population: 62 million

Currency: Philippine peso
Size: 300,000 square km
Climate: Tropical
National Airline: Philippine Airlines

General information
The Spanish colonised this archipelago of over 7000 islands in 1565 and in 1898 they were ceded to the USA. During the Second World War the country was occupied by the Japanese and in 1946 the Philippines became an independent republic. The early years of independence saw little improvement in the country's fortunes but this changed in 1965 when Ferdinand Marcos was elected president. He brought economic development and increased prosperity to the country. Despite this there was unrest and in 1972 a state of martial law was declared. This lasted until 1981 but when the leader of the opposition was assassinated in 1983 the unrest resurfaced. In 1986 Marcos was exiled to the USA in disgrace and Cory Aquino became president. She survived several coup attempts by supporters of Marcos and introduced a number of reforms, including a new constitution.

Food and drink
Food from around the world is available in the Philippines – from Egyptian to Japanese and from Mexican to Mongolian. Filipino food tends to take the best from several types of cooking and so you will come across roast pig, spicy curries, noodle soup, chicken marinaded in soy sauce and a huge array of sweets and desserts. Rice is the basis of many meals and tropical fruits are plentiful and exotic.

Internal transport
Internal flights are good value for a bit of island hopping but if you have time to spare then there are frequent boat services to most popular destinations. Bus services are efficient and cheap and there is a large number of companies to choose from. There are also three railway lines in the country. For shorter journeys and in cities the local form of transport is the jeepney – converted US army jeeps that are packed to bursting point and driven by maniacs.

Things to see
Manila, Luzon Island. The main entry point to the country and a city that offers some worthwhile historical sites and a thriving nightlife. Luzon island itself has several places of interest.

Of the other 7000 islands some of the ones worth a visit are: Samar, Leyte, Bohol, Cebu, Negros, Panay and Romblon.

Useful addresses
Embassy of the Philippines, 17 Albemarle Street, London W1X 7HA. Tel: (0171) 499 5443.
British Embassy (PO Box 1970 MCC) Electra House, 115-117 Esteban Street, Legaspi Village, Metro Manila.
British Council (PO Box AC 168 Cubao), 73rd Street, New Manila, Quezon City, Metro Manila.

SINGAPORE

Capital: Singapore
Type of Government: Republic
Official languages: Chinese, English, Malay and Tamil
National Airline: Singapore Airlines

Currency: Singapore dollar
Size: 602 square km
Climate: Tropical
Population: 3 million

General information
In 1811 Singapore was resettled by 100 Malays and in 1819 the Englishman Sir Stamford Raffles arrived at the Singapore River. He decided that the area would make an excellent British trading base. He established a station of the British East India Company here and in 1824 it was ceded to Britain as part of the Straits Settlement. Singapore thrived for the next 100 years and became one of the main trading centres in southeast Asia.

The Second World War brought an end to Singapore's prosperity and in 1942 the island was taken over by the invading Japanese. At the end of the war Singapore decided to fight for its own independence and this was achieved in 1959. After brief membership of the Federation of Malaysia, Singapore became an independent republic in 1965. Since then the country has consolidated its trading position and also established itself as a major centre for tourism, finance and international investment.

Food and drink
Singapore is one of the great culinary countries of the world. There is a wide variety of national cuisines from which to choose: Singaporean, Chinese, Malaysian, Indonesian, Indian, Japanese, Korean, Vietnamese and Western. Seafood and fresh fruit come in many exotic shapes and sizes. One of the best ways to enjoy food in Singapore is at one of the numerous food centres, or hawker centres. These are informal food markets, frequently in the open air, that have dozens of stalls all serving different types of food. There are an equivalent variety of drinks available but tradition dictates that you must have a

Singapore Sling at the Raffles Hotel.

Internal transport
Singapore offers a second to none internal transport system. Buses are clean, fast and appear at very frequent intervals. The Mass Rapid Transit (MRT) system is the local version of the underground, only better. There are over 10,000 taxis in the city and the road system ensures that travel throughout the island is relaxed and quick.

Things to see
Jurong Birdpark. Hundreds of exotic tropical birds in pleasant surroundings.
    Bird Singing Concert, corner of Tiong Bahru. Every Sunday the locals bring their caged birds to this corner to let them sing to their heart's content.
    Chinatown. The old and the new rub shoulders in central Singapore.
    Chinese and Japanese Gardens. Delicate evocation of the Oriental way of life.
    Mandai Orchid Gardens. A paradise for all flower lovers.
    Sentosa Island. Take the cable car ride to this island which boasts displays of the Japanese invasion of the island, three museums, nature walks and Underwater World.
    Singapore Zoo. A zoo where the animals actually have some space to walk around.
    Singapore is also a great centre for shopping.

Useful addresses
Singapore High Commission, 9 Wilton Crescent, London SW1X 8SA. Tel: (0171) 235 8315.
British High Commission, Tanglin Circus (PO Box 19), Singapore 10.
British Council, Singapore Rubber House, Collyer Quay, Singapore 0104.
Tourist Information Centre, 1-119 Raffles City Tower, Singapore.

THAILAND

Capital: Bangkok	Currency: Baht
Type of Government: Kingdom	Size: 514,000 square km
Official language: Thai (English is also	Climate: Tropical
widely spoken and understood)	National Airline: Thai Airways
Population: 57 million	International

General information
The Khmers ruled much of the country for hundreds of years and in 1767 the Thai capital, Auytthaya, was destroyed by invaders. Although this was a great blow to the Thais they soon struck back. The Burmese were expelled from the country and in 1782 King Rama I established a new capital named Bangkok. Throughout the 19th century western powers made various attempts to colonise Thailand but these efforts were thwarted, principally by two monarchs, Rama IV and Rama V.
    In 1932 Thailand (named Siam until 1939) replaced its absolute monarchy

with a constitutional monarchy. Since then the country has experienced varying fortunes, matched by political and social upheavals. In the Second World War Thailand was occupied by the Japanese.

In 1970 Thailand developed closer links with its neighbours but relations soon deteriorated with both Vietnam and Laos. In 1992 there were demonstrations against one of the many military governments which have been in power over the years. This resulted in free elections and Chuan Leekpal was elected as the democratic prime minister.

Thailand operates a very severe anti-drugs policy – which includes the death penalty for trafficking in drugs such as heroin.

Food and drink
Thai food combines the best aspects of Chinese and Indian food. It is spicy and full of flavour and can be very hot – look out for anything that has hot red chillies as an ingredient. Seafood is a speciality, while noodles, rice, curries and sweet and sour are widely available. There is also a wide range of international cuisine to be found including Chinese, Indian, Indonesian, Malay, Japanese and Western. Tropical fruits are plentiful and include such delights as mangoes, mangosteens, durians, rambutans, longans, lychee, tamarinds, pomeloes, jackfruit, jujubes and over 20 kinds of bananas. One of the local drinks is Mekong whisky which should be treated with respect.

Internal transport
Transport within Thailand is both cheap and efficient. Thai Airways International flies to over 15 destinations throughout the country and prices are reasonable. The rail system connects all parts of the country and there are first, second and third-class carriages. Some slower trains have only third-class. The road system in Thailand is of a good standard and local bus services are a quick way of getting around. There are also air conditioned coaches which offer a bit more luxury such as on-board videos. Even so they are remarkably good value.

In Bangkok taxis and tuk-tuks (three-wheel motorbike taxis) are a cheap way to get around but always make sure you know what the fare is going to be before you get in. There are also river taxis on the waterways and the same rule applies to them.

Things to see
Bangkok. A vivacious capital that is a paradise for eating, shopping and sightseeing. Shoppers should always be careful when buying gem stones and do not go to any shops if you are approached to do so by someone you meet in a restaurant or in the street.

Nakhon Pathom, 60 km west of Bangkok. Home of the world's tallest Buddhist monument.

Ayutthaya, 70 km north of Bangkok, the old capital of Siam.

Chiang Mai, northern Thailand. The main city in the north of the country. Famous for historic temples, trekking, festivals and handicrafts.

Chiang Rai, northern Thailand. Notable for its scenery and the hilltribe villages.

Khao Yai National Park, northeast Thailand. Contains many protected species including deer, bears, tigers, elephants, giant hornbills, sunbirds and silver pheasants.

Pattaya, eastern Thailand. One of the top beach resorts in the country and very popular with tourists.

Ko Samui, southern Thailand. The second largest island in the country and one of great beauty and hospitality. A popular tourist destination.

Phuket, southern Thailand. Thailand's largest island and its beaches and local seafood ensure that it is one of the most popular tourist areas in the southeast of Asia.

Useful addresses
Royal Thai Embassy, 29-30 Queen's Gate, London SW7 5JB. Tel: (0171) 589 2944.
Tourism Authority of Thailand, 49 Albemarle Street, London W1X 3FE. Tel: (0171) 499 7679/3297.
British Embassy, Ploenchit Road, Bangkok.
British Council, 428 Rama I Road, Siam Square, Bangkok 10500.
Tourism Authority of Thailand, 372 Bamrung Muang Road, Bangkok 10100. Tel: (02) 225 0060.

VIETNAM

Capital: Hanoi
Type of Government: Democratic Republic
Official language: Vietnamese
National Airline: Air Vietnam

Currency: Dong
Size: 329,466 square km
Climate: Tropical
Population: 70 million

General information
In 1802 a Vietnamese empire was created and shortly after this the French occupied the area. During the Second World War the country was occupied by the Japanese, during which an independence movement was formed by Ho Chi Minh. The French did not recognise his calls for freedom and this led to war between 1946-54. The French were eventually defeated and in 1954 Vietnam was divided in North and South. This only resulted in civil war and in 1961 the United States offered their assistance to the South. This proved to be a fateful decision and until their withdrawal in 1973 the Americans fought a bitter and unpopular rearguard action. In 1975 the North won the war and declared a united Socialist Republic of Vietnam. In 1979 the Chinese invaded Vietnam which resulted in thousands of people trying to flee the country. In recent years Vietnam has been trying to rebuild its fractured tourist industry but it is a good idea to get in touch with the Vietnam Embassy if you are planning to visit here.

Food and drink
Similar to Thai cuisine, with a bit of Chinese thrown in, the emphasis is on fresh ingredients, quick cooking and, of course, chillies. Street stalls sell an array of

tempting dishes; beef wrapped in vine leaves and deep fried, prawn and lotus-shoot salad and pancakes filled with prawn, beansprouts and pork fat.

Internal transport
After years of debilitating fighting the internal transport system is still in the process of getting back on its feet. Trains and buses are slow and uncomfortable and the internal air service is expensive. If you are not in a hurry the train is probably the best bet.

Things to see
Hanoi, north Vietnam. An attractive and surprisingly quiet capital.There are some pleasant lakes in the city centre. The tomb of Ho Chi Minh is in the main square.

Ho Chi Minh City, south Vietnam. Formerly called Saigon this is a vibrant city that has markets, a cathedral, a palace, several temples and a zoo.

Cu Chi, south Vietnam. An area where heavy fighting took place and now is a form of living museum.

Danang, central Vietnam. An area where local tribes can be seen and there are also marble-faced caves and temples with a mountain.

Useful addresses
Vietnamese Embassy, 12-14 Victoria Road, London W8 5RD. Tel: (0171) 937 1912.
British Embassy, 16 Pho Ly Kiet, Hanoi.

16
West Asia

AFGHANISTAN

Capital: Kabul
Type of Government: Republic
Official languages: Pushtu and
  Dari Persian

Currency: Afghani
Size: 657,500 square km
Climate: Hot and dry
Population: 17 million

General information
The country became independent in 1747 and during the 19th century it was a political pawn as Britain and Russia fought for control of central Asia. In 1921 Afghanistan declared itself independent from the British.

Since the Second World War Afghanistan has suffered several military coups and border frictions with Pakistan. In the 1980s the Soviet Union invaded Afghanistan, an occupation that lasted until 1989. Since then there has been fierce fighting between Mujahidin rebels in the country. The situation remains fraught and travellers should try and avoid going there.

Useful address
Afghanistan Embassy, 31 Prince's Gate, London SW7 1QQ.

BANGLADESH

Capital: Dhaka
Type of Government: Republic
Official language: Bengali
National Airline: Bangladesh Biman

Population: 115 million
Currency: Taka
Size: 142,797 square km

Climate
Cool and dry from November to March, April and September are hot and it is hot and wet during the monsoon season from mid-May to October.

General information
The area was conquered by the Afghans in the 12th century and this led to the growth of the Islamic religion. From 1857 Bangladesh was part of British India and in 1947 it became part of Pakistan as East Pakistan. However, it was thought within the country that they were getting the rough end of the deal and

this led to civil war in 1971. Independence for Bangladesh came the following year. Natural disasters and military coups have plagued the country since then and it was not until 1991 that free democratic elections were held.

Food and drink
Very similar to the cuisine found in India. The emphasis is on curry, rice, various breads and dhal but a variety of fish can also be found, as can lobster and prawns.

Internal transport
Internal flights are cheap but their safety record is poor. There is a good rail system and this can be very cheap if you go 3rd class. Even 1st and 2nd are good value. Road travel can be undertaken in a selection of weird and wonderful contraptions. Boat travel is one of the best ways to see the country.

Things to see
Dhaka, central Bangladesh. Known as the 'city of mosques', the city's history dates back hundreds of years.
   Chittagong Hill Tracts, southeast Bangladesh. Hill tracts in a jungle area where there are Buddhist hill tribes. Some areas are restricted.
   Cox's Bazar, southeast Bangladesh. Several different nationalities and cultures and 110 km of unbroken beach.

Useful address
Bangladesh High Commission, 28 Queen's Gate, London SW7 5JA. Tel: (0171) 584 0081.
British High Commission (PO Box 90), Dilkusha, Dhaka 2.
British Council (PO Box 161), 5 Fuller Road, Ramna, Dhaka 2.

BHUTAN

Capital: Thimphu   Population: 1.6 million
Type of Government: Kingdom   Currency: Ngultrum
Official language: Dzonghka Bhutanese   Climate: Monsoons interspersed
                                              with warmer and drier weather

General information
Due to its proximity to India part of Bhutan was annexed by Britain in 1865. In 1910 a treaty was signed whereby Britain agreed not to interfere with the country's internal affairs. This coincided with the first maharaja (now the king) being installed. In the 1950s and 1960s the country underwent major social changes and the current king has to tread warily between neighbouring India and Tibet.

Food and drink
Very similar to the cuisine in India.

Internal transport
Road travel is the main way to get around but the road system is basic, as is much of the transport.

Things to see
Thimphu, west Bhutan. A new town that has an impressive palace and an interesting bazaar.
Paro, west Bhutan. Impressive temples and monasteries.
Phutsholing, southwest Bhutan. A journey to this town offers some stunning mountain scenery, dotted with the mountain strongholds of feudal lords.

INDIA

Capital: New Delhi   Currency: Indian rupee
Type of Government: Federal Republic   Size: 3,287,590 square km
Official languages: Hindi and English   Population: 853 million
National Airline: Air India

Climate
Generally tropical. There are regional variations but basically the weather can be split into three seasons: cool and dry, hot and dry, and hot and wet. In the north of the country it can get very cold and there is a lot of snow.

General information
The Hindu culture in the area saw its beginnings in the 4th-6th centuries AD with the flourishing of the Gupta dynasty. In the 10th century the Muslims raided the area and set up a sultanate based on Delhi in 1129. In the 16th century there was another Muslim invasion and this resulted in the establishment of the influential Mogul Empire in 1526.

Also during the 16th century Europeans were beginning to explore India. The British East India Company was a powerful force and when the Mogul Empire was declining in influence in the 18th century the British fought with French traders for dominance of the area. In 1757 Robert Clive achieved an important victory at Plassey and thereafter British influence increased. Some parts of the country were renamed British India while others were run by local princes under British supervision.

Due to economic problems there was general unrest in the 19th century and this resulted in the Indian Mutiny (1857-59) which led to reforms and greater Indian involvement in the running of the country. However, this led to calls for complete independence and Mahatma Gandhi led a campaign of civil disobedience aimed at achieving this goal. In 1947, following a period of imprisonment, Gandhi and his supporters had their wishes granted and India became independent. In the same year Pakistan was created as a Muslim state, a move which has caused considerable friction in the last forty years.

As well as disputes with Pakistan, particularly over the Kashmir border, there have been internal problems with various separatist movements calling for autonomy for their region. In 1984 the prime minister, Indira Gandhi, dealt firmly with Sikh separatists but she was assassinated in the same year as a result. In 1991 her son, Rajiv, suffered the same fate. Since then internal affairs have stabilised and, being a nuclear power, India has an important role in world affairs.

Food and drink

Curry is king in India and there are a wide range on offer. Not all of them are explosively hot and the emphasis is on flavour rather than incineration – up to 25 spices are used in the production of a good curry. Vegetables, chicken, lamb and fish will all appear in curries. In terms of strength they range from *vindaloos* to the milder *kormas*. In the more remote regions it is usually a case of eating what is offered and more often than not this will be dhal and rice. Breads are also an important part of the Indian diet and these range from *chapatis* and *paratha* to the thicker *nan*. This is also a wide range of desserts, the most common a local version of ice cream that goes by the name of *kulfi*. Indian tea, or *chai* is served in small cups and is very syrupy sweet. Indian beer is welcoming if you have come from a Muslim country.

Internal transport

India is rightly famous for its rail network (over 60,000 km of track) and it is still the best way to travel around the country. There is a booklet called *Trains at a Glance* which is a timetable of all the major rail routes. There are trains to most parts of the country and there are two main classes – 1st and 2nd. If possible it is a good idea to go for reserved seats – Indian trains are very crowded and sometimes you have to have the qualities of a rugby player to get on board and find a seat. Train travel is cheap and Indrail passes can make it even cheaper if you are doing a lot of travelling.

Other forms of travel include an extensive air network, a bus network that operates throughout the country (although you need strong nerves on some of the vehicles) and in the cities taxis and rickshaws are a cheap and quick way to get around.

Things to see

Travellers can spend a lifetime in India (and some do) and still not see everything that this expansive country has to offer. This is just a brief selection of some of the delights that await the visitor.

North India

Delhi. Impressive Moghul architecture of Old Delhi contrasts with the more spacious streets of New Delhi. Local handicrafts are plentiful here.

Agra. Home of the world renowned Taj Mahal.

Rajasthan. An exotic region that contains the magnificent cities of Jaipur and Jaisalmer and the lakes of Udaipur.

The Ganges. The spiritual heart of India. There are a number of holy cities that are dotted along its banks – Varanasi (the eternal city), Allahabad, Rishikesh and Hardwar.

The Himalayas. Some of the most impressive mountains in the world and including Kashmir, Shimla and the Kulu Valley. Trekking is a popular pastime here and houseboats are popular places to stay.

West India

Bombay. A modern city that offers everything from a hanging garden to a magnificent racecourse to the impressive Gateway to India.

Gujarat. This region includes the birthplace of Mahatma Gandhi – Porbandar.

Gir Forest. The last refuge of the Asian lions.

Ahmedabad. Well known for its textile industry.

Maharashtra. Thirty Buddhist caves cut into a rock gorge.

Goa. India's most famous tourist area – 100 km of sandy coastline and plenty of Western inspired nightlife. There are also wildlife sanctuaries with wild boar and sambar.

South India

Madras. The former home of the ancient Dravidian civilisation and the city is rich in architecture. It is the centre of the Hindu tradition of classical dance.

Andaman Islands. An archipelago famous for its coral and water-sports.

Mahabalipuram, Chidambaram, Tanjore and Madurai. Religion plays a very important role here and these towns have a remarkable array of temples.

Mysore. Known as the sandalwood city and the smell of incense is everywhere.

Kerala. With sea and surf on one side and spice plantations on the other this is an area where cultures and nationalities mix happily.

Kanya Kumari. India's Lands End, where the railway line ends (and begins) and you can see the moon set and rise at the same time.

East India

Calcutta. One of India's most fascinating cities. Underneath the poverty, overcrowding and squalor is a city that shows all sides of India – it is certainly never dull.

Darjeeling. An area of great beauty with stunning mountain views and spectacular sunrises. Famous for its tea plantations.

Kalimpong. Situated in the foothills of the Himalayas this bazaar town is a stepping off point for numerous climbs and treks.

Assam. A state that is famous for its tea and also has impressive wildlife reserves, particularly the tiger reserve of Manas.

Bhubaneswar, Puri and Konark. A 'Gold Triangle' of towns renowned for their glorious temples.

Useful addresses

Indian High Commission, India House, Aldwych, London WC2B 4NA. Tel: (0171) 836 8484.

Indian Tourist Office, 7 Cork Street, London W1X 1PB. Tel: (0171) 812 0929.

British High Commission and British Council, AIFACS Building, Rafi Marg, New Delhi 110/001.

THE MALDIVES

Capital: Male
Type of Government: Republic
Official language : Divehi
Population: 220,000

Currency: Rufiyaa
Size: 298 square km
Climate: Tropical

General information
An Islamic country that was a British protectorate from 1887 to 1965. In 1968 the country became a republic and in 1988 there was a failed coup attempt.

Food and drink
Fish, seafood and fresh fruit are the best local produce, but most of the food on the islands is imported.

Internal transport
Since the Maldives is a collection of islands the main way of getting around is by ferry from island to island. In Male there are a few taxis but bicycle is the best way to get around.

Things to see
Male, central Maldives. A charming capital with a market, a museum and several mosques.
    Resort Islands. The Maldives are dotted with island resorts, many of which are located near the Male Atoll.

NEPAL

Capital: Kathmandu
Type of Government: Kingdom
Official language: Nepali
Population: 19.5 million

Currency: Nepalese rupee
Size: 141,400 square km
National Airline: Royal Nepal
    Airlines

Climate
Hot and dry from April to June, monsoon from June to October, warm and pleasant from October to April. However, it can get very cold up in the mountains.

General information
The Gurkas conquered the region in the 18th century and since then the country has been ruled by the Shah family and then the Rana. Although a new constitution was agreed in 1959 this was abolished by the king three years later. In 1989 there was a considerable degree of tension with neighbouring India and this led to an economic blockade. In 1990 demonstrations heralded a more democratic regime.

Food and drink
The staple fare is lentils, rice and curried vegetables. However, for some strange

reason Kathmandu has a restaurant for virtually every type of cuisine in the world, from Russian to Italian. Since it is a Hindu country there is no beef to be found – buffalo tends to be a prolific substitute. The local brew is *chang*, Tibetan-style beer.

Internal transport
Bicycle is a good way to see the areas around Kathmandu, but you will have to be fit to negotiate some of the hills. For destinations out of pedalling distances buses operate, but be prepared for a bumpy ride.

Things to see
Kathmandu, central Nepal. One of the great historic cities in the world and the centre point of Kathmandu Valley. Some of the highlights include Durbar Square, Hanuman Dhoka (the royal palace), Swayambhunath (the 'monkey temple'), Bodnath (a huge Buddhist stupa) and Gokarna (the royal game reserve).

Patan, central Nepal. Close to Kathmandu and offering similar attractions.

Bhaktapur, central Nepal. The third major city in the valley and its slightly basic nature only adds to its charm.

Pokhara, west Nepal. The main attraction here is the scenery – some of the best mountain views in the world and also the picturesque Phewa Lake.

Trekking. Nepal is one of the premier trekking locations in the world. Everest is the best known and the longest (over a month – but you do not go to the top of the mountain!), but other popular treks are Helambu, Langtang, Annapurna Sanctuary and Jomosom and Muktinath.

Treks can be undertaken in an organised group or as a freelance project but it is advised that you go with a group of people and do not trek alone.

Useful addresses
Nepal Embassy, 12A Kensington Palace Gardens, London W8 4QU. Tel: (0171) 229 1594.
British Embassy (PO Box 106), Lainchaur, Kathmandu.
British Council (PO Box 640), Kantipath, Kathmandu.

PAKISTAN

Capital: Islamabad
Type of Government: Republic
National Airline: Pakistan International Airways

Currency: Pakistan rupee
Size: 796,000 square km
Population: 120.84 million
Official language: Urdu

Climate
Hot and dry in the south but significantly colder in the mountainous northern regions. Monsoon season is from mid-July to mid-September.

General information
The Islamic Republic of Pakistan came into being as an independent state on 14

August 1947. This followed years of political struggle to create a Muslim state that was independent from the predominantly Hindu India. However, there was friction within Pakistan and with India. The most common cause of dispute was the region of Kashmir – an area that is administered by India, even though it is populated mostly by Muslims. There was also a veiled hostility between East and West Pakistan – two separate areas, split by India.

In 1953 the military took control of the country. This lasted until 1970 when a democratic election was held. However, the results were catastrophic: the friction between east and west erupted and a civil war ensued. India stepped in to restore order and defeated the Pakistan Army. As a result East Pakistan became the independent state of Bangladesh.

In 1971 Zulfikar Bhutto came to power. His rule lasted until 1977 when the military, in the form of General Zia ul Haq, once more took control and executed Bhutto in 1979. In 1988 Zia was killed in a plane crash and the country reverted to democratic rule. The balance of power turned full circle when Zulfikar Bhutto's daughter, Benazir, was elected as the democratic president of Pakistan in 1988. Although she briefly lost power she was re-elected in 1993 and the country is now consolidating a delicate democracy.

Food and drink
Curries are the basic fare throughout Pakistan but they are not always of the mouth-burning variety, unless you want them to be. Tandoori cooking is a speciality and in the northern areas there is the influence of Middle East cooking – kebabs and suchlike. Breads, such as nan, are also a common part of the diet. Being a strict Muslim country alcohol is banned (although Westerners can get drinks in some of the larger hotels). Tea (*char*) is the most common drink and this is served from street corners to restaurants as a strong, sweet concoction that comes in small cups.

Internal transport
The railway system is the way to travel long distances. The rail network is extensive and the trains are well used – even to the point of people sitting on the roof. Local minibuses are a cheap way to get around but you need strong nerves to put up with some of the driving techniques.

Things to see
Moenjodaro, Sind region. A ruined city that was the pride of the ancient Indus civilisation.

Lahore, Punjab region. One of Pakistan's most interesting cities. Some of the features worth seeing are: Lahore Fort; Badshahi Mosque; Mosque of Wazir Khan; and the Shalimar Gardens.

Peshawar, North-West Frontier Province. A proud and defiant frontier town.

Darra, North-West Frontier Province. A small town that specialises in making its own guns.

Khyber Pass, North-West Frontier Province. Worth a visit to say that you have been there.

Gilgit and Hunza, the Northern Territory. Two delightful towns in the mountainous north of Pakistan. Mount Rakaposhi is the dominant peak in the area and trekking is a popular pastime.

Chitral, the Northern Territory. Situated in the west of the country and a good area for trekking.

Useful addresses

Pakistan Embassy, 36 Lowndes Square, London SW1X 9JN. Tel: (0171) 235 2044.

British Embassy, Diplomatic Enclave, Ramma 5 (PO Box 1122), Islamabad.

British Council, 23 87th Street G 6/3, (PO Box 1135) Islamabad.

Pakistan Tourism Development Corporation (Information Service) House 2, Street 61, F 7/4 (PO Box 1465), Islamabad.

How to Master Languages

Roger Jones

With the expansion of international travel and the advent of the global market, languages are more valuable than ever before. Written for business people, students and others, this book explains: why learn a language, which language to choose, language training and where to find it, getting down to language learning, children and languages, and language training in organisations. A big reference section completes the book, giving information on an enormous variety of courses, guides and study material, providing an overview of the world's myriad languages and their use today. Roger Jones DipTESL is himself an experienced linguist, writer and educational consultant.

£8.99, 160pp illus. 1 85703 092 3

Please add postage & packing (UK £1 per copy. Europe £2 per copy. World £3 per copy airmail).

**How To Books Ltd,
Plymbridge House, Estover Road,
Plymouth PL6 7PZ
Tel: (01752) 697545. Fax: (01752) 695699. Telex: 45635.**

17
South America

ARGENTINA

Capital: Buenos Aires
Type of Government: Republic
Official language: Spanish
National Airline: Argentinian Airways

Currency: Argentinian peso
Size: 3,761,274 square km
  (including Antarctic territory)
Population: 32.3 million

Climate
Due to its size there is a wide variety of climate. This ranges from the ski resorts of the Andes (17 in total) to the tropics.

General information
Spanish settlers formed the first permanent settlement at Buenos Aires in 1580. In 1778 Buenos Aires was allowed to take part in overseas trade and in 1816 Argentina established its independence from its colonial rulers. In 1946 Colonel Juan Domingo Peron came to power and began a period of intense nationalisation. Peron was overthrown by the military in 1955 but in free elections in 1973 Peron was swept back to power, only for the military to intervene again three years later. In 1983 democracy was restored and the country currently enjoys a period of relatively stable government.

Food and drink
Argentinian beef is among the best in the world and features heavily in the local diet. This is frequently served in restaurants called 'parillas'. Maize is also an important ingredient in local cuisine and dishes using this are most frequently found in the northwest. Argentinian wine is also well worth trying.

Internal transport
Good railway system and local air transport. Road transport can be erratic and many of the country's roads need renewing.

Things to see
The Iguazu Falls, part of the Iguazu National Park, Misiones region. Impressive waterfalls in a stunning surrounding.
    Cardones National Park, northern Argentina. Dramatic scenery featuring giant cacti and natural stone sculptures.

Patagonian Andes, southern Argentina. A wide variety of attractions – ski resorts, prairies, glaciers, forests and lakes.

La Pampa, central Argentina, west of Buenos Aires. Cowboy country, Argentinian style.

Buenos Aires. One of the great capitals of the world. Varied, vibrant and distinctly Latin American.

Useful addresses

Embassy of the Argentine Republic, 53 Hans Place, London SW1X 0LA. Tel: (0171) 584 6494.

UK Government Representative, Dr. Luis Agote 2412/52 1425, Buenos Aires.

Secretariat for Tourism, Avenida Santa Fe 883, 1368 Buenos Aires. Tel: 3122232/3125550.

BOLIVIA

Capital: La Paz
Type of Government: Republic
National Airline: Lloyd Aereo Boliviano
   (LAB)
Currency: Boliviano

Official languages: Spanish, Quechu
   and Aymara
Population: 7.4 million
Size: 1,098,580 square km

Climate

Hot and humid on the low lying plains but cool to cold in the mountainous regions.

General information

Ruins found in the country indicate a civilisation in the area dating back to the 10th century. This later became part of the Inca Empire and then fell to the Spanish in the 16th century when it became known as Upper Peru.

At the beginning of the 19th century the call for freedom began to be heard. A long and bloody guerrilla war was conducted for nearly 20 years, until Bolivia achieved independence in 1825. However, there were many disputes with neighbouring countries and as a result Bolivia lost a quarter of its territory. In 1971 General Hugo Suarez came to power following a military coup. He was deposed in the same fashion in 1978. Since then events in the country have remained volatile. There are still disputes with Peru and Chile over access to the Pacific.

Food and drink

Soup, rice and beef are the staple dishes in Bolivia. Red peppers are used frequently in cooking so most of the food is quite spicy. Fried trout is a speciality in the area around Lake Titicaca. Although beef is plentiful a good alternative is *pacumutu* (grilled skewered meat). The water should not be used for drinking if possible and fruit should be peeled. One local drink is *api*, which is fermented from corn and sold on street corners and markets.

Internal transport
Internal flights in Bolivia are cheap but consequently much used so advance booking is advisable. Transport between villages is frequently undertaken by buses and trucks, which is very cheap but uncomfortable and unreliable. The rail system has improved in recent years but only runs between the major cities.

Things to see:
La Paz, western Bolivia. The altitude is a drawback in this cosmopolitan capital city (11,900 feet above sea level), but this is offset by majestic mountains and pre-Inca ruins.

Orturo, 130 miles southeast of La Paz. Well known for its Carnival which starts on the Saturday before Ash Wednesday.

Cochabamba, western Bolivia. A city which has stunning views and still maintains much of the traditions of the country.

Potosi. One of the first great cities of the Americas based on the silver found in Cerro Rico ('Rich Mountain').

Tarija, southern Bolivia. A valley renowned for its fine wines, folklore and traditional costumes.

Useful addresses
Bolivian Embassy, 106 Eaton Square, London SW1W 9AD, Tel: (0171) 235 4248/2257.
British Consulate and Embassy, (Casilla 694), 2732 Av. Arce, La Paz.

BRAZIL

Capital: Brasilia	Currency: Cruzado
Type of Government: Federal Republic	Size: 8,511,965 square km
Official language: Portuguese	Population: 150 million
National Airline: Varig Brazilian Airlines	

Climate
Varied – tropical in the north, temperate in the Brazilian Highlands in the south and arid in the southwest plains.

General information
Brazil was discovered in 1500 by the Portuguese navigator Pedro Alves Cabral. For the next four hundred years the fate of the country was dependent on its natural resources. Wood, sugar cane, gold, diamonds, coffee and rubber all played a part in the country's history and established it as a major exporter of these items.

At the beginning of the 19th century the King of Portugal, Dom Joao VI, moved his court to Brazil and in 1815 it was made a kingdom. However, this could not halt the push for independence which was declared in 1822 by Dom Pedro I, first Emperor of Brazil. In 1869 the country was declared a Republic.

Throughout the 20th century Brazil was ruled by a mixture of democratic and military governments. In 1985 elections were held to end 20 years of military rule. In 1992 President Fernando Collor de Melo resigned following corruption charges and Itamar Franco took over the presidency. The position remains unpredictable today.

Food and drink
In the south prime beef is the staple diet and one of the most popular places to eat it is the *Rodizho* restaurants. In the Amazon area fish, fruit and rice is the staple diet. Other areas have their own unique cuisines including seafood in the northeast based on African recipes and black bean and meat stew in the southeast of the country. There is good local beer and wine in Brazil and the national drink is *cachaca*, a potent rum made from sugar cane.

Internal transport
Internal air transport is well developed and serves most parts of the country. There are also numerous bus companies and this is one of the cheapest ways to travel. There is an internal railway system but this can be sparse and erratic. Travel by car is not recommended and hitchhiking should not be undertaken.

Things to see
Rio de Janeiro. A thriving, schizophrenic city. Slick hotels contrast sharply with the depressing shanty towns. Sites worth visiting include Sugarloaf Mountain, the beaches of Copacabana, Mount Corcovado and its statue of Jesus.

Iguazu Falls, southern Brazil. One of the largest and most impressive waterfalls in the world. Located on the border with Argentina.

Salvador, northeast Brazil. A city where African folklore based on slavery has been preserved.

The Amazon Basin, northern Brazil. Still one of the great wilderness areas on earth. Manaus, in the northwest, is a good point for jungle excursions.

Useful addresses
Brazilian Embassy, 32 Green Street, London W1Y 3FD. Tel: (0171) 499 0877.
Brazilian Consulate, 6 St Albans Street, London SW1Y 4SG. Tel: (0171) 930 9055.
British Embassy, Avenida das Nacoes Lote 8, Caixa Postal 586, Brasilia DF.
British Council, (Caixa Postal 6104), SCRN 708/9 Nos. 1/3, 70.740, Brasilia DF.

CHILE

Capital: Santiago
Type of Government: Republic
Official language: Spanish
Population: 13 million

Currency: Chilean peso
Size: 741,767 square km
National Airline: LAN Chile

Climate
Arid in the south, Mediterranean in type in the central valley, temperate in the forest and lake districts and cold in the south of the country.

General information

Southern Chile was populated by the Mapuche Indians and northern Chile was populated by the Atacama Indians. They were conquered by the Incas in the 15th century who were then conquered by the Spaniards in 1532. In 1541 a Spanish colony was founded in Santiago.

At the beginning of the 19th century the indigenous population revolted against their Spanish masters. In 1818 the Republic of Chile was established and a period of prosperity followed based on copper production. During the 20th century this economic prosperity declined. In 1970 Salvador Allende became the first democratically elected Marxist head of state. However, three years later he was overthrown by a military coup led by General Pinochet. For 15 years Pinochet led a harsh, right wing regime and in 1988 he was finally ousted in a democratic election. In 1990 Patricio Aylwin became President.

Food and drink

Seafood is of high quality in Chile and the best bet for the culinary traveller. There is also an ample supply of fresh meat. Chilean wines are excellent and plentiful.

Internal transport

There are five railway networks throughout Chile but some of them only take freight. The Pan-American is the foundation of the road system and while this is good the buses and taxis which travel on it are often old and unreliable. Long distance coaches are a better bet. Two airlines, LAN Chile and Ladeco, provide air transport throughout the country and shipping is a popular form of transport along the lengthy west coast.

Things to see

Vina del Mar. A picturesque town with impressive beaches.

Portillo. Chile's best ski area.

Arica. On the northern border, a popular resort town.

Parque Nacional Lauca. A national park on a plateau in the snow-capped Andes.

Temuco. One of Chile's 'young' cities, there are seven national parks in the vicinity.

Patagonia and Tierra del Feugo. In the far south of the country is a region of icebergs, fjords, lakes, lagoons and ice fields.

Useful addresses

Chilean Embassy, 12 Devonshire Street, London W1N 2DS. Tel: (0171) 580 6392.

British Embassy, (Casilla 72-D), La Concepcion Av. 77, Providencia, Santiago.

British Council, (Casilla 15 T), Eliodora Yanez 832, Tajamar, Santiago.

National Tourist Board, Sernatur, Servicio Nacional de Turismo, Av. Providencia 1550, Santiago.

COLOMBIA

Capital: Bogota
Type of Government: Republic
Official language: Spanish
Population: 33 million
National Airline: Avianca

Currency: Colombian peso
Size: 1,138,914 square km
Climate: Varied – from tropical to
   temperate

General information

Indian tribes were the original inhabitants of this country, but they suffered at the hands of Spanish colonisers in the 16th century. In 1819 the famous freedom fighter, Simon Bolivar, achieved independence for Greater Colombia, an area that comprised Colombia, Panama, Venezuela and Ecuador. In 1830 Venezuela and Ecuador broke away and in 1903 Panama became independent.

In the 1950s Colombia suffered from civil war and there was a brief period of military rule. In the last twenty years the country has been plagued by political and social unrest. Much of this is the result of the country's lucrative drugs trade. Because of the violence connected with this travellers should be very careful when in Colombia.

Food and drink

Beef, chicken and seafood form the basis of most meals and some popular dishes are: chicken with rice, chicken and potato ragoût, rice with crab, smoked fish with salad, steak topped with a fried egg, beef stew and pork with red beans. Soups are also filling and tasty. Coffee is the national drink and several varieties of rum are produced.

Internal transport

Bus services on the main routes are reasonable but on the smaller roads it is a lot less satisfactory. Be careful with your luggage and be prepared for some hairy driving. The rail system is old and slow.

Things to see

Bogota, central Colombia. Combines all facets of South American life.

The Caribbean Coast, north Colombia. A beautiful coast, ringed by dramatic mountains.

Cartagena, northwest Colombia. A city rich in colonial history.

Santa Marta, northwest Colombia. A popular sun and sea resort.

San Agustin, southwest Colombia. The site of important Andean archaeological remains.

Useful addresses

Colombian Embassy, 3 Hans Crescent, London SW1 0LR. Tel: (0171) 589 9177.
British Embassy, (Apartado Aereo 4508), Calle 38, 13-35 Pisos 9-11, Bogota.
British Council, (Apartado Aereo 089231), Calle 87 No. 12-79, Bogota.

ECUADOR

Capital: Quito
Type of Government: Republic
Official language: Spanish – Quechua
  is widely spoken
Population: 11 million

Currency: Sucre
Size: 270,670 square km
Climate: Equatorial. Hot at the coast
  and cooler in the mountains
National Airline: Ecuatoriana

General information
The Spanish established a colony here in 1532. In 1821 there were revolts led by Marshal Sucre and this led to independence. In 1961 the president was overthrown by a military coup; he returned to power a few years later but the military again ousted him. After a few years of being ruled by a military junta democratic elections were held in 1984. In recent years Ecuador and Peru have been involved in border disputes.

Food and drink
In the larger cities you will be able to find Chinese, French, Middle Eastern and Western cuisine. Local food includes fish and seafood in tomato sauce, cream of potato soup and pork with corn bread and bananas.

Internal transport
The bus system is a good way to travel around the country. The roads are good and the buses are usually cheap, efficient and reasonably comfortable. The trains are slower and generally uncomfortable. Taxis and minibuses are cheap in the cities.

Things to see
Quito, central Ecuador. A tranquil and slow-paced capital, with magnificent views and architecture.
   The Galapagos Islands, west coast of Ecuador. Home of hundreds of rare plants and animals including the unique giant tortoises.
   Guayaquil to Quito. It is worth taking the train between Ecuador's two main cities – you will be rewarded with magnificent views of the Andes.
   El Oriente, east Colombia. A remote jungle area where the way of life of the indigenous Indians has been preserved.

Useful addresses
Ecuador Embassy, 3 Hans Crescent, London SW1X 0LS. Tel: (0171) 584 1367.
British Embassy, (Casilla 314), Gonzalez Suarez, 111 Quito.
British Council, (Casilla 8829), Av. Amazonas 1646, Quito.

GUYANA

Capital: Georgetown
Type of Government: Cooperative

Currency: Guyana dollar
Size: 214,969 square km

Republic
Official language: English
National Airline: Guyana Airways

Climate: Tropical
Population: 800,000

General information
The Spanish first explored the area in 1499 but the Dutch made the first settlements in the 17th century. After periods of occupation the country was ceded to Britain in 1831. Guyana became independent in 1966 and a strain has been placed on the economy in recent years because of the refugees from Surinam.

Food and drink
There is a wide choice of Indian curries and also African cuisine such as plantains made into cakes and fruit in coconut milk. Other specialities include Portuguese garlic pork and American pepperpot. Local beer and rum are popular.

Internal transport
The Guyana Transport Company runs buses to various parts of the country but these are usually crowded. There are no passenger trains and boats are a popular way of getting around the country's many waterways.

Things to see
Georgetown, north Guyana. A laid-back combination of colonial architecture, flora and theatre.
    Bartica, north Guyana. A stepping-off point for gold and diamond fields.
    Kaieteur National Park, central Guyana. A variety of wildlife and the stunning Kaieteur Falls.

Useful addresses
High Commission of Guyana, 3 Palace Court, Bayswater Road, London W2 4LP. Tel: (0171) 229 7684.
British High Commission (PO Box 10849), 44 Main Street, Georgetown.

PARAGUAY

Capital: Asuncion
Type of Government: Republic
Official Language: Spanish – Guarani
    is widely spoken
National Airline: LAP

Currency: Guarani
Size: 406,752 square km
Climate: Tropical
Population: 4.5 million

General information
The Spanish were the first European settlers and the country became a Spanish colony in the 16th century. It became part of the vice-royalty of Peru and then, in 1776, part of the vice-royalty of Rio de la Plata. In 1811 Paraguay became independent. The country suffered badly during the War of the Triple Alliance (1865-70) against Brazil, Argentina and Uruguay. During the early 20th century the country suffered periods of political unrest. In 1954 General Stroessner came

to power but his regime was frequently accused of human rights violations. In 1989 Stroessner was overthrown in a coup.

Food and drink
Meat is of a very high quality and soup is also a popular staple meal. For a snack you could try *chipas*, a cornmeal dough cake that is mixed with cheese and egg.

Internal transport
Buses in all shapes and forms are the most common form of transport. The standard of driving and conditions on board are equally variable.

Things to see
Asuncion, southwest Paraguay. An interesting capital that has retained much of its history and traditional way of life.
   San Bernardino, southwest Paraguay. A popular resort town.
   Itaugua, southwest Paraguay. A centre for genuine local handicrafts.

Useful addresses
Paraguay Embassy, Braemar Lodge, Cornwall Gardens, London SW7 4AQ. Tel:
   (0171) 937 1253.
British Embassy, (Casilla de Correo 404), Calle Presidente Franco 706,
   Asuncion.

PERU

Capital: Lima
Type of Government: Republic
Official languages: Spanish and Quechua
Population: 23 million

Currency: Sol
Size: 1,285,215 square km
Climate: Tropical
National Airline: Aero Peru

General information
Before the first Europeans landed in Peru the land was occupied by first the Chimu and then the Inca tribes of South American Indians but they could not withstand the might of the Spanish when they arrived in 1533. The Spanish viceroy established his headquarters in Lima and this was a period of great activity and, for the Spanish, prosperity.
   In 1821 Peru became the last of Spain's American colonies to declare its independence. For the next fifty years the country enjoyed considerable stability and prosperity. However, this was weakened during the War of the Pacific and, after their opposition to Germany in the Second World War, Peru has been dependent on the USA for aid. There have also been several years of political unrest. During the 1980s 10,000 people died in civil unrest. Despite promises of free-market policies Congress was dissolved in 1992. Due to the volatile situation in the country travellers should exercise caution when in Peru.

Food and drink
Chicken, fish and beef make up the majority of local dishes and cheap meals can be bought at the marketplaces and street stalls. Two popular dishes are *cebiche*, raw

fish with lemon and onion, *chicharrones de pollo*, grilled chicken. There are plenty of restaurants offering Chinese food and sweets and cakes are something of a delicacy. The national drink is called *pisco* – a fiery brandy that is drunk copiously.

Internal transport
Local buses and trucks are the most common way to get around the country. However road conditions are often only moderate at best and the buses are overcrowded and badly maintained. Trains operate in the south of the country and although they are slow they are cheap and generally more comfortable than the buses. In Lima you can travel by buses, minibuses or *colectivos*.

Things to see
Lima, west Peru. One of the most important cities in South America. It is a fascinating mix of colonial history and 20th century modernisation.

Huaraz, west Peru. An internationally renowned centre for climbers and trekkers.

The Amazon Basin, north Peru. The area still has a kind of mythical effect on travellers and, despite modern abuses, it is still one of the great unspoilt jungle areas in the world.

Cuzco, south Peru. The capital of the Inca empire and bursting with Inca history, endeavour and architecture.

Machu-Picchu, south Peru. Situated in Cuzco this is probably the most famous of the Inca creations. It is the site of the Lost City, the only Inca city that survived the Spanish occupation and remained intact.

Lake Titicaca, south Peru. The world's largest navigable lake with regular transport.

Useful addresses
Peruvian Embassy, 52 Sloane Street, London SW1X 9SP. Tel: (0171) 235 1917.
Peruvian Tourist Office, 10 Grosvenor Gardens, London SW1W 0BD. Tel: (0171) 824 8693.
British Embassy, (Apartado 854), Edificio Pacifico-Washington, Plaza Washington, Avenida Arequipe, Lima.
British Council, (Apartado 14-0114), Calle Alberto Lynch 110, San Isidro, Lima 1.

SURINAM

Capital: Paramaribo	Currency: Surinam guilder
Type of Government: Republic	Size: 163,265 square km
Official language: Surinamese	Climate: Tropical
Population: 450,000	National Airline: Surinam Airways

General information
The British were the first Europeans to establish a settlement here, in 1650, and in 1667 the country was ceded to the Netherlands. Following periods of control by Britain and the Netherlands again, Surinam became independent in 1975,

causing 40,000 Surinamers to emigrate. Since then the country has been plagued by military coups and guerrilla action.

Food and drink
A wide range of international cuisines is on offer – European, Indonesian, Creole, Chinese and Indian.

Internal transport
There are buses to most parts of the country and one rail service.

Things to see
Paramaribo, north Surinam. A relaxed city with a Dutch colonial flavour.
   The scenery and tropical vegetation are the main attractions outside the capital.

Useful address
British Honorary Consulate, c/o VSH United Buildings, PO Box 1300, Van't, Hogerhuysstraat, Paramaribo.

URUGUAY

Capital: Montevideo	Currency: New Uruguayan peso
Type of Government: Republic	Size: 186,926 square km
Official language: Spanish	Climate: Sub-tropical
Population: 3 million	National Airline: Pluna

General information
The Spanish established their dominance here in the 18th century and in 1776 Uruguay became part of the vice-royalty of Rio de la Plata. It was only with British help that Uruguay achieved independence in 1828. During the 1960s there was considerable guerrilla activity in the country but this was crushed in 1973. The new regime was repressive and attracted international condemnation. Military rule was finally ended in 1985.

Food and drink
Similar to Argentinian cuisine – some of the local dishes include sausage baked in dough, spicy oxtail soup and a variety of cuts of beef.

Internal transport
There is a frequent national bus service and there are several rail routes although they tend to be slow and uncomfortable. In the cities there are plenty of cheap buses, minibuses and taxis.

Things to see
Montevideo, south Uruguay. The main tourist location in the country. Its attractions include white beaches and good tourist facilities.
   Punta del Este, east Uruguay. The country's most popular tourist resort – sun, sand etc.

Useful addresses
Uruguay Embassy, 140 Brompton Road, London SW3 1HY. Tel: (0171) 589
    8835 or (0171) 589 8735.
British Embassy, Calle Marco Bruto 1073, Montevideo.

VENEZUELA

Capital: Caracas   Currency: Bolivar
Type of Government: Republic   Size: 912,050 square km
Official language: Spanish   Climate: Tropical
Population: 20 million   National Airline: Viasa

General information
Columbus was the first European to sight the country and in 1499 it was named
Venezuela (little Venice) by an Italian explorer, Vespucci. The Spanish then
controlled the country until Simon Bolivar brought freedom to the area in 1821.
Until after the Second World War the country was ruled by a succession of
dictators. Since then oil revenue helped produce reasonable stability in the
country but this evaporated in the 1980s and in 1992 there were two failed coup
attempts.

Food and drink
The quality of food is high in Venezuela and there are hundreds of excellent
local and international restaurants in Caracas. Beef is the country's speciality
and this is usually served with chips or rice. Cornflour rolls with beef and
vegetables are sold at street stalls. Cakes and fresh fruit are also plentiful and
exotic.

Internal transport
Local buses are cheap and efficient and the roads are generally good. The
exception to this is buses in the mountain areas. In Caracas the best way to get
around is on the modern subway.

Things to see
Caracas, northeast Venezuela. A very modern capital that reflects the years when
the oil revenue was pouring in. There are impressive beaches nearby.
    Angel Falls, southeast Venezuela. The world's largest waterfall – seventeen
times higher than Victoria Falls.
    The Orinoco Delta, southeast Venezuela. Local villages and traditional ways
of life are dotted along this massive delta.

Useful addresses
Venezuela Embassy, 1 Cromwell Road, London SW7. Tel: (0171) 584 4206.
British Embassy, (Apartado 1246), Avenida La Estancia No. 10, Ciudad
    Comercial, Tamanaco, Caracas.
British Council, (Apartado 1246) Torre La Noria, Piso 6, Paseo Enrique Eraso,
    Sector San Roman, Las Mercedes, Caracas.

18
The Middle East

BAHRAIN

Capital: Manama
Type of Government: Absolute
  monarchy
Population: 550,000

Currency: Bahrain dinar
Size: 660 square km
Official language: Arabic – English
  is widely spoken

Climate
Generally very hot although cooler from November to March.

General information
With its history dating back to 6000 BC Bahrain was a popular stopover for Alexander the Great as he was trying to unify the Middle East. Islam was introduced in the 7th century and then came under the control of successive Persian and Ottoman rulers. From 1521 to 1602 the Portuguese took control and the Arabs then had brief control until the powerful Al Khalifa dynasty took over. From 1861 to 1971, when independence was achieved, Bahrain was a British protectorate. Since independence the country has enjoyed a successful and stable period, due largely to the country's supplies of oil.

Food and drink
Generally Middle East cuisine and there are also a number of Indian, Chinese and Thai restaurants. Beer is available and is best served very cold due to the heat.

Internal transport
Bus is the most practical way of getting around and there is a reasonably good network. The larger towns have taxis but they do not have meters so agree a fare first.

Things to see
Manama, north Bahrain. A new capital that has the National Museum, an impressive modern mosque and an interesting dhow-building yard.
    Bahrain Fort, north Bahrain. The country's most impressive archaeological site – there are four main excavations.
    Ad-Diraz and Barbar Temples, north Bahrain. Temples dating back thousands of years.

Suq-al-Khamis Mosque, north Bahrain. The oldest mosque in the country.

Tree of Life, southeast Bahrain. Claimed to be at the centre of the Garden of Eden. Very remote and difficult to get to.

Muhurraq Island, northeast Bahrain. The country's second most important island and with valuable architecture and remains.

Useful addresses
Bahrain Embassy, 98 Gloucester Road, London SW7. Tel: (0171) 370 5132.
British Embassy (PO Box 114), Government Road, North Manama.
British Council (PO Box 452), 21 Government Avenue, Manama 306.
Bahrain Directorate of Tourism, PO Box 26613, Manama.

IRAN

Capital: Tehran
Type of Government: Islamic Republic
Official language: Persian (Farsi)
Population: 64 million
National Airline: Iran Air

Currency: Iranian rial
Size: 1,648,000 square km
Climate: Hot and dry in summer
    and cool and dry in winter.

General information
Islam was established in the area by the Arabs and following periods of rule by the Turks and then the Mongols the Persian Safavid Dynasty came to power from 1587 to 1736. After their power declined the British and the Russians showed an interest in the area and during the 19th century this caused internal unrest. This unrest continued through the 20th century, culminating in 1979 with the Islamic Revolution led by the Ayatollah Khomeini. This hardline and extreme regime has led to deteriorating relations with the West and Iran remains a place where travellers should take great care. Islam is taken very seriously here and visitors are expected to follow the rules. This means that both men and women should dress in a very conservative fashion with no unnecessary bare flesh showing. However, if you make the effort then you will be accepted a lot more readily.

Food and drink
Fresh ingredients are favoured and rice, bread, vegetables, herbs and fruit are plentiful. Lamb and chicken are the most common meats and are often served as kebabs, marinated and then grilled. Local soups and omelettes are also available and both are filling and very tasty. A national delicacy is *fesenjun*, a stew of duck, goose, chicken or quail cooked in a pomegranate sauce. Tea is the most popular drink and it is something of a social occasion in the (all male) tea houses. There is a black market in alcohol but this is best avoided.

Internal transport
There is an extensive network of internal air flights and the prices are very low. However, many flights are booked up weeks in advance so it is a case of planning well and booking early. There are dozens of bus companies and they offer lux and super class services (super is the superior version). Fares are very

cheap, as are the local minibuses, but on long trips it is worth booking ahead. Iranian roads are generally very good. The rail network covers much of the country and is very cheap – first and second class seats are available.

Things to see
Tehran, north Iran. Not a great city but interesting as an illustration of the extremes of the Islamic Revolution.

Esfahan, central Iran. An architectural feast with the greatest number of Islamic buildings in the country.

Shiraz, south Iran. A former Persian capital and one of the country's most pleasant large cities, dotted with mosques, forts and bazaars.

Persian Gulf Islands, south Iran. There are 16 islands, 11 of which are inhabited, and they offer rugged scenery, historical value and also the chance to sit back and relax.

Caspian Region, north Iran. Site of the Caspian Sea (actually the world's largest lake) that is ringed by resort towns and impressive scenery.

Useful addresses
Iranian Embassy, 27 Prince's Gate, London SW7 1PX. Tel: (0171) 584 8101.
Iranian Consulate, 50 Kensington Court, London W8 5DD. Tel: (0171) 937 5225.
British Embassy (PO Box 1513), Avenue Ferdowsi, Tehran.

IRAQ

Since the Gulf War in 1991 Western visitors have not been given visas for Iraq and it is not recommended that travellers try and visit this volatile country.

ISRAEL

Capital: Jerusalem
Type of Government: Republic
Official languages: Arabic and Hebrew
Population: 6 million

Currency: Israeli shekel
Size: 20,700 square km
Climate: Temperate
National Airline: El Al

General information
Throughout history Israel, or Palestine as it was formerly, has been a vital religious and political area, keenly disputed by Jews, Muslims and Christians.

Israel came into being in 1948 when the UN recommended that Palestine be divided into a Jewish state, an Arab state and an internationally administered zone around Jerusalem. Arab forces immediately invaded but they were repulsed by the Israelis who then took over the majority of Palestine while the remainder was annexed between Jordan and Egypt. These areas, the West Bank and the Gaza Strip, have been the cause of much fighting between Israelis and the Arab allies of Egypt, Syria and Jordan. The Palestinian Liberation Organization (PLO) also fought a terrorist campaign against what they saw as the Israeli invaders and this came to a head in 1988 when PLO protestors fought bitterly over disputed territory.

In 1994 a peace agreement was signed by the Palestinians and the Israelis agreeing to return land for peace. At the time of writing the situation remains tense but signs of a lasting peace are emerging.

Travellers should keep the political and religious situations in mind when in Israel.

Food and drink

Felafel, hummus and kebabs are common, cheap meals and there is also western food such as hamburgers and pizzas. *Kosher* food is that which is 'ritually acceptable' according to Jewish law. This means that foods such as pork are forbidden and others have to be prepared in a certain fashion. There are numerous restaurants that are devoted to *kosher* food. A variety of breads and fresh fruit is one of the delights of the local cuisine. Tea and coffee are drunk widely and beer is the main alcoholic tipple.

Internal transport

The road system is very well developed and buses are the best way to get around. The Jewish buses are more comfortable but the Arab ones are cheaper and safer. There is a limited rail network and although it is cheap it is not very convenient. Shared taxis (*sherut*) are the best way for shorter distances.

Things to see

Jerusalem, central Israel. One of the most historic and holiest cities in the world. Weeks rather than days should be devoted to all that Jerusalem has to offer.

Tel Aviv, west Israel. More a business centre but there are some superb beaches nearby.

Galilee, north Israel. An area of great religious significance and natural beauty. Nazareth is the most important of the religious sites. The Sea of Galilee is a major tourist spot.

The Dead Sea, east Israel. Renowned for its high level of salt which enables people to float in its waters.

Eilat, south Israel. A major tourist resort on the Red Sea but keep a close eye on your valuables.

Jericho and Bethlehem, central Israel. Two of the country's most important religious sites but check out the political situation before you go due to their historical role in the Occupied Territories.

Useful addresses

Israeli Embassy, 2 Palace Green, London W8 4QB. Tel: (0171) 957 9500.
British Embassy, 193 Hayarkon Street, Tel Aviv 63405.
British Council (PO Box 3302), 140 Hayarkon Street, Tel Aviv 61032.

JORDAN

Capital: Amman
Type of Government: Constitutional
  Monarchy

Currency: Jordanian dinar
Size: 97,740 square km
Climate: Very hot and dry in the

Official language: Arabic
National Airline: Royal Jordanian

summer; cooler in winter.
Population: 4 million

General information
The area was part of the Roman Empire and then successively ruled by the Arabs, the Crusaders and the Turks. Following its independence in 1946 Jordan fell into conflict with Israel over the occupation of the West Bank, which it felt should be ruled by the Palestinians. During the Gulf War in 1991 Jordan supported Iraq which led to international sanctions being imposed. Since then Jordan has re-established itself as an important player in the complex politics of the Middle East.

Food and drink
Standard Middle East fare with lamb being the most common meat. *Felafel* (chick-pea and salad sandwiches), *shawarma* (spiced lamb) and *khobz* (flat bread made with yoghurt) are all cheap and can be bought from the numerous foodstalls. Local beer and wine is also available.

Internal transport
Buses and minibuses are common and they offer services that vary in both cost and reliability. The most popular form of transport is service taxis – customized Peugeots and Mercedes.

Things to see
Amman, north Jordan. One of the most ancient cities in the world, with archaeological remains dating back to 3000 BC.
    Petra, south Jordan. A lost city that remained hidden for over 1000 years. One of the most spectacular sights in the Middle East.
    Jerash, north Jordan. The site of a preserved Roman city.
    The Dead Sea, west Jordan. Famous for its salty, buoyant water.
    Wadi Rum, south Jordan. Dramatic desert scenery.

Useful addresses
Jordanian Embassy, 6 Upper Phillimore Gardens, London W8 7HB. Tel: (0171) 937 3685.
Jordanian Tourist Office, 211 Regent Street, London W1. Tel: (0171) 437 9465.
British Embassy (PO Box 87), Abdoun, Amman.
British Council (PO Box 634), Rainbow Street, off First Circle, Jabla Amman, Amman.

KUWAIT

Capital: Kuwait City
Type of Government: National Assembly
Official language: Arabic
Climate: Warm, hot and very hot

Currency: Kuwait dinar
Size: 24,286 square km
Population: 2 million

General information
After originally being settled by Arabic nomads Kuwait became a British protectorate at the outbreak of the First World War. Oil was discovered in 1938 and this transformed the country's economy. Independence was achieved in 1961 and since then they have experienced aggressive overtures by Iraq. This culminated in an Iraqi invasion in 1990, which subsequently led to the Gulf War. Travellers should be wary of going too close to the Iraqi border.

Food and drink
Indian food is prevalent in the country and there is also a large quantity of western style pizza, hamburgers etc. Alcohol is not allowed in Kuwait.

Internal transport
Many internal bus routes have not been restored following the Gulf War and travel is a slow process. Taxis are readily available in Kuwait City.

Things to see
Kuwait City, east Kuwait. Still recovering from the Gulf War.
   Failaka Island, east Kuwait. The country's most important archaeological site.

Useful addresses
Kuwait Embassy, 45-46 Queen's Gate, London SW7. Tel: (0171) 589 4533.
British Embassy, Arabian Gulf Street, Amman.

LEBANON

Capital: Beirut
Type of Government: Republic
Official language: Arabic
National Airline: Middle East Airlines

Currency: Lebanese pound
Size: 10,452 square km
Population: 3 million

Climate
Hot and dry in the summer and cool and wet in the winter – 300 days of sun a year.

General information
Following almost 20 years of bitter civil war Lebanon is slowly returning to something approaching normality. However, travellers should exercise caution when visiting this country which used to be one of the most popular in the Middle East.

Food and drink
A good selection of kebabs, salads, breads and *mezze* (hors d'oeuvres) are popular throughout the country and syrupy desserts are common. Alcohol is widely available and there is a good selection.

Internal transport
The only realistic way of getting around is by road and buses, taxis and service taxis (usually old Mercedes) are the preferred modes of transport. Driving standards can be erratic.

Things to see
Beirut, west Lebanon. A once beautiful city that has been scarred badly by the civil war.

Tripoli, northwest Lebanon. A main port that has the mark of the Crusaders on it.

Byblos, west Lebanon. Impressive ruins and a scenic port.

The Bekaa valley, central Lebanon. Two important sites to visit are Baalbeck and Heliopolis.

Useful addresses
Lebanese Embassy, 21 Kensington Palace Gardens, London W8 4QM. Tel: (0171) 229 765.
Lebanese Tourist Office, 90 Piccadilly, London W1. Tel: (0171) 409 2031.
British Embassy, Shamma Building, Rawche, Beirut.

OMAN

Capital: Muscat
Type of Government: Sultanate
Official language: Arabic
National Airline: Oman Aviation

Currency: Rial Omani
Size: 300,000 square km
Population: 1.5 million

Climate
Tropical in the south and cooler in the mountainous interior.

General information
In the 16th century Oman was settled by the Portuguese, the Dutch and the English. Since the 19th century Britain has had considerable influence in the country and the current sultan, Qaboos Bin Said, was educated at Sandhurst. He has tried to develop his country while at the same time maintain many of the traditional features.

Food and drink
As well as traditional Middle East cuisine Indian food is the most common and curry can be found in most restaurants and foodstalls. Some alcohol is available but usually only in the larger restaurants and hotels.

Internal transport
Buses are the best way to get from town to town and because this is cheap, it is a good idea to book tickets in advance. There are occasionally service taxis to get around the country but the bus service is usually a better bet.

Things to see
Muscat, northeast Oman. A delightful capital that offers many of the original charms of the Gulf area.

Sur, northeast Oman. Good beaches and a dhow builder's yard.

Salalah, south Oman. A lush contrast to the rest of the country. Stunning beaches and picturesque mountain scenery are the main attractions.

Useful addresses
Omani Embassy, 44A Montpelier Square, London SW7 1JJ. Tel: (0171) 584 6782.
British Embassy (PO Box 6898), Ruwi, Muscat.
British Council (PO Box 7090 Jibroo), Road One, Medinat Qaboos West, Muscat.

QATAR

Capital: Doha
Type of Government: Absolute
   Monarchy
Climate: Very hot and humid in the
   summer and warm in the winter.

Currency: Qatar riyal
Size: 11,000 square km
Population: 400,000
Official language: Arabic

General information
For much of the 19th and 20th centuries Qatar was reliant on Britain and in 1916 it became a British protectorate. Qatar became independent in 1971. In recent years Qatar has had close ties with Saudi Arabia and, more recently, Iran.

Food and drink
Western food and Indian curries are the most common types of cuisine. The larger hotels sell alcohol if you are desperate for a drink.

Internal transport
Since there are no buses or service taxis, regular taxis and rented cars are the only viable method of getting around.

Things to see
Doha, east Qatar. A pleasant capital but with little to see except a museum, a fort and a zoo. There are also a few sites of interest within a couple of hours drive to Doha, most notably Umm Silal Mohammed and Umm Silal Ali.

Useful addresses
Embassy of Qatar, 27 Chesham Place, London SW1X 8HG. Tel: (0171) 235 0851.
British Embassy (PO Box 3), Doha.
British Council (PO Box 2992), Ras Abu Aboud Road, Doha.

SAUDI ARABIA

Capital: Riyadh
Type of Government: Kingdom
Official language: Arabic
National Airline: Saudi Arabian Airlines

Currency: Riyal
Size: 2,400,000 square km
Population: 15 million

Climate
Since most of the country is desert the temperatures in the summer are ferocious. In winter they become pleasantly warm.

General information
Saudi Arabia came into being in 1932 as a result of the Saud family trying to dominate the warring tribes of the Arabia peninsula and wrest control from Turkey. Due to large oil deposits the country discovered considerable economic power. During the Gulf War in 1991 international forces were stationed in Saudi Arabia following Iraqi rocket attacks on Saudi cities. The Saudi royal family continues to have a powerful hold over the country.

Food and drink
Western inspired fast food and Indian curries are most common in cities and grilled chicken and beans is the staple diet further afield. There is no alcohol allowed in the country and this should be adhered to.

Internal transport
Buses are reasonably priced, comfortable and usually punctual. There is also a rail line connecting the main centres and it is efficient; 2nd class is cheaper than the bus. There is an internal air network but this is quite expensive.

Things to see
Riyadh, central Saudi Arabia. A new city and most of the interesting ruins are outside the city.

Jeddah, southwest Saudi Arabia. Combines thousands of years of history with a thriving modern city. The Old City is of particular interest.

Abha, southwest Saudi Arabia. A popular resort town with picturesque mountain scenery.

Asir National Park, southwest Saudi Arabia. Dramatic mountains in the north contrast with the southerly plains.

Madain Salah, west Saudi Arabia. The country's best archaeological site consisting of excellent rock tombs.

Useful addresses
Saudi Arabian Embassy, 30 Belgrave Square, London SW1X 8QB. Tel: (0171) 235 0831.
British Embassy (PO Box 94351), Riyadh 11693.
British Council (PO Box 2701), Dabab Street, off Washem Street, Mura'aba, Riyadh 11461.

SYRIA

Capital: Damascus
Type of Government: Republic
Official language: Arabic
National Airline: Syrian National
    Airlines

Currency: Syrian pound
Size: 185,680 square km
Climate: Mediterranean
Population: 12.2 million

General information
From 1517 until the First World War Syria was part of the Ottoman Empire. In 1920 it came under limited French control and in 1946 the country became independent. Since then there have been troubled alliances with fellow Arab countries, economic growth and several military coups. Despite an international image for unrest and trouble it is a relatively easy country in which to travel but travellers should always keep their wits about them.

Food and drink
Standard Middle East cuisine is available in most part of Syria.

Internal transport
The bus network is well developed, cheap and generally efficient. The types of buses vary from the standard microbuses to the more luxurious Pullman and Karnak buses. The rail network is also good but the stations are invariably inconveniently placed. Service taxis and hitching are also useful ways to get around.

Things to see
Damascus, south Syria. Claims to be the oldest continuously inhabited city in the world and a fascinating place to spend a few days. The medieval city and the Omayyad Mosque are a must.

Aleppo, north Syria. A romantic town that rivals the delights of the medieval city of Damascus.

Crac de Chevaliers, west Syria. One of the country's best tourist attractions featuring a magnificent fort built by the Crusaders.

Palmyra, central Syria. An oasis in the desert that contains one of the great historical sites in the world – a ruined city dating back to the 2nd century AD.

Useful addresses
Syrian Embassy, 8 Belgrave Square, London SW1 8PH. Tel: (0171) 245 9012.
British Embassy, Malki Quarter, 11 Mohammed Kurd Ali Street, Imm Kotob,
    Damascus.

TURKEY

Capital: Ankara
Type of Government: Republic
Official languages: Arabic and Kurdish

Currency: Turkish lira
Size: 779,452 square km
National Airline: Turkish Airlines

Population: 59 million

Climate
Mediterranean in the north, cool in the central region and very hot in the southeast.

General information
The Ottoman Empire (1300-1922) was one of the most powerful in the world but when the country became a republic in 1923 many western ideas and customs were adopted. Following the Second World War the country became more democratic but this was coupled with increasing instability, leading to military coups and the imposition of martial law in the 1960s and the 1970s. There have also been problems with Greece and the Kurds and some of these frictions remain today.

Food and drink
Similar to Greek food and some of the local dishes are shish kebab, doner kebab, Turkish pizza, *meze* (hors d'oeuvres) and lamb in a variety of guises. Turkish coffee is excellent as is the local raki (aniseed firewater).

Internal transport
The bus services are excellent and the long distance ones are very comfortable. Some companies offer non-smoking services. The rail service is invariably slower but it is cheap and a good way to see the country if you have plenty of time. Taxis are readily available in the big cities but beware of rip-offs, particularly in Istanbul.

Things to see
Istanbul, central Turkey. A city rich in eastern history, full of mosques, ruins and local bazaars. Old Istanbul is where many of the local delights can be found.
   Gallipoli, northwest Turkey. Site of a tragic First World War battle and the war graves bring the point home.
   Troy, northwest Turkey. An historic site and it is thought that up to nine cities have been built on the site.
   Selcuk and Epheses, west Turkey. The site of impressive Roman ruins.
   Beach resorts include Bodrum, Patara and Antalya.

Useful addresses
Turkish Embassy, 43 Belgrave Square, London SW1X 8PA. Tel: (0171) 235 5222.
Turkish Tourist Office, 170-173 Piccadilly, London W1V 9DD. Tel: (0171) 734 8681.
British Embassy, Sehit Ersan Caddesi 46A, Cankaya, Ankara.
British Council, Kirlingic Sokak 9, Gazi Osman Pasa, Ankara.

UNITED ARAB EMIRATES

Capital: Abu Dhabi   Currency: Dirham
Type of Government: Federal   Size: 83,650 square km
  Government   Population: 2 million
Official language: Arabic

Climate
Very hot although it can get quite cold in the desert areas during the winter.

General information
This union of seven sheikdoms was first arranged in 1820 but it was not until 1971 that it became a formal federation of states. The discovery of oil has made the country one of the richest per capita in the world.

Food and drink
Indian, Pakistani, Lebanese and western food is common throughout the country. Alcohol is sold only in the larger hotels.

Internal transport
Since there are no air or bus services between the emirates the only practical way to get around is by service taxis. These are vehicles that carry up to seven people and leave when full.

Things to see
Abu Dhabi, north UAE. A city that shows what the influence of oil can be.
    Dubai, north UAE. A shining example of Middle East capitalism – the area is rich and proud of it.
    Sharjah, north UAE. The third largest of the emirates and the home of some interesting architecture.

Useful addresses
UAE Embassy, 30 Prince's Gate, London SW7 1PT. Tel: (0171) 581 1281.
British Embassy, Khalid Bin Al-Waleed Street, Abu Dhabi.
British Council (PO Box 248), Al-Jabar Building, First Floor, Sheikh Zayed I Street, Abu Dhabi.

YEMEN

At the time of writing the civil war in Yemen dictates that it is not a viable destination for travellers.

19
Australasia and the
South Pacific

AUSTRALIA

Capital: Canberra
Type of Government: Parliamentary
  democracy – a member of the
  Commonwealth
Official language: English
National Airline: Qantas

Currency: Australian dollar
Size: 7,686,884 square km
Climate: Varied – tropical in the
  north, temperate in the south
Population: 18 million

General information

Aborigines from southeast Asia inhabited the country over 20,000 years ago. The Portuguese were the first Europeans to arrive in the 16th century, and they were followed by the Dutch in the 17th century. In 1770 Captain Cook landed on the east coast and claimed it for Britain. Initially it was used for convicts from Britain who were sent there as an alternative to the death penalty. Due to farming possibilities a civilian population was slowly built up in the country.

By 1829 the whole country had become a British dependency and the discovery of gold in Victoria in 1851 attracted more settlers. In 1901 the six separate colonies became an independent dominion of the British Empire. Despite measures to restrict non-white immigrants a wide range of nationalities settled in Australia.

During both World Wars Australia supported the Allies and played a significant role, particularly in the First World War at Gallipoli. Since the Second World War though closer links have been formed with Asia, and Japan is now a major trading partner.

In 1986 constitutional links between Australia and Britain were formally cut and in recent years there has been a strong movement towards forming a Republic. This had been led by the Prime Minister Paul Keating.

Food and drink

Almost any type of international cuisine can be found in Australia due to a wide selection of ethnic groups in the country – from Greek to Vietnamese and Indonesian to Mexican. If you cannot find a type of cooking in Australia then it probably does not exist. Standard Australian cooking is based on the meat pie and chips mentality and all varieties of fast food are popular, as is the ubiquitous barbecue. Seafood is one of the great delights of Australian cooking and includes lobster, tiger prawns, monkfish and mud crabs.

Some of the best wine in the world is made in Australia and it is also relatively cheap. Beer is the most common drink and is always drunk ice-cold. The national spirit is Bundaberg Rum (Bundy) and in some quarters it is considered un-Australian to drink anything else.

Internal transport
There is an excellent internal coach service with Deluxe, Ansett, Australian Coachlines and Greyhound being the main companies. Because of the size of the country some journeys take several days but all of the coaches are air conditioned and most of them have videos. All of the main companies offer travel cards for varying lengths of time and these are very good value if you are planning on doing a lot of coach travel. The internal air network covers most of the country but it is expensive in comparison with coaches. Trains operate in most regions but they are better for short, local journeys. The long distance trains tend to take the least direct route and can take days rather than hours to get to their destination.

Things to see
Sydney, New South Wales. The Sydney Harbour Bridge and the Opera House are just two of the attractions of this cosmopolitan city.

The Great Barrier Reef, off the Queensland Coast. One of the memorable tourist attractions in the world. A few days, minimum, are needed to experience fully the wonders of the Reef and a diving course is recommended.

North Queensland. Rainforests, beaches and lush scenery are abundant in this wilderness region. Cairns and Port Douglas are two of the most popular tourist areas in the country.

The Gold Coast, Queensland. The St Tropez of Australia – beaches and sunshine by day, casinos and nightclubs by night.

Alice Springs, Northern Territory. An outback town, literally in the middle of nowhere.

Ayers Rock and the Olgas, Northern Territory. Five hundred kilometres from Alice Springs, Ayers Rock rises magnificently out of the red desert sand. The nearby Olgas are a voluptuous contrast.

Darwin, Northern Territory. A tropical town near the stunning Kakadu National Park.

Kimberleys, Western Australia. Dramatic mountain range in the far north.

Broome, Western Australia. A former pearl town which has a distinctly Asian air.

Coober Pedy, South Australia. An opal-mining town where many of the houses are built underground to escape from the searing heat.

Hobart, Tasmania. A quieter pace of life than some of the mainland cities.

Melbourne, Victoria. One of the country's most cosmopolitan cities.

Useful addresses
Australian High Commission, Australia House, The Strand, London WC2B 4LA. Tel: (0171) 379 4334.
Australian Consulate, Chatsworth House, Lever Street, Manchester M1 2D1.

Tel: (0161) 228 1344.
Australian Tourist Commission, 10 Putney Hill, London SW15 6AA. Tel:
(0181) 780 2227.
British High Commission, Commonwealth Avenue, Canberra ACT 2600.

NEW ZEALAND

Capital: Wellington

Type of Government: Parliamentary
democracy – a member of the
Commonwealth

Population: 3.8 million

Currency: New Zealand dollar

Size: 268,704 square km

Climate: Varied – sub-tropical in the
north, temperate in the south

National Airline: Air New Zealand

General information
Inhabited by the Maoris from the 14th century – the first Europeans landed in
1642. Captain Cook arrived in 1769 and during the 19th century it was used as
a whaling and trading base. In 1840 the country became a British colony,
attracting settlers who wanted to turn their hand to sheep farming. There were
two disputes with the Maoris over land rights but these were settled in 1871.
The country had a very advanced social policy and it was the first country in the
world to give women the vote. New Zealand became independent in 1931 and
since then has been working to forge closer ties with Asian countries. In recent
years the country has experienced a severe recession.

Food and drink
While the range of New Zealand cuisine is not stunning it is the quality of food
that is special. Fresh meat such as lamb, pork and venison is among some of the
best in the world as is the seafood – salmon, lobster, oysters, mussels and
scallops. There is also a wide range of fruit and vegetables – avocado,
asparagus, sweet potato, kiwi fruit and boysenberries – and New Zealand
cheeses have won awards around the world. New Zealand wine is very good,
particularly the sparkling varieties.

Internal transport
There is a good internal coach network and travel passes are available from most
companies. The rail network runs to all main centres in the country and the air
network covers most of the country but it can be an expensive way to get around.

Things to see
Wellington, north island. A superb harbour and also good museums, botanic
gardens and cathedrals.
  Christchurch, south island. A pleasant city with interesting aspects of New
Zealand culture.
  Auckland, north island. An impressive harbour city with a zoo, an
underwater world, several museums and a nearby vineyard tour.
  Dunedin, south island. A city with a distinctly Scottish atmosphere.
  Milford, south island. Milford Sound is one of the great scenic experiences in

New Zealand.

Queenstown, south island. A year-round resort with ski-ing in the winter and magnificent scenery all year.

Wanaka, south island. Scenic lake mountains – whitewater rafting is a popular pastime.

Greymouth, south island. Displays much of the early history of the country.

Rotorua, north island. Famous for its magnificent thermal springs.

Mount Cook, south island. Stunning peaks where people can climb, walk, ski or just look at the scenery.

Useful addresses

New Zealand High Commission, New Zealand House, Haymarket, London SW1Y 4TQ. Tel: (0171) 930 8422.

New Zealand Tourist Board, PO Box 239, Weybridge, Surrey KT13 8YT.

British High Commission, Norwich Union Building, 179 Queen Street, Auckland 1.

SOUTH PACIFIC ISLANDS

The South Pacific Islands are a collection of independent nations and international dependencies. The dependencies are:

UK: Pitcairn Islands.

USA: American Samoa, Marshall Islands, Federation States, Belau, Guam and the Northern Marianas.

New Zealand: Cook Islands, Niue and Tokelau.

France: Tahiti-Polynesia, Wallis and Futuna, New Caledonia.

Chile: Easter Island.

Ecuador: Galapagos.

Indonesia: Irian Jaya.

The independent countries are:

Fiji, Kiribati, Nauru, Solomon Islands, Tonga, Tuvalu, Vanuatu, Western Samoa.

In many ways the South Pacific Islands have a lot in common – idyllic beaches, pleasant tropical climates and a combination of watersports and fascinating coral reefs. It is an excellent area for island-hopping and it is an area to be explored at a leisurely pace.

Local cuisine includes vegetables such as taro, yams, cassava, breadfruit and sweet potato, tropical fruits, lagoon fish and the occasional pig for special functions.

People who visit Australia and New Zealand should make every effort to take in at least a few of the South Pacific Islands. The experience will be a rewarding one and you will be following in the footsteps of such notable names as Robert Louis Stevenson and W Somerset Maugham.

20
North and Central America

NORTH AMERICA

CANADA

Capital: Ottawa
Type of Government: Federal democracy
   within the Commonwealth
Official languages: English and French
Population: 28 million

Currency: Canadian dollar
Size: 9,976,169 square km
Climate: Hot and dry in summer,
   very cold in winter
National Airline: Air Canada

General information

It appears that there were Viking settlements here as early as 1000 AD but it was not until 1497 that the first Europeans appeared in Canada. In 1608 the Frenchman Champlain established a permanent settlement at Quebec and this became known as New France. The British also became interested in the area, particularly for the lucrative fur trade, and they set up the Hudson Bay Company in 1670. Over the next 100 years the British and French fought over the country and in 1763 it was ceded to Britain.

In 1791 Quebec was divided into French-speaking Lower Quebec and English-speaking Upper Quebec. They were reunited in 1867 and by 1905 Canada was a confederation of nine states. In 1931 the country was defined as an independent constitutional monarchy in the British Commonwealth. In 1982 Queen Elizabeth II signed a new constitution for Canada.

The French problem has refused to go away for Canada and the French-speaking population have long been agitating for an independent Quebec. This remains a political and social issue and one that still divides the country.

Food and drink

A more refined version of the excesses of American cuisine. Due to its large ethnic population there is a wide choice of cuisine available.

Internal transport

Canada is a vast country and if you are going from coast to coast then serious consideration should be given to flying. A rail service operates across the country and although it is a romantic notion to travel in this fashion much of the terrain is flat and featureless. Coaches are a good way to get around in individual states.

Things to see

Ottawa, east Canada. An uninspiring capital but the home of some of the country's oldest architecture.

Montreal, east Canada. A vibrant city that has more than a little French flair.

Quebec, east Canada. The city that has caused so many problems for Canada but it is a lively and historic place.

Niagara Falls, east Canada. The world's most famous waterfall – it is even more impressive in the winter than it is in the summer.

Vancouver, west Canada. A relaxed city that is Canada's version of San Francisco.

The Rocky Mountains, west Canada. A towering mountain range that is a haven for walkers, climbers and nature lovers.

The Prairie, central Canada. Occupying thousands of miles it is quite a sight just to see so much wheat.

Northwest Territories. Home of the local Inuit Indians and one of the world's last great wilderness regions.

Useful addresses

Canadian High Commission, Macdonald House, 38 Grosvenor Street, London W1X 0AA.

British High Commission, Elgin Street, Ottawa, Ontario K1P 5KY. Tel: 0613 237 1530.

MEXICO

Capital: Mexico City	Currency: Mexican peso
Type of Government: Federal Republic	Size: 1,967,183 square km
Official language: Spanish	Climate: Sub-tropical
Population: 90 million	National Airlines: Aerovias de Mexico and Mexicana

General information

The Mayan Indians occupied the country from the 2nd to the 13th century, with a 400 year break when the Toltecs were in control. The Aztecs flourished in the 14th and 15th centuries. In 1521 the Spanish arrived and Mexico became part of the Spanish vice-royalty of New Spain. For 300 years the locals were subjugated but in 1821 this ended with the coming of independence. There then followed a period of civil war and revolution, culminating in the Mexican constitution which was written in 1917. Despite democratic aims the country is now a one-party state and has suffered great economic difficulties in the last 15 years. Large Mexican debts have been rescheduled and written off.

Food and drink

Mexican food is generally meat based and hot and spicy. The staples are *tortillas*, *enchiladas*, *tacos* and *tamales* (maize pancakes cooked in a variety of fashions and filled with chicken, pork, vegetables or cheese). Other dishes such as *guacamole* (avocado sauce) and *turkey mole* (a mixture of chilli, tomato, peanuts, chocolate, almonds, onion and garlic) are also popular accompaniments. Tequila (made from cactus) is the national drink and the local beer is very good.

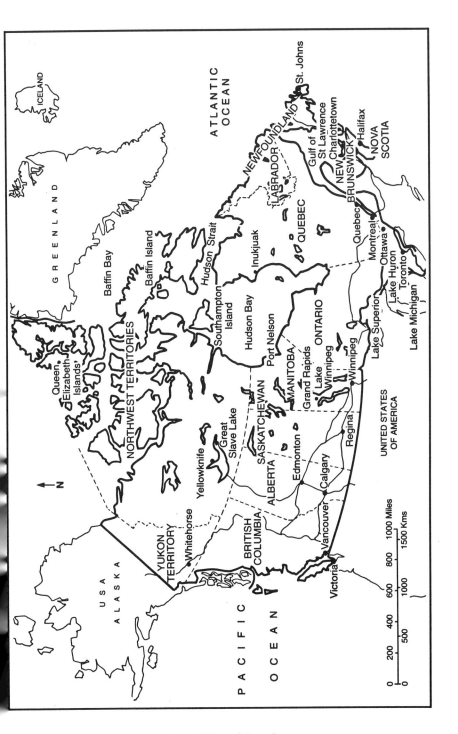

Fig. 3. Map of Canada.

195

Internal transport
There is an extensive bus system including first-class, deluxe and ordinary services. They cover most parts of the country but some of the drivers seem to think they are in control of racing cars. The rail network is good but is more expensive and less flexible than the buses. Internal flights are frequent but expensive.

Things to see
Mexico City, south Mexico. A sprawling, polluted capital that can be slightly overpowering.
San Miguel de Allende, central Mexico. An elegant colonial town that is classified as a national monument.
Mitla, south Mexico. The home of valuable Mixtec remains.
San Cristobal de las Casas, south Mexico. An impressive collection of colonial architecture and arts.
Chichen-Itza, south Mexico. A famous Mayan archaeological site.
Acapulco, south Mexico. The country's premier beach resort.

Useful addresses
Mexican Embassy, 42 Hertford Street, London W1Y 7TF. Tel: (0171) 499 8586.
Mexican Tourist Office, 60 Trafalgar Square, London WC2N 5DS. Tel: (0171) 734 1058.
British Embassy (PO Box 90 Bis), Rio Lerma 71, Col Cuauhtemoc, Mexico City 06500 DF.
British Council (Apdo Postal 30-588), Maestro Antonio Caso 127, Col San Rafael, Mexico City 06470 DF.

UNITED STATES OF AMERICA

Capital: Washington DC
Type of Government: Federal Republic
Official language: English
National Airline: Continental,
     American Airlines

Currency: American dollar
Size: 9,363,123 square km
Population: 250 million

Climate
Varied – generally hot and dry in the summer and very cold in the winter, particularly in the north.

General information
Discovered by Columbus in 1492, the country was explored and settled by several nations including the British, the French and the Spanish. The British established colonies in the east and in the 18th century this caused frictions and the 13 colonies achieved independence following the American Revolution (1754-63). At the same time the west of the country was being settled, and this process was accelerated by the discovery of gold in California.
    In the 19th century there was conflict over slavery between the cotton growing Southern states and the industrial North. This led to the Civil War (1861-65)

which was won by the North and resulted in the abolition of slavery. In 1867 Alaska was bought and in 1898 Hawaii was annexed. During this time America was enjoying considerable economic and territorial expansion and this continued after the First World War. This ended in 1929 with the Wall Street Crash and the subsequent Depression.

America contributed to the Allied effort in the Second World War, after the Japanese bombing of Pearl Harbour. Since then the USA have been one of the major world powers and for several decades pursued a relentless policy of anti-communism. This led to their intervention in the Vietnam War (1961-75) which resulted in a humiliating climbdown.

In recent years the USA has contributed to improved relations with the former Soviet Union but in 1991 they showed that they were still willing to use military power when they attacked Iraq during the Gulf War. During the 1990s America has experienced a serious economic recession which now seems to be easing.

Food and drink
The home of fast food and it is a case of being able to find just about anything you want. The quantity of food is almost as impressive as the quality – even small portions would appear large to most non-Americans.

Internal transport
There is an excellent internal air network and in some cases it can be the cheapest form of transport. The coach network is efficient and wide ranging but it is worth bearing in mind that some journeys can take days rather than hours. Greyhound is the major coach company and something of an American institution. The rail network is extensive but not as flexible or as cheap as coach travel. Being the land of the motor car America is a good place to buy or rent a car for travelling.

Things to see
There is enough to see and do in America to keep travellers occupied for a lifetime. Below is just a selection of places and areas to visit.

North East: Boston, New York, Washington, New England, Cape Cod, Vermont, Niagara Falls and Gettysburg.

The West: San Francisco, Los Angeles, Las Vegas, Arizona, Hawaii, the Grand Canyon, Yosemite National Park, Death Valley, the Rockies.

North West: Seattle and Alaska.

The South: New Orleans, Atlanta, Dallas, Memphis, Nashville and Chattanooga.

Useful addresses
United States Embassy, 24 Grosvenor Square, London W1A 2JB. Tel: (0171) 499 9000.

United States Travel & Tourism Administration, PO Box 1EN, London W1A 1AE. Tel: (0171) 495 4466.

British Embassy, 3100 Massachusetts Avenue NW, Washington DC 20009.

CENTRAL AMERICA

BELIZE

Capital: Belmopan
Type of Government: Parliamentary
  democracy
Official language: English – Spanish is
  widely spoken
Population: 205,000

Currency: Belize dollar
Size: 23,000 square km
Climate: Sub-tropical
National Airline: Belize Transair
  from USA

General information
The first recorded European settlement was in 1638 when some British sailors were shipwrecked in the area. As the settlement tried to establish itself it suffered numerous attacks from neighbouring Spanish settlements. It was finally resolved in 1798 when the British settlers won a decisive victory. In 1871 British Honduras was declared a British colony. In 1981 Belize achieved independence. The area is susceptible to hurricanes, one of which severely damaged the former capital, Belize City.

Food and drink
Fresh fruit and vegetables are of a distinctly tropical nature and fresh fish and seafood is the speciality of several parts of the country.

Internal transport
There are four main roads in the country and these connect all the major towns and population centres. There are regular bus services and also internal flights to most parts of the country. Taxis operate in the towns and they usually have fixed rates.

Things to see
Mundo Maya. Tourism has been developed in conjunction with neighbouring countries; it is designed to promote the Maya Indian culture and heritage.
   Community Baboon Sanctuary, central Belize. A wildlife park set up to protect the endangered black howler monkey.
   Hol Chan Marine Preserve. An area designed to protect the world's second largest coral reef.
   The Blue Hole. An exceptional diving site on the reef.
   Altun Ha, northeast Belize. The most extensively excavated of all the Maya sites.

Useful addresses
Belize High Commission, 10 Harcourt House, 19A Cavendish Square, London W1M 9AD.
British High Commission, PO Box 91, Belmopan.

COSTA RICA

Capital: San José
Type of Government: Republic
Official language: Spanish
Population: 3.5 million

Currency: Colon
Size: 50,900 square km
Climate: Tropical
National Airline: LACSA

General information
The country was discovered by Columbus in 1502 and he was followed by Spanish settlers who virtually wiped out the indigenous Indian population. Little development was undertaken and this stagnation eventually led to the rise of the independence movement which achieved its aim in 1821. The powerful coffee-growers were the first group to hold power and this led to periods of dictatorial rule. In 1948, following weeks of civil conflict, the National Liberation Party came to power and introduced a more democratic style of government and took some of the power from the military. Since then Costa Rica has enjoyed more stability than some of its neighbours.

Food and drink
Local cuisine borrows heavily from Mexican and some of the most popular dishes include *gallo pinto* (rice and black beans, usually served for breakfast with sour cream or fried eggs), *tortillas* (corn pancakes or omelettes), *casado* (rice, black beans, fried plantain, beef and chopped cabbage), *palmitos* (hearts of palms served with salad and a vinegar dressing), *arroz con pollo* (rice and chicken), and *elote* (corn on the cob). There are five local beers and rum is good and cheap.

Internal transport
Buses operate to most parts of the country, centring on San José. There are two types – direct, which are quicker and more expensive, and normal services. Some routes are very crowded. There is a limited rail service which is cheaper but slower than the buses. There is also an internal air network but you need to book well in advance. The 'Jungle Train' which runs from San José to the Caribbean coast travels through a fine cross section of the country's scenery.

Things to see
San José, north Costa Rica. A cosmopolitan city that has more in common with North than Central America.

Poas Volcano National Park, central Costa Rica. An impressive volcano (last active in 1954) is the main attraction of the park.

Braulio Carrillo National Park, central Costa Rica. Areas of protected virgin rainforest.

Fortuna, northwest Costa Rica. An excellent viewpoint for the Arenal Volcano.

Tortuguero National Park, east Costa Rica. An important breeding ground for the green sea turtle.

Useful addresses
Costa Rican Embassy, 36 Upper Brook Street, London W1Y 1PE. Tel: (0171)
    495 3985.
British Embassy, Paseo Colon, Calle 38 and 40, San José.

EL SALVADOR

Capital: San Salvador	Currency: Colon
Type of Government: Republic	Size: 21,393 square km
Official language: Spanish	Climate: Tropical
Population: 5.5 million	National Airline: TACA

General information
The Spanish arrived here in 1526 and quickly overran the local Aztec
population. It took 300 years for the grip of Spanish rule to be broken and
from 1823-38 El Salvador formed part of the Central American Federation. The
country became independent in 1841 and during the 1960s there were two
periods of war with Honduras. The 1970s and 1980s were marked by repressive
rulers and internal violence. In 1991 a peace agreement was signed and this has
been reasonably effective but travellers should still exercise caution.

Food and drink
Rice, beans and salad are the basic fare and the local *pupusa* (a thick tortilla
filled with sausage, cheese or beans) is a popular snack or meal. Local beer is in
plentiful supply.

Internal transport
Since there is no passenger rail network, buses are the best way to get around.
There are a lot of them but they are invariably very crowded. This is explained
by the fact that they are very cheap. A more expensive option is the internal air
network. All large towns have a plentiful supply of taxis.

Things to see
San Salvador, central El Salvador. The country's capital and focal point. In the
shadow of a volcano it has some fine colonial buildings and a good nightlife.
    Los Chorros, central El Salvador. A picturesque park with refreshing pools
and wildlife.
    Montecristo Cloud Forest, northwest El Salvador. An international nature
reserve with an extraordinary variety of flora and fauna.
    Tazumal Ruins, west El Salvador. The most important Mayan Indian ruins in
the country.
    Cerro Verde National Park, west El Salvador. A national park on top of a
volcano with birds and wildlife. A popular area for hikers.

Useful addresses
El Salvador Embassy, 5 Great James Street, London WC1 3DA. Tel: (0171) 432
    2141.
British Embassy, 4828 Paseo General Escalon, San Salvador.

GUATEMALA

Capital: Guatemala City
Type of Government: Republic
Official language: Spanish
Population: 10 million

Currency: Quetzal
Size: 108,889 square km
Climate: Tropical
National Airline: Aviateca

General information
The Maya Indians and the Aztecs inhabited this area before the Spanish arrived in 1524. They soon conquered the local tribes and had control of the country until 1821 when it formed the main part of the Central American Federation. Guatemala became independent in 1839. Its recent history has been marked by military dictatorships and political instability. In recent years there have been questions about the country's civil rights record and there have even been some attacks on foreign tourists.

Food and drink
A mixture of Mexican and American food. Beer and rum are the most popular drinks.

Internal transport
The bus system is moderate but the only other alternative is the expensive air network.

Things to see
Antigua Guatemala, south Guatemala. The site of some of the country's best colonial buildings.
    Western Guatemala. The country's highland region and its most picturesque. Always check the local political situation before you travel here.
    Central and Eastern Guatemala. Mountain scenery contrasts with the local Mayan ruins in the region.

Useful addresses
Guatemalan Embassy, 73 Rue de Courcelles, 75008 Paris.
British Embassy, 7a Avenida 5-10, Zona 4 (7th Floor), Guatemala City.

HONDURAS

Capital: Tegucigalpa
Type of Government: Republic
Official language: Spanish
Population: 5.1 million
National Airline: Tab/SAHSA

Currency: Lempira
Size: 112,088 square km
Climate: Tropical – cooler in the
    inland mountain regions

General information
Initially settled by the Mayan Indians, the area was conquered by the Spanish and then gained independence in 1821. The country's recent history has been of

internal and external conflicts, particularly with El Salvador and Nicaragua. In 1988 the USA sent troops to stop incursions by Nicaragua. Travellers should monitor the current political situation.

Food and drink
The staple diet consists of beans, rice, tortillas, fried bananas, meat, potatoes, yucca, cheese and vegetables. On the coasts the fish is good. Beer is widely available.

Internal transport
Buses are cheap and frequent and internal air flights offer reasonable value. Passenger train services can be found in the north of the country and hitching is fairly easy. Boats can also be taken along the Caribbean Coast.

Things to see
Tegucigalpa, southwest Honduras. A refreshing capital that is a good stepping stone to other parts of the country.
   Western Honduras. Notable for its Mayan ruins, particularly at Copan. There are also some fine lakes and two national parks.
   Northern Honduras. The main feature is the Caribbean coast which offers excellent beaches and delicious seafood.
   Bay Islands, north coast. Three islands, Roatan, Guanaja and Utila, that offer first class diving and snorkeling. The coral reef is the main attraction.

Useful addresses
Honduran Embassy, 115 Gloucester Place, London W1H 3PJ. Tel: (0171) 486 4880.
British Embassy, Colonia Palmira, Edificio Palmira, 3rd Storey, opposite Hotel Honduras Mayua, Tegucigalpa.

NICARAGUA

Capital: Managua
Type of Government: Republic
Official language: Spanish
Population: 4 million
National Airline: AeroNica

Currency: Cordoba
Size: 148,000 square km
Climate: Tropical – cooler in the
   mountainous north

General information
Following Spanish dominance from 1522 Nicaragua achieved independence in 1838. From 1916 the USA had close links with the country but this could not prevent internal strife and civil war. During the 1980s there was a fierce struggle between the rival Sandinista and Contra groups. The USA supported the Contras, and despite allegations of corruption, the Sandinistas were defeated. In 1990 there was a free election and since then some stability has returned to the country but the situation is fragile and should be monitored by travellers.

Food and drink
Similar fare to the rest of central America – beans, rice, fried bananas, cabbage and tomato salad, and tortillas filled with cheese, chicken, beef or pork. Local beer and rum are produced.

Internal transport
Buses are cheap, frequent and crowded. Keep an eye on your luggage and beware of pickpockets. There is one main train line and the trains are cheaper than the buses but you should look after your belongings. Some parts of the country are only accessible by boat.

Things to see
Managua, west Nicaragua. Although there is some interesting architecture and markets the main function of the capital is for official matters.

Volcan Masaya National Park, west Nicaragua. A large volcano that is classified as being active.

Lago de Nicaragua, southwest Nicaragua. The 10th largest freshwater lake in the world.

Caribbean Coast, east Nicaragua. An 640 kilometre stretch of coast with large areas of tropical rainforest.

Useful addresses
Nicaraguan Embassy, 8 Gloucester Road, London SW7 4PP. Tel: (0171) 584 3231.
British Embassy, Entrada Principal de la Primera Etapa, Los Robles, Managua.

PANAMA

Capital: Panama City	Currency: Balboa
Type of Government: Republic	Size: 78,046 square km
Official language: Spanish	Climate: Tropical
Population: 2.5 million	National Airline: COPA

General information
The area was conquered by the Spanish in 1502 and when it broke free from its colonial masters Panama became part of the newly independent Colombia in 1821. In 1903 it became independent, supported by the USA. Although recent political events have been turbulent a reasonable amount of stability is provided by American interests.

Food and drink
A good variety of local and international cuisine. The indigenous food is a tasty combination of Mexican and Caribbean flavours. Seafood is very common and of an excellent standard.

Internal transport
Buses are the best way to get around although some areas of the country can

only be reached by boat.

Things to see
Panama City, central Panama. An administrative centre but with some worthwhile architecture. Nearby is the famous Panama Canal.

Soberania National Park, central Panama. The country's most accessible area of tropical rainforest.

Peninsula de Azuero, south Panama. An area with top-class beaches.

Chiriqui, west Panama. A picturesque area with a volcano, hot springs and beaches.

Useful addresses
Panamanian Embassy, 24 Tudor Court, London EC4Y. Tel: (0171) 353 4792.
British Embassy, Calle 53, Edificio Swissbank, Marbella, Panama City.

Applying for a United States Visa
A practical guide to the new immigration law
Richard Fleischer

Major changes have affected the process of obtaining visas to the USA in the wake of the 1990 Immigration Act, and not until 1992 were some of the procedures officially clarified, and the application forms published. This new book meets an urgent need for up-to-date detailed and practical information on how to apply for a United States visa. It covers immigration visa categories (employment, investor, family), and the complete range of non-immigrant visa categories (prefix letters, B, H, L, E, Q, P, R, F, and J).

This is the most recent and authoritative guide on the market; with its valuable professional advice and comprehensive forms, it will be the one essential reference for all US visa applicants, their families, employers and professional advisers.

Richard I Fleischer has been practising imigration law since 1973. The clients he represents include multi-national, medium and small companies, universities, government officials and individuals, foreign ambassadors, cabinet-ministers, sports professionals and famous and ordinary people from 110 countries.

£15.99 hardback, 192pp illus. 1 85876 000 3.

Please add postage & packing (UK £2 per copy.
Europe £3 per copy. World £5 per copy airmail).

Plymbridge Distributors Ltd, Plymbridge House, Estover Road,
Plymouth, PL6 7PZ, United Kingdom.
Tel: (01752) 695745. Fax: (01752) 695699. Telex: 45635.

21
The Caribbean

To many people the image of the Caribbean is one of palm-fringed beaches and relaxing cocktails by the pool. In many respects this is true and the islands of the West Indies are the perfect place to relax and put your feet up for a while. However, there is a lot more to these islands than mere sun worshipping; all of them have interesting colonial history attached and some of the inland scenery is well worth dragging yourself off the beach to see.

International cuisine is available throughout the islands. Local delicacies include lobster, red snapper, goat water, ducana, fungi and saltfish. Tropical fruit is in abundance. Cocktails with fresh fruit are a popular drink and the local rum punch should be sampled.

The weather is pleasantly sub-tropical all year round – sea breezes ensure that the summers are not too hot and in the winter the temperature at night might drop to a pleasant 60 degrees.

The Caribbean is a perfect place for a spot of island hopping as there are numerous yachts that sail around the area and it is relatively easy to hitch a ride or work your passage through the islands.

There are dozens of islands throughout the Caribbean and they each have their own individual character. The main areas are made up of the Greater Antilles, the Lesser Antilles, Trinidad and Tobago and the Bahamas. Between them they offer a wide range of activities from diving and sailing to fishing and sun worshipping.

BAHAMAS

Capital: Nassau
Type of Government: Commonwealth
Official language: English

Population: 270,000
Currency: Bahamian dollar
Size: 13,864 square km

General information
After Columbus discovered this collection of over 700 islands it became a British crown colony in 1717. Britain had control of the islands until 1973 when it achieved full independence in the Commonwealth.

Useful addresses
Bahamas High Commission, 10 Chesterfield Street, London W1X 8AH. Tel: (0171) 408 4488.

British High Commission (PO Box 676C), Barclays Building, Roebuck Street, Bridgetown.

GREATER ANTILLES

CUBA

Capital: Havana
Type of Government: Republic
Official language: Spanish

Population: 10.6 million
Currency: Cuban peso
Size: 148,124 square km

General information
Christopher Columbus arrived in Cuba in 1492 and the following century the Spanish colonised Cuba and subjected the area to a brutal regime of slavery and repression. In 1902 Cuba was declared an independent republic.

In 1940 Batista was elected President but his regime was corrupt and this gave rise to a revolutionary movement led by Fidel Castro. In 1953 Castro staged a failed coup but in 1959 he was more successful: he overthrew the government and replaced it with his Russian supported communist regime. Once Castro took power relations with America deteriorated and in 1961 a global crisis was narrowly averted during the Bay of Pigs incident.

In 1976 a socialist constitution was approved by a referendum. Since then economic conditions have led to considerable hardship for the people of Cuba.

Useful addresses
Cuban Embassy, 167 High Holborn, London WC1V 6PA. Tel: (0171) 240 2488.
Cuban Consular Section, 15 Grape Street, London WC2 8DR. Tel: (0171) 836 7618.
British Embassy, Edifico Bolivar, Capdevila 101-103, Morro y Prado, Havana.

DOMINICAN REPUBLIC

Capital: San Domingo
Type of Government: Republic
Official language: Spanish

Population: 7.5 million
Size: 48,442 square km
Currency: Dominican Republic peso

General information
Discovered in 1492 by Columbus the island became a Spanish colony and achieved independence in 1821. Haiti and the USA have occupied the country since then and its recent history has been marked by internal instability, closely monitored by the USA.

Useful address
Dominican Republic Honorary Consulate, Queens Mansions, Brook Green, London W6 7EB. Tel: (0171) 602 1885.

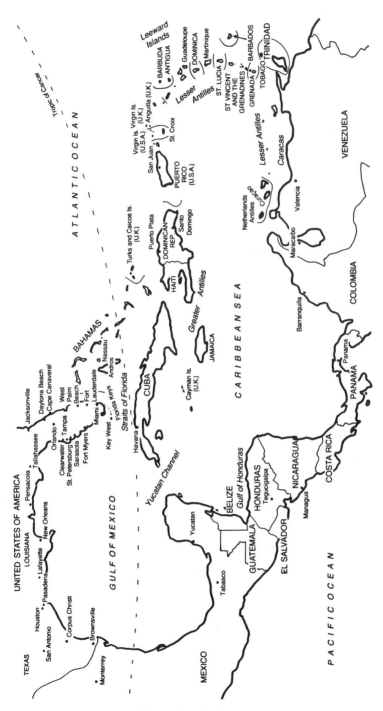

Fig. 4. The Caribbean.

207

HAITI

Capital: Port-au-Prince	Population: 6 million
Type of Government: Republic	Currency: Gourde
Official language: French – Creole is	Size: 27,750 square km
widely spoken	Climate: Sub-tropical

General information
The island was discovered by Columbus in 1492 and soon became a Spanish colony. The native Indian population were treated harshly and hundreds of slaves were brought to the island. In 1804 Haiti became independent and since then the island has been plagued by internal problems. In recent years there have been several military coups and the position remains fragile, with the USA taking a close interest in affairs.

Useful address
Haiti Support Group, 90 Hodford Road, London NW11 8EG. Tel: (0181) 201 9878.

JAMAICA

Capital: Kingston	Population: 2.5 million
Type of Government: Parliamentary	Currency: Jamaican dollar
democracy within the Commonwealth	Size: 10,991 square km
Official language: English	

General information
Discovered in 1494 the Spanish soon took control and destroyed the local Arawak population. In 1655 it became a British colony and was subsequently a centre for the slave trade until 1833. In 1962 Jamaica became independent within the Commonwealth and since then there have been periods of conflict between the two main political parties.

Useful addresses
Jamaican High Commission, 1 Prince Consort Road, London SW7 2BQ. Tel: (0171) 823 9911.
British High Commission (PO Box 575), Trafalgar Road, Kingston 10.

PUERTO RICO

Capital: San Juan	Population: 3.5 million
Type of Government: Commonwealth	Currency: US dollar
Official language: Spanish – English is	Size: 8674 square km
also widely spoken	

General information
The island was discovered by Columbus in 1508 and after 400 years of Spanish rule it was ceded to the USA in 1898. Since then it has maintained the status of a

self-governing commonwealth in association with the USA.

LESSER ANTILLES

The nature of these islands reflects in part their colonial history: the British, the French, the Dutch and the USA have all played an important role in the area. Some countries are independent while others are dependencies. There are two groups of islands within the Lesser Antilles, the Windward Islands and the Leeward Islands.

ANTIGUA AND BARBUDA

Capital: St John's
Population: 68,000
Currency: dollar
Size: 440 square km

BARBADOS

Capital: Bridgetown
Official language: English
Population: 270,000
Currency: Barbados dollar
Size: 430 square km

CURACAO

Main town: Willemstad
Population: 180,000
Size: 444 square km

DOMINICA

Capital: Roseau
Population: 85,000
Official language: English
Currency: East Caribbean dollar
Size: 728 square km

GRENADA

Capital: St George's
Official language: English
Population: 90,000
Currency: East Caribbean dollar
Size: 344 square km

GUADELOUPE

Capital: Basse-Terre
Population: 350,000
Size: 1780 square km

MARTINIQUE

Capital: Fort-de-France
Population: 350,000
Size: 1090 square km

ST KITTS-NEVIS

Capital: Basseterre
Population: 45,000
Currency: East Caribbean dollar
Size: 262 square km

ST LUCIA

Capital: Castries
Population: 150,000
Currency: East Caribbean dollar
Size: 616 square km

ST VINCENT AND THE GRENADINES

Capital: Kingstown
Population: 120,000
Size: 390 square km
Currency: East Caribbean dollar

Useful addresses

Barbados High Commission, 1 Great Russell Street, London WC1B 3NH. Tel: (0171) 631 4975.

Eastern Caribbean Commission, 10 Kensington Court, London W8 5DL. Tel: (0171) 937 9522.

Grenada High Commission, 1 Collingham Gardens, London SW5 0HW. Tel: (0171) 373 7808.

TRINIDAD AND TOBAGO

Capital: Port-of-Spain
Type of Government: Republic
Official language: English
Size: 5128 square km

Currency: Trinidad and Tobago dollar
Population: 1.5 million
Climate: Tropical

General information

Originally occupied by Arawak and Carib Indians the islands were a Spanish colony from the 16th century until 1809. The country was a member of the Federation of the West Indies from 1958-1961 and became independent in 1962. Since then there have been periods of political instability but a military coup in 1990 was defeated.

Useful addresses

Trinidad and Tobago High Commission, 42 Belgrave Square, London SW1X 8NT. Tel: (0171) 245 9351.

British High Commission (PO Box 225), Furness House, Independence Square, Port-of-Spain.

22
Europe

Due to its close proximity to Britain, and the increasing tendency to look at the countries of Europe as having a lot in common, the individual European countries will not be looked at in great depth. Many people travelling around the world will want to cast their eyes further afield and try to find some more unusual and exotic locations. This is not to say that travelling round Europe is not an exhilarating and stimulating experience – it definitely is, and there is enough material there for a whole book on its own!

Austria
Austrian Embassy, 18 Belgrave Mews West, London SW1X 8HU. Tel: (0171) 235 3731.

Belarus
Consulate of Belarus, 1 St Stephen's Crecent, Bayswater, London W2 5QT. Tel: (0171) 221 3941.

Belgium
Belgian Embassy, 103 Eaton Square, London SW1W 9AB. Tel: (0171) 235 5422.

Bulgaria
Bulgarian Embassy, 186-188 Queen's Gate, London SW7 3HL. Tel: (0171) 584 9400

Croatia
Croatian Embassy, 18-21 Jermyn Street, London SW1Y 6HP. Tel: (0171) 434 2946.

Cyprus
Cypriot Embassy, 98 Park Street, London W1Y 4ET. Tel: (0171) 499 8272.

Czech Republic
Czech Republic Embassy, 23 Kensington Palace Gardens, London W8 4QY. Tel: (0171) 229 1255.

Denmark
Danish Embassy, 55 Sloane Street, London SW1X 9SR, Tel: (0171) 235 1255.

Estonia
Estonian Embassy, 16 Hyde Park Gate, London SW7 5DG. Tel: (0171) 589 3428.

Finland
Finnish Embassy, 38 Chesham Place, London SW1X 8HW. Tel: (0171) 235 9531.

France
French Embassy, 58 Knightsbridge, London SW1X 7JT. Tel: (0171) 201 1000.

Germany
German Embassy, 23 Belgrave Square, London SW1X 8PZ. Tel: (0171) 235 5033.

Greece
Greek Embassy, 1A Holland Park, London W11 3TP. Tel: (0171) 221 6467.

Hungary
Hungarian Embassy, 35 Eaton Place, London SW1. Tel: (0171) 235 4048.

Iceland
Icelandic Embassy, 1 Eaton Terrace, London SW1W 8EY Tel: (0171) 730 5131.

Italy
Italian Embassy, 14 Three Kings Yard, London W1Y 2EH. Tel: (0171) 629 8200.

Latvia
Latvian Embassy, 72 Queensborough Terrace, London W2 3SP. Tel: (0171) 727 1698.

Lithuania
Lithuanian Embassy, 17 Essex Villas, London W8 7BP. Tel: (0171) 938 2481.

Luxembourg
Luxembourg Embassy, 27 Wilton Crescent, London SW1X 8DS. Tel: (0171) 235 6961.

Malta
Maltese Embassy, 16 Kensginton Square, London W8 5HH. Tel: (0171) 938 1712.

Netherlands
Netherlands Embassy, 38 Hyde Park Gate, London SW7 5DP. Tel: (0171) 584 5040.

Norway
Norwegian Embassy, 25 Belgrave Square, London SW1X 8QD. Tel: (0171) 235 7151.

Poland
Polish Embassy, 47 Portland Place, London W1N 3AG. Tel: (0171) 580 4324.

Portugal
Portuguese Embassy, 62 Brompton Road, London SW3 1BJ. Tel: (0171) 581 8722.

Romania
Romanian Embassy, 4 Palace Green, London W8 4QD. Tel: (0171) 937 9666.

Russian Federation
Russian Federation Embassy, 13 Kensington Palace Gardens, London W8 4QS. Tel: (0171) 229 8027.

Slovak Republic
Slovak Embassy, 25 Kensington Palace Gardens, London W8 4QY. Tel: (0171) 243 0803.

Slovenia
Slovenian Embassy, Sute 1, Cavendish Court, 11-15 Wigmore Street, London W1H 9LA. Tel: (0171) 495 7775.

Spain
Spanish Embassy, 24 Belgrave Square, London SW1X 8QA. Tel: (0171) 235 5555.

Sweden
Swedish Embassy, 11 Montagu Place, London W1H 2AL. Tel: (0171) 724 2101.

Switzerland
Swiss Embassy, 16-18 Montagu Place, London W1H 2BQ. Tel: (0171) 723 0701.

Ukraine
Ukrainian Embassy, 78 Kensington Park Road, London W11 2PL. Tel: (0171) 727 6312.

Useful Addresses

GENERAL

Berghaus, 34 Dean Street, Newcastle-upon-Tyne NE1 1PG. Tel: (0191) 232 3561.

Careers Research and Advisory Centre (CRAC), Bateman Street, Cambridge CB2 1LZ.

Central Bureau for Educational Visits and Exchanges, Seymour Mews House, Seymour Mews, London W1H 9PE. Tel: (0171) 486 5101.

International Voluntary Services (IVS), Old Hall, East Bergholt, Colchester, Essex CO7 6TQ.

Karrimor, 19 Avenue Parade, Accrington, Lancs BB5 6PR. Tel: (01254) 385911.

Kibbutz Representatives, 1A Accommodation Road, London NW11. Tel: (0181) 458 9235.

Rohan, 30 Maryland Road, Tongwell, Milton Keynes MK14 8HB. Tel: (01908) 618888.

Royal Geographical Society, 1 Kensington Gore, London SW7. Tel: (0171) 589 5466.

Trailfinders, 42-50 Earls Court Road, London W8 6EJ Tel: (0171) 938 3366.

Vacation Work, 9 Park End Street, Oxford OX1 1HJ. Tel: (01865) 241978.

Vango, 70 East Hamilton Street, Ladyburn, Greenock PA15 2HB. Tel: (01475) 744122.

Voluntary Service Overseas (VSO), 317 Putney Bridge Road, London SW15 2PN. Tel: (0181) 780 2266.

Volunteer Centre, 29 Lower King's Road, Berkhamstead, Herts HP4 2AE.

WEXAS International Ltd, 45-49 Brompton Road, London SW3 1DE.

Youth Hostel Association, Trevelyan House, 8 St Stephen's Hill, St Albans, Herts AL1 2DY. Tel: (01727) 55215.

HEALTH

British Airways Travel Centre, 156 Regent Street, London W1. Tel: (0171) 439 9584.

Communicable Disease Surveillance Centre, 61 Colindale Avenue, London NW9 5EQ. Tel: (0181) 200 6868.

Department of Infections and Tropical Medicine, East Birmingham Hospital,

Bordesley Green East, Birmingham B9 5ST. Tel: (0121) 6611.

Hospital for Tropical Diseases, 4 St Pancras Way, London NW1 0PE. Tel: (0171) 387 4411 or (0171) 388 8989/9600 (travel clinic) or (0893) 337722 (pre-recorded healthline).

Department of Infection and Tropical Medicine, Ruchill Hospital, Glasgow G20 9NB. Tel: (0141) 946 7120.

Medical Advisory Centre for Travellers Abroad (MASTA), London School of Hygiene and Tropical Medicine, Keppel Street, London WC1E 7H1. Tel: (0171) 631 4408.

Further Reading

GENERAL

Airports Guide – Europe (Thomas Cook).
The Budget Travel Handbook (Horizon, Plymbridge House, Estover Road, Plymouth PL6 7PZ).
An Explorer's Handbook (Hodder & Stoughton).
The Flier's Handbook (Pan).
Handbook for Women Travellers (Piatkus).
Home from Home (Central Bureau).
How To Books. For list see front of this book (page 2).
International Directory of Voluntary Work (Vacation Work).
Kibbutz Volunteer (Vacation Work).
Lonely Planet Guides, PO Box 617, Hawthorn, Victoria 3122, Australia.
Nothing Ventured – Disabled People Travel the World (Rough Guide).
Overseas Timetable – Railway, Road and Shipping (Thomas Cook).
Rough Guides, 1 Mercer Street, London WC2H 9QJ.
The Round the Word Air Guide (Fontana).
The Student Handbook (Macmillan Publishers Ltd).
Summer Jobs Abroad (Vacation Work).
Travel with Children (Lonely Planet).
The Travellers Handbook (WEXAS).
The Vegetarian Traveller (Grafton).
Women Travel (Rough Guide).
The World Train Travel Guide (Kuperard).
Work Your Way Around the World (Vacation Work).

HEALTH

ABC of Healthy Travel (BMJ Publications).
International Travel and Health: vaccination requirements and health advice (World Health Oganisation).
Traveller's Health: How to Stay Healthy Abroad (OUP).
The Traveller's Health Guide (Lascelles).

Index